BLUE HELMET

BLUE HELMET

My Year as a UN Peacekeeper in South Sudan

EDWARD H. CARPENTER

Foreword by A. K. Bardalai

Potomac Books | *An imprint of the University of Nebraska Press*

Library of Congress Cataloging-in-Publication Data
Names: Carpenter, Edward H., author. | Bardalai, A. K.
(Apurva Kumar), writer of foreword.
Title: Blue helmet: my year as a UN peacekeeper in South
Sudan / Edward H. Carpenter; foreword by A. K. Bardalai.
Description: Lincoln: Potomac Books, an imprint
of the University of Nebraska Press, 2025. | Includes
bibliographical references and index.
Identifiers: LCCN 2024038867
ISBN 9781640125995 (hardback)
ISBN 9781640126497 (epub)
ISBN 9781640126503 (pdf)
Subjects: LCSH: United Nations Mission in South
Sudan. | United Nations—Peacekeeping forces—South
Sudan. | Marines—Biography. | South Sudan—Politics
and government—2011– | BISAC: BIOGRAPHY &
AUTOBIOGRAPHY / Military | HISTORY / Africa / East |
LCGFT: Autobiographies.
Classification: LCC JZ6377.U6 C365 2025 |
DDC 355.35709629—dc23/eng/20240821
LC record available at https://lccn.loc.gov/2024038867

Designed and set in Minion Pro by A. Shahan.

The views expressed in this publication are those of the
author and do not necessarily reflect the official policy
or position of the Department of Defense or the U.S.
government—nor do they necessarily reflect the official
policy or position of the United Nations Mission in
South Sudan or the United Nations.

The public release clearance of this publication by the
Department of Defense does not imply Department of
Defense endorsement or factual accuracy of the material.

This book is dedicated to all of the women and men of the United Nations Mission in South Sudan, especially to the 141 who have made the ultimate sacrifice in the cause of peace, and to the people of South Sudan, who deserved better than I gave them.

Contents

Part 3. The Ordeal

Part 4. The Long Road Back

Illustrations

Foreword

As a retired major general from the Indian Army, I have served in my share of conflicts, but since 1992, my professional passion has been the pursuit of peace. This was born from my personal experience serving as a United Nations (UN) observer in Angola, working to bring about the end of what was then the African continent's longest-running civil war. Serving as the deputy head of mission and deputy force commander in the United Nations Interim Force in Lebanon, attaining a doctorate in UN peace operations, and writing extensively on this subject over the years have required me to read many, many books about peacekeeping.

Among them all, *Blue Helmet* stands out to me. It is one of the rare accounts of modern peacekeeping in which the author writes from his personal experience, nothing more and nothing less. This book does not follow the traditional academic format; rather, it is a memoir that describes a human journey, revealing events as they unfolded. It reads as a spontaneous flow from his heart, and one that gives a refreshingly honest account. The author does not hesitate to criticize even his own country, the United States of America, for its failures to empathize with the suffering of South Sudan and to fund the programs that could mitigate it.

The South Sudanese people have endured one of the longest political and military struggles in modern history, characterized by the horrors of war, famine, and disease. When the latest peace treaty was signed in 2018, it was a cause for hope, but since that time, thousands of innocent civilians have been massacred by their armed countrymen and their own government. Why is this happening? What can be done about it? Those are the questions for which *Blue Helmet*'s author provides uncomfortable answers.

Edward Carpenter is a retired Marine officer who served with the United Nations Mission in South Sudan (UNMISS) and sought to rectify its deplorable status as not only the largest and most expensive peacekeeping mission in the world but also the one least likely to act forcefully to protect civilians.

His account dispels the commonly held myth that peacekeepers, as individuals and tactical units, shy away from using force to protect civilians either due to national caveats or because they fear taking fatal casualties in confrontations with armed groups. Instead, he shows that it is risk-averse senior mission leaders, operating without oversight, who are responsible for the current crisis in UN peace operations. The main thrust of *Blue Helmet* is that UNMISS can and should do much more to protect civilians than it has between 2012 and 2024. If it does not, I am afraid it may suffer the same fate as similar missions in Mali and the Democratic Republic of the Congo that were asked to leave after failing to protect civilians in accordance with their mandates.

Blue Helmet is a must-read for peacekeepers and policymakers, for academics seeking primary source material, and for all those who are keen to make a virtual journey to a country few would otherwise get to see. It is a book sure to elicit strong emotional reactions by portraying peacekeeping at its best and worst, by calling out prejudice and profiteering, and by giving candid recommendations for what individuals and their political institutions must do to reform UN peacekeeping and make good on organization's determination to save succeeding generations from the scourge of war.

Maj. Gen. (Ret.) (Dr.) A. K. Bardalai
Former peacekeeper

Preface

For the dead, this book surely comes too late. The United Nations has repeatedly failed to prevent violence in countries where it had active missions, even when the warning signs were there—in Rwanda, in Bosnia, and in South Sudan on multiple occasions since 2011. But for the living, I believe there might still be time—time to reunite abducted women and children with their families, time to break the cycles of violence in South Sudan.

For the civilians and humanitarians who will come under threat in future conflict zones and look to peacekeepers to protect them, there is still time—but only if we make fundamental reforms in how and where we deploy our missions, how we equip and organize them to best protect the most vulnerable, and how we hold senior leaders accountable if they fail to protect civilians from death, torture, sexual violence, and abduction at the hands of armed men.

Blue Helmet: My Year as a UN Peacekeeper in South Sudan is about good intentions, broken systems, and the people working to make a difference in the lives of others during the founding of a nation. It is my personal account of a year that encompassed the best and worst moments in a career that has spanned three decades, two wars, and five continents. It seeks to answer important questions: Why is it so important that we get peacekeeping right? What does it look like when we get it wrong? And what must we do better?

I wrote this book because I felt a responsibility to say what others could not. As a retired officer, I can speak more freely than many of my colleagues in the UN who continue to serve. The diverse agencies of the UN have done a great deal of good in conflict zones, but they have also done harm—sometimes through their actions but more often by their failures to act.

Abbreviations

APC	armored personnel carrier
ATV	all terrain vehicle
AU	African Union
C2	command and control; refers to the organizational practice that guides the employment of forces in support of objectives
CAR	Central African Republic
CDF	chief of defense forces
CIMIC	civil military coordination
COA	course of action
CTSAMVM	Ceasefire and Transitional Security Arrangements Monitoring and Verification Mechanism
DDR	disarmament, demobilization, and reintegration
DRC	Democratic Republic of the Congo
ECAC	evasion and conduct after capture
ENDEX	end of exercise
EU	European Union
FAO	UN Food and Agriculture Organization
FHQ	force headquarters
HOFO	head of field office, the senior UNMISS civilian in a region
HRD	Human Rights Division
ICRC	International Committee of the Red Cross
IDP(s)	internally displaced person(s)
IED	improvised explosive device

IGAD Intergovernmental Authority on Development, an eight-nation bloc in East Africa consisting of Djibouti, Ethiopia, Somalia, Eritrea, Sudan, South Sudan, Kenya, and Uganda

JMAC Joint Mission Analysis Center

JMCC Joint Military Ceasefire Commission

JTSC Joint Transitional Security Committee

MSF Médecins Sans Frontières, also known as "Doctors Without Borders," an independent humanitarian organisation that delivers emergency medical aid to people around the world who are affected by armed conflict, epidemics, natural disasters, and exclusion from healthcare

NGO nongovernmental organization

NPTC National Pre-Transitional Committee

NSS National Security Service

NUF Necessary Unified Forces

OCHA UN Office for the Coordination of Humanitarian Affairs

OHCHR UN Office of the High Commissioner for Human Rights

POC protection of civilians

PTSD post-traumatic stress disorder

QIP quick impact project

R&R rest and recuperation, a means by which some UN staff members can take time away from their duty station and get a break from the stresses of the conditions under which they serve without being charged annual leave

RJMEC Reconstituted Joint Monitoring and Evaluation Commission

SOI sharing of information

SPLA Sudan People's Liberation Army

SPLA-iO Sudan People's Liberation Army-in-Opposition

SRSG special representative of the secretary-general

SSPDF South Sudan People's Defense Forces

SSR   security sector reform

SUV   sport utility vehicle

U5   Policy and Plans Branch

UAV   unmanned aerial vehicle

UN   United Nations

UNISFA   United Nations Interim Security Force for Abyei

UNMISS   United Nations Mission in South Sudan

UNPOL   United Nations Police

USMOG   U.S. Military Observer Group

VA   Department of Veterans Affairs

WFP   World Food Programme

WHO   World Health Organization

Military Ranks

Lt. Gen.   lieutenant general (three stars)

Maj. Gen.   major general (two stars)

Brig. Gen.   brigadier general (one star)

Col.   colonel

Lt. Col.   lieutenant colonel

Maj.   major

Capt.   captain

Sgt.   sergeant

BLUE HELMET

SOUTH SUDAN – JUNE 2019

SECURITY SITUATION

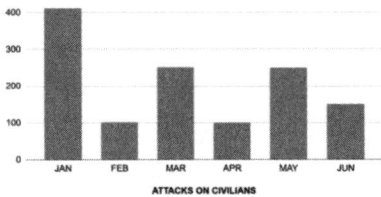

ATTACKS ON CIVILIANS

UN efforts to protect civilians had failed to prevent over 900 separate attacks, which were the cause of –

627 Killings – **123 Abductions** – **84 Cases of Conflict-Related**
15% of victims were children
Children were the most commonly abducted, followed by women.
Sexual Violence (CRSV)
5% of the victims were children

HUMANITARIAN SITUATION

7.2M PEOPLE IN NEED

→1.83M INTERNALLY DISPLACED PERSONS (IDPs)

184K IDPs IN "PROTECTION OF CIVILIANS" SITES

6.96M SEVERELY "FOOD INSECURE" *

597K MALNOURISHED WOMEN

860K MALNOURISHED CHILDREN

2019 HUMANITARIAN RESPONSE PLAN
Funding Required – $1.5B USD
Funding Provided at Mid-Year - $345M

BARELY 23% FUNDED

* These figures included 21,000 civilians who were suffering in what the World Food Program deemed 'famine' conditions – people dying from starvation and disease due to "a complete lack of access to food and other basic needs."

1. South Sudan's human security situation, June 2019. Created by author based on United Nations map data, information from OCHA/ReliefWeb, and public domain statistics from the UNMISS Human Rights Division and the World Food Programme.

PART 1

The Call to Adventure

1   The Worst Day

Only the dead have seen the end of war.

—GEORGE SANTAYANA

10 April 2019. Our mission—to visit a government official at his country estate to gain insight into human rights violations reported in the area—was fairly routine. Traveling in a pair of white sport utility vehicles (SUVs) with a local doctor as our liaison and wearing the traditional blue helmets of United Nations (UN) peacekeepers, we passed through the first several checkpoints with ease. These roadblocks were a ubiquitous sight in this war-ravaged nation. They were usually manned by police or soldiers in and around the capital, but out here in the countryside, the guards wore the mismatched uniforms characteristic of the local militia. We weren't hassled for bribes, but once we were asked for food. "*As'eef,*" I said in my poorly accented Juba Arabic.[1] *Sorry.* The man shrugged and waved us on.

As we approached the turnoff for the official's residence—a big house set in a wooded area about a quarter mile off the main road—we passed through a checkpoint that was unmanned. The circumstance was odd enough that I halted our little convoy and called our headquarters for guidance, which was—unsurprisingly—to continue our mission. As we turned onto the narrow dirt road leading into the wooded area surrounding the house, my mind was already moving ahead. *Would our contact have the information we needed? How would his armed guards react to a half dozen blue helmets walking up to the door? Would he c—*

The improvised explosive device (IED) exploded to our left, shearing the front axle and slamming our vehicle to a halt. Even though my ears were still ringing from the blast, I could hear bullets hitting the right side of the SUV. I shouted, "Bail out left!"

If it hadn't been for the lessons drilled into me in our pre-deployment training, I would have followed my instincts and made my exit in the opposite direction—away from the blast, the fire, and the smoke. Going left was a dice roll, but it was still a better choice because the vehicle gave us a little more protection from the incoming rifle fire.

A quick count of the team confirmed my four peacekeepers were up—alive, uninjured, and returning fire. Our helmets and body armor had done their jobs. The doctor was not so lucky; his body had been thrown clear of the vehicle and lay a few feet away, his left leg partially severed. Blood was soaking his shirt from some upper body trauma. I had no idea what exactly.

I shouted at the team to lay down covering fire, grabbed my buddy Mack, and sprinted toward the doctor. He was not a small man, and the weight of his unconscious body, slick with blood, defied our first attempt to lift him. Forced to settle for an undignified drag, we managed to get him back to the cover of the vehicle, where we put a tourniquet on his leg and strapped him to a stretcher made of flexible plastic that could be hauled across the ground.

Kneeling over our doctor-turned-patient, I also realized that we were outgunned and running low on ammunition. I had already handed both of my extra magazines to the other peacekeepers who were still returning fire. This wasn't supposed to be happening. We were here as observers, and most of our colleagues traveled unarmed. We Americans, Canadians, Australians, and Germans were the only ones who carried weapons, which were nothing more threatening than pistols.

Bullets continued to hum through the air above us and smack into the side of our vehicle as we crouched behind it in a slick mixture of blood and sweat. We had to get to a more defensible position and quickly. Frantically scanning for an escape, I glimpsed a house on the other side of the road we'd just left. Shouting an order to pull back, I drew my pistol and led the way at a sprint. Mack and Danny followed, dragging the doctor on the stretcher, and behind them—still firing their pistols toward the muzzle flashes in the trees—came Christopher and Emm.

We made it to the building, cleared and occupied a room, and treated the doctor. We applied a chest seal to plug the wound in his right side; performed an essential, albeit gruesome needle decompression to allow his collapsed lung to expand; and ran a nasopharyngeal airway down his nose and into his throat to help him breathe easier. I had just called for the quick reaction force and a medevac helicopter when I heard our instructors shouting, "ENDEX! ENDEX! ENDEX!" The exercise was over. This "worst day" was just to prepare us for the real thing.

* *

Well, it wasn't *quite* over. Although we had done many things right, our colonel thought we needed to run through the scenario again. And again. Military training was often repetitive. Even once we had a general idea of what was about to happen, the stress and unpredictability meant that every iteration was different. Someone's gun jammed, someone twisted an ankle, someone got hit by simulated (sim) munitions and had to be treated as a casualty. And of course, as we got increasingly tired and frustrated, the same exact exercise became even harder.

"How long do you think you guys were in the kill zone?" asked one of our instructors, a tall, ex–special forces medic who went by the call sign "Clocktower."

I looked at the team. "A couple of minutes, tops," I replied, as they nodded in agreement.

"Check this out," Clocktower said, and we huddled around his cell phone. We watched the simulated IED blast and saw our vehicle swerve to a stop. Thirty seconds. Watched ourselves bail out, start to return fire, sprint to the casualty. A minute ticked by. Mack and I wrestled with the heavy "body." We dragged it toward the vehicle. Struggled to get a tourniquet on its leg. Strapped the dummy to the stretcher. Three minutes. Four. At last, we started to move toward the buildings, away from the gunfight. It had taken five long minutes.

Clocktower shook his head. "Five minutes, bro. What the fuck were you thinking?"

* *

We finally performed the culminating exercise to the satisfaction of the senior evaluator and headed back to our ready room to shed our gear and clean the paint and powder residue from the sim munitions that we had fired in training. The next time we loaded our magazines it would be with live rounds.

Today's worst day was over, but it was not the only one we experienced in our month of training prior to deployment. We were treated to simulated mortar attacks, hostage situations, and a staff exercise where a stable, peaceful country began to melt into chaos due to the twin threats of a spreading cholera epidemic and fighting between government and opposition forces. All these exercises were intended to ensure that we were mentally and physically conditioned to survive and lead through the worst things that might potentially happen on our assignments as UN peacekeepers.

This training was conducted by the U.S. Military Observer Group (USMOG), an organization that traced its history to the early days of UN peacekeeping. Lt. Col. Chris Matherne, the director of operations for USMOG, addressed us all during our first day of training in a classroom on the seventh floor of the Taylor Building in Arlington, Virginia. "You're going to go out and do great work—maybe even earn some medals," he said. "But a year or two from now, I don't want to remember any of you. Because there's only one officer that we remember at USMOG, and that officer is Colonel William Higgins."

                    ∗ ∗

Col. William "Rich" Higgins was a rising star in the Marine Corps in 1987 when he was selected to serve in Lebanon as the senior military observer for the United Nations Truce Supervision Organization, one of the UN's oldest peacekeeping missions.

As he was driving alone on the coastal highway between Tyre and Naqoura in southern Lebanon, his vehicle was stopped at a checkpoint, and members of the Islamist militant group Hezbollah kidnapped him. Higgins remained in captivity for over a year—interrogated, tortured—and his captors eventually executed him. As a result of this tragedy, USMOG was created to ensure that American officers bound for peacekeeping assignments received special training prior to their departure and that their whereabouts were tracked while they carried out their assignments.

Our three weeks of training—"book work" in Arlington, an urban survival and escape practicum, and this "high-risk operator" course—together with our updated equipment, were intended to prevent any of us from ending up like Colonel Higgins.

                    ∗ ∗

The USMOG commanding officer, Col. Allen J. Pepper, spoke briefly before our classes started in earnest. He warned us to expect a very different level of organization and a slower pace of progress than we might be used to. He also suggested that we should all invoke the "Serenity Prayer" and ask for the courage to change the things we could, the serenity to accept the things we couldn't, and the wisdom to know the difference.

He also reminded us that going forward, we would be ambassadors for our country. While the United States put a lot of money into supporting the un's peacekeeping efforts, it contributed very few military personnel.[2] We would be a distinct minority in each of our missions and often the only member of the U.S. military that any of our peers might ever meet. As such, our colleagues would judge the U.S. military—and Americans in general— based on what they saw of us, and so would the people of our host nations.

In the big peacekeeping missions, military forces made up the greatest number of un staff. Its 110,000 soldiers were supported by hundreds of aircraft and thousands of ground vehicles, all of them painted in the universally recognizable color scheme of plain white with "un" stenciled on them in large black letters. Out of all those familiar blue helmets that one often saw in the media, there were exactly thirty-eight American officers, eight of whom were U.S. Marines. So how did I, out of the all the eighteen thousand officers in the Marine Corps, end up here—just days away from departing for the world's newest and most dangerous nation?[3]

2 Origin Story

I have an idea that some men are born out of their due place. . . .
They are strangers in their birthplace. . . . Perhaps it is this sense of
strangeness that sends men far and wide in the search for something
permanent, to which they may attach themselves . . . urges the wanderer
back to lands which his ancestors left in the dim beginnings of history.
—SOMERSET MAUGHAM

1 August 2018. When I first joined the Marine Corps, my goal was to become
a fighter pilot. After completing the six-month program of infantry training
that every Marine officer starts their career with, I spent six months in San
Diego working as the ground safety officer for a fighter squadron while I
waited for my spot in flight school to open. My time in the squadron reinforced my conviction that the fighter pilot's lifestyle was what I wanted. A
backseat ride in an F/A-18D fighter jet was exhilarating. Picking up the pieces
from a squadron-mate's crash landing in the Arizona desert was sobering,
but it didn't change my mind about my chosen profession. Military aviation
was inherently dangerous, but it was also a family tradition.

As life often goes, my dream job was not the one I'd end up in. My
instructors didn't think my landings were up to par. I argued that I'd never
made a landing I couldn't walk away from but to no avail. I was reclassified
as an aviation supply officer, and it would take a while to discover what a
blessing in disguise that had been.

In the eighteen years that followed, I'd spend as much time abroad as I
had in the United States. I served in Operation Iraqi Freedom and Operation
Enduring Freedom; spent years in Saudi Arabia, Japan, and Indonesia; rose to
the rank of lieutenant colonel; and ultimately commanded my own aviation
logistics squadron. On paper, I appeared to be a model officer—with high
marks on all my performance evaluations; a serious, square-jawed appearance
in my official photos; and a long list of specialized qualifications—but I'd

always felt something had set me apart from my peers. Although I'd served in two wars, I was morally opposed to the institution of warfare, especially as it was practiced in the modern age.

I had been homeschooled by a hero-turned-hippie. My father had piloted U.S. Army Air Corps c-47 transport planes over the Himalayas—"The Hump"—from India to China during World War II. Then he gave up on the capitalist system in general and the military-industrial complex in particular to raise a dozen kids, most of us growing up on a secluded eight-hundred-acre tract of forests and pastures in the Ozark mountains of northwestern Arkansas.

I became an avid reader at an early age. The limited space in the tumbledown two-bedroom shack where I spent my early years was largely filled with shelves of books, which made up in part for the lack of indoor plumbing and toys. One of the volumes that would strongly influence my young psyche was T. H. White's *The Once and Future King*.

It was a riveting adaptation of *Le Morte d'Arthur*, and one philosophical element stood out to me. White's version of the legendary king had all the advantages that had allowed real-world nobles to plant their iron-shod boots on the firmament of history, trampling nameless millions into the dust in their quest for land, wealth, fame, and occasionally the glory of whatever gods they claimed to worship. But White's king used his power and privilege to defend and help the weak, not to bend them to his will. The idea of "might for right" instead of "might makes right" resonated with me, as did one of my father's favorite sayings, "Service before self."[1]

Military service was in my blood. In my mind, I imagined it to encompass virtuous ideals of fighting not only the good fight but also the fair fight, of saving the lives of the innocent, and of bringing freedom to the oppressed. I was young—just seventeen years old—and very naive when I enlisted in the U.S. Army on the day that Operation Desert Shield began in 1990.

I wanted to help liberate the innocent and unprepared citizens of Kuwait from the grip of their Iraqi conquerors despite the grim assessments that U.S. casualties would be high, but the war ended before my two-month stint in boot camp did. I went on to advanced training, learned to repair helicopters, and spent the next few years going to college and working as a crew chief on old uh-1 "Huey" helicopters for the New Mexico Army National Guard on the weekends.

Those vintage aircraft had been the standard in Vietnam, and many of the pilots in my unit were veterans of that war. I enjoyed riding along in the crew chief's seat in the rear of the helicopter—manning the door guns, loading stretchers, and handling the preflight and postflight maintenance— but I aspired to be a pilot like my father.

Only one branch of the military had offered a direct and guaranteed path to flight school—the Marine Corps. Or at least that's what the recruiting officer said. The path wasn't direct, and it wasn't easy, but that was how I had ended up in the Marines during one of the most peaceful interludes in its history. That period of relative calm ended abruptly on 11 September 2001, and I would go on to serve in both theaters of America's long wars in Iraq and Afghanistan.

I contemplated getting out of the Marines when my minimum service requirement was up. I was a young captain, serving in Japan at the time, and I knew that with my degree in engineering and experience in logistics, I could make a lot more money in the "real world." I'd also seen enough to know that the U.S. military was falling far short of fulfilling the vision of T. H. White's fictional king.

But I had come to believe there was a need for people like me to try to change the system from the inside. The U.S. military didn't always use its might for right, but as an insider, I would be in a position to attempt to change this—however minutely. Also, regardless of whether I was able to effect much difference in the military, it would improve my credentials to advocate for changes once I rejoined the civilian world. Political hawks easily dismissed as "bleeding-heart liberals" those who approached issues of political, military, and social reform from a background of academia or humanitarian work, but I thought they would find it much more difficult to use that approach to sideline a retired military officer.[2]

That said, idealism was not the only force that drove me. As did many young American men who came from poor, rural backgrounds, I knew that the military represented one of the few ways to break out of the class into which I had been born. There was still truth in the observation of the Enlightenment-era writer Samuel Johnson that military officers were "much more respected than any other man who has as little money." The U.S. military asked a lot of its young officers, but the institution also had a great deal to offer in return: leadership experience and opportunities to travel, to learn, and to teach. It also gave me some more intangible benefits.

My childhood had ended early, as my mother had died in a car accident when I was eight years old. While I believe my father and stepmother did love us children, their relationship had its own challenges, and my formative years were characterized by significant levels of physical abuse and neglect. With seven younger siblings to care for, I changed a lot of diapers and cooked a lot of meals.

I began working in the food service industry at fourteen and discovered that while my insular homeschooling may have made me book smart, it had left my social skills with much to be desired. I also was acutely conscious of my family's poverty, especially in the status symbol–loving society of America, where the media and marketers drummed out a constant message that self-worth and social position were measured in brands of clothes and cars and beer.

The military had helped me escape that mindset when we were given our clothes, which all looked identical. For the first time I ate well and trained a great deal—all new experiences for a skinny kid who'd never played team sports. Military service forced me out of my tendency to introversion and gave me a framework to make friends; changing duty stations every few years also gave me the perfect out for my noncommittal tendencies. I never had to settle down—not with a partner and not with a job—and I could and did work as a supply officer, a tactics adviser, a foreign area officer, a military professor, and a fellow in a strategic think tank.

* *

My ultimate goal had been to attain the position of a squadron commander— the role where, in my opinion, a Marine officer could do the greatest good for the most Marines and have the best chance of influencing the institution. I accomplished that milestone in 2016 and spent the next two years leading 575 Marines of Marine Aviation Logistics Squadron 26. Rather than retiring after my command tour, I then chose to stay and serve in one more uniquely challenging and influential role—that of a Marine attaché.

Attaché officers serve in U.S. embassies around the world both as the military advisers to America's ambassadors and as the eyes and ears of the Marine Corps Intelligence Activity. I had been selected to serve as an attaché in Indonesia, but an intermediary assignment at the Pentagon opened my eyes to the toxic work conditions in the upper echelons of the Department of Defense. That experience convinced me that spending another three years in uniform was not what I wanted to do with my life, so I looked for a final overseas assignment, preferably a short tour of only a year.

Such postings were hard to come by for Marines, and most were in Asia, where I'd already spent over a quarter of my career. While I had always been drawn to Europe and Africa, both were largely the domain of the U.S. Army, so I'd never had a chance to serve in either region. *Now*, I thought, *I might know someone who could make it happen.*

* *

A few months earlier, during the administrative in-processing that accompanies any move to a new duty station in the Marine Corps, I'd met a fellow Marine officer, Maj. Ania "Koz" Driscoll, who had also just arrived in Washington. As we chatted about where we'd be working, Koz told me that she would be the Marine liaison for USMOG and that based on my background and interests, she thought I'd make a great peacekeeper. I told her that I was slated for service as an attaché, but she'd handed me her card anyway. "Call me if the situation changes," she'd said, and now it had.

Koz was still looking for a lieutenant colonel to serve as the senior U.S. officer in the United Nations Mission in South Sudan (UNMISS), and it sounded like my kind of assignment—overseas and in the field. A final tour as a peacekeeper would definitely check a block for "new experiences," and perhaps in South Sudan I could make up for the damage that I'd helped do in Iraq and Afghanistan.

Afterward I could retire with my honor redeemed, with my horizons broadened, and with dust on my boots. I could leave the military with greater credentials to advocate for positive change in the world. What better way to end my career as a Marine officer?

3   Big Men, Strong Women

The power of the proverbial African big man depends on his ability
to feed his followers; his girth advertises the wealth he has to share.
—DEBORAH SCROGGINS

21 November 2018. It was something of a trope that Americans in general
knew little about the world's second-largest land mass, often referring to its
many countries as though they were one big nation—"Africa"—and thinking
of its people as a homogenous group, "Africans," defined in large part by
the color of their skin. There wasn't much to excuse this lack of awareness
regarding the continent overall, but for South Sudan, the ignorance was a
perhaps a bit more understandable. The landlocked nation was rarely visited
even by the most adventurous tourists, but I was luckier to know a little
more about both the country and the continent than many Americans did.

I had visited Africa twice before—spending time in Ghana, Namibia,
Botswana, and Zimbabwe—and had studied the security situation in South
Sudan as part of my coursework at the U.S. Air Force's Air War College a
few years earlier. But I hadn't really heard much about the country since
then—no news reports or magazine articles, no tweets or Facebook posts.
When I'd used it as a case study on implementing a notional U.S. "whole-
of-government engagement strategy" in 2015, South Sudan had just been
emerging from a civil war. Now as I began to research the nature of my
new assignment, I quickly discovered that peace had not lasted very long
and that politics was still very personal in South Sudan.

One thing that set South Sudan apart from its neighbors was its lack of
a visionary leader. As I started my training, the most influential leaders
in East Africa—Uganda's Yoweri Museveni, Rwanda's Paul Kagame, and
Kenya's Uhura Kenyatta—all headed political organizations that were (at
best) weak democracies and (at worst) benevolent dictatorships, but all
three men had long nourished and pursued distinctive visions for their

nations. Unsurprisingly, these men and their inner circles had profited greatly in the process, but they had brought their countries forward into the twenty-first century, nurturing tourism, education, infrastructure, and medicine. Unfortunately for South Sudan, its own visionary leader, John Garang, had been killed in a plane crash on 30 July 2005, just three weeks after cementing the deal that would lead to his country's gaining its independence from Sudan.[1]

Since that time, a diverse cast of characters had attempted to fill the power vacuum. Salva Kiir Mayardit had been called "the good soldier," but he was never meant to be a president. Throughout the long wars for South Sudan's independence, he had been Garang's right-hand man, unswerving in his loyalty and quick to carry out orders. Kiir was a reliable military general, but he lacked Garang's vision and sense of a destiny for the country. One South Sudanese journalist, Daniel Akech Thiong, called him "the pawn who became a king." But Kiir was Garang's appointed successor and had held on to the top political job in South Sudan since the country's formation despite repeated challenges from political and military opponents, chief among them being Dr. Riek Machar Teny.

Machar—whose followers often call "Dr. Riek"—was the twenty-sixth son of a village chief, and his name in the Nuer language was synonymous with "trouble." Some thought his name was prophetic. A heavy-set man, with a gap in his teeth and a lazy eye, he had been leading opposition forces in South Sudan, one way or another, for nearly thirty years. He had fought first for, then against, and then again for John Garang; likewise, he had served Salva Kiir as vice president and had then gone to war against him—twice.

Machar's first wife, Angelina Teny, was sophisticated, intelligent, fluent in Arabic and English, and had spent years abroad, living in the United Kingdom and obtaining her master of business administration degree from Oxford. By blood, she was linked to several of her political allies and to some of her opponents. In a time and place where many women's roles were defined by their husbands, Teny had become a power in her own right, and since 2015 she had served as the minister of defense for the opposition.

"Madam Angelina" was not the only woman to hold such senior roles. John Garang's wife, Rebecca Nyandeng, had been a member of the same rebel army that her husband led to help gain South Sudan's independence. "Mama Rebecca" was known to be hard on her female troops but was well respected. An outspoken advocate for the rights of women in general, she stood up for female veterans in particular. Like Machar, she had been accused by President Kiir of fomenting a coup, but rather than resort to violence, Nyandeng used soft power from afar, working for years from exile in neighboring Kenya to achieve peace through political means.

While they were some of the biggest players, they were not the only ones. One particularly dedicated individual in South Sudan occasionally sent out an unofficial visual guide that listed the current movers and shakers in South Sudanese politics and military affairs, and he updated it whenever the power dynamics shifted. At the time I started my training, it contained dozens of political parties, some with a single notable member, some with many more.

All these 131 people had been united—more or less—by their fight for independence, but since it had been achieved, their struggles had been against each other. As I was headed to South Sudan in part to help create the conditions for their peaceful reunification, it made intuitive sense to me that I should learn about them even though nothing in our training curriculum required me to do so.

The great historical strategist Sun Tzu had observed that a leader who understood all sides in a conflict, including his or her own, would have nothing to fear from the result of a hundred battles. More through luck and personal interest than by design, my understanding of South Sudan's major political and military actors extended beyond the limited information found in USMOG's standard training materials. But I didn't know anything about the personalities on my own side. Had I been as familiar with the careers of my senior UN leaders as I was with those of their South Sudanese counterparts, I might have been better prepared for what lay ahead. Unfortunately, it was not something that USMOG had a plan to teach us, and it was not something I thought to research for myself.

4 A Short History of South Sudan

What is known as the Southern Sudan today has
no history before AD 1821.

—A. J. ARKELL, BRITISH ARCHAEOLOGIST

15 February 2019. As a prolific reader and an occasional writer, I had learned
that the setting of a story may often be imbued with as much character as the
protagonists themselves. There were places in the world where the geography
and the weather were simply a backdrop and where history was something
too distant to be much considered in daily life. Other locales featured factors
that could be dangerous and even deadly. Deserts and jungles were just such
naturally occurring antagonists, while cities in the grip of war or under the
sway of criminal elements were their man-made equivalents. As I studied
the material that USMOG provided on South Sudan, I noted that the country
seemed to possess a combination of hazards both elemental and human that
had the potential to make it a doubly dangerous character in this chapter
of my life.

The area was subject to the monsoon cycle—hot, wet summers and hot,
dry winters—and was cursed by mosquitoes bearing malaria and by tsetse
flies carrying sleeping sickness. But it was also blessed over most of its
expanse with rich soil well suited for agriculture. In many places, that soil
was also rich in oil, gold, and other valuable deposits—resources that had
proved a curse for its current inhabitants.

But sadly, outsiders had long considered South Sudan's most valuable
commodity to be its human capital. Slave traders from the north had raided
the region since the Bronze Age, taking men, women, and children to sell to
the empires of Egypt, Greece, Rome, and India, as well as to the Ottomans
and the Mamluks, the French, and, yes, the Americans. Along with slaves,
the traders also took ivory, cattle, and gum Arabic, along with wild beasts
for menageries and fighting pits. But mostly, they took human beings. Pre-

dominantly their captives were the tall, Nilotic people of the Nuer, the Dinka, and the Shilluk tribes that inhabited the regions that were most accessible to raiders traveling the Nile on boats or crossing the Sahara on camels. The ancient kingdoms of Meroe, Napata, and Kush were some of the Sudanese realms that had prospered from the lucrative slave trade between Egypt and sub-Saharan Africa. With the rise of Islam and its spread in North Africa in the seventh century AD, Arabs came to predominate the slave traders, and their customers spread beyond Egypt and the Indian Ocean to Morocco and the kingdoms of Arabia.

South Sudan was a borderland, a place at the far edge of the empires, where the desert gave way first to savannas and then to jungle, and where Islam met and mixed with animist and Christian faiths. In this region, Arab peoples and culture bumped up against those of "black Africa"—that is, the nomadic pastoralist tribes of the Dinka, the Nuer, the Murle, and the Shilluk people, and the many smaller, more agrarian groups that populated the Equatorias. The latter groups had their own royal legacies such as the kingdom of the Azande, which had lasted until the colonial era.

Contrary to the opinions of ethnocentric Englishmen, South Sudan had a long history, which had been characterized by centuries of exploitation, first by Egyptian and Arab slavers and then by British colonial administrators. From the time of the pharaohs, Egypt had exercised varying degrees of influence over the region, and in 1820 the Egyptian ruler Muhammad Ali Pasha established dominion over it for the purpose of obtaining ivory and slaves. When the opening of the Suez Canal in 1869 attracted the attention of the Great Powers, Britain entered into a condominium with Egypt to administer the region under Anglo-Egyptian rule. Formally, a governor-general appointed by Egypt with British consent ruled the territory, but in practice, it became another British imperial possession, where the English practiced their usual policy of divide and rule.

By 1924 the country was functionally divided into a pair of separate territories—the Muslim, Arabic-speaking north and the African south, where missionaries from around the world encouraged Christianity and English. Beyond bringing religion and taking resources, the British made little effort to develop the southern reaches of the Sudan when they occupied it from 1899 to 1956. They only laid one rail line and few roads. They made even less effort to foster diplomatic relations with the Nilotic tribes, and when the people rebelled against British attempts to impress them for labor, they were brutally subjugated, their long spears being no match for the colonials' machine guns and the newest development in warfare—aerial bombing.

* *

Thus, the British Empire wrote the first draft of the tragedy that would play out repeatedly in South Sudan over the next 120 years. Its simple plot had terrible outcomes for its cast of millions. There was always a government force that ruled from stronghold cities, exploiting the resources while the majority of people lived in poverty. Opposition forces rose in the countryside, supported by outsiders with their own agendas. The government forces dropped bombs, burned villages, and forced the common people from their homes. The opposition moved like mercury, slipping this way and that, never definitively pinned down. Eventually those forces became the government and took their turn to exploit the land and its people, and when others rebelled against them, those rebels-turned-governments also took their turn to bomb and burn. The British did this as did the northerners from Khartoum. When the Sudan People's Liberation Movement (SPLM) came to power, it pursued the same strategies from the same places against the same people. Once it might have been fairly said that only the names changed in this tragedy, but the pace of history had so accelerated that for forty years, even the names stayed the same, and only their roles in the bloody drama differed. In 1993 Salva Kiir was the chief of staff for the Sudan People's Liberation Army (SPLA), dodging bombs dropped by the Sudanese Air Force. In 2013 it was Kiir who directed bombing runs against his fellow southerners in Bor and who ordered Equatorian villages burned in 2017.

* *

The British Empire had taken gold, timber, and ivory from South Sudan over its six decades of occupation. When the United Kingdom formally relinquished its hold on the region in 1956, it took South Sudanese autonomy as well, ceding control of the south not to the region's indigenous leaders but to the distant and disliked Arab administrators in Khartoum.

This sparked the first civil war between the Arab north and the African south; it lasted until 1972 when the Addis Ababa Agreement was signed, granting the south considerable autonomy and a share of the natural resources. Ten years of peace followed, but when oil was discovered in Southern Sudan, the Arab government in Khartoum attempted to redraw state boundaries so that the oil fields would fall under its control. When this strategy failed politically, it attempted to use force, sparking the second round of the civil war. In 1983 after the Sudanese government declared the Addis Ababa Agreement dissolved and attempted to Islamize the south, John Garang formed the SPLM and SPLA to oppose Arab rule. Two decades of war followed, and the twin specters of slavery and famine returned to the region.

In 2005 the SPLM and the Sudanese government signed the Nairobi Comprehensive Peace Agreement, a new peace treaty that granted autonomy to the south for a six-year trial period, after which the southern states were to hold a referendum on remaining united with the north or forming its own nation. The agreement called for a ceasefire, the sharing of oil revenues, and Islamic law remaining in effect in the north with the south being free to institute its own laws. Under the agreement, John Garang, leader of the southern rebels, was to hold the office of vice president of Sudan until the referendum.

Garang, however, died in a helicopter crash just three weeks after taking that office, and his deputy, Salva Kiir, took his place. Six years passed peacefully, and the referendum held in 2011 yielded an unsurprising result: an overwhelming majority of southerners voted to break ties with the north and form an independent state. The Republic of South Sudan joined the United Nations as the world's 193rd sovereign state, with Salva Kiir as its first president.

Still, the coalition of rebel groups that had banded together in the fight for independence was fraught with conflicting tribal allegiances. Riek Machar, leader of one of the largest factions, was chosen to be vice president, but political tensions increased nonetheless. In 2012 Machar and others accused Kiir of having dictatorial ambitions—a charge that President Kiir seemed to confirm by dismissing Machar and the entire cabinet of ministers in 2013, claiming that they were planning a coup.

Fighting had broken out between forces loyal to both the president and the former vice president, and the country suffered through three bloody years of civil war. The UN Mission in South Sudan, which was originally intended to help the country manage its transition to sovereign status, pivoted to the tasks of trying to protect civilians from the fighting, to facilitate the distribution of humanitarian aid, and to reconcile the warring factions.

In 2015 a ceasefire was reached, and Riek Machar returned to the capital of Juba to again take up the mantle of vice president. But within a year, Juba was again rocked by gunfire as fighting broke out between the rival forces aligned with the country's two senior leaders. Machar fled Juba once more, and the civil war reignited. It continued until the signing of the latest peace deal in 2018 that called for a ceasefire, a unification of the armed forces, and the formation of a transitional government with Machar again serving as vice president.

That was the way things stood in 2019 as I began the training that would prepare me to serve as one of the peacekeepers tasked with helping to "create a durable peace" in a country that for over a century had gone without peace of any kind.

5 Africa Wants to Kill You

Do not travel to South Sudan due to crime and armed conflict.
Violent crime, such as carjackings, shootings, ambushes, assaults,
robberies, and kidnappings[,] is common throughout South
Sudan, including Juba. Armed conflict is ongoing throughout the
country and includes fighting between various political and ethnic
groups, and weapons are readily available to the population.

—U.S. STATE DEPARTMENT TRAVEL ADVISORY, JUNE 2018

10 March 2019. During our week of classroom work in Arlington, Lieutenant Colonel Matherne taught several modules himself, and a consistent
thread ran through his various presentations that was summarized in his
first words: "Africa wants to kill you." He listed some of the many ways that
could happen: The water and food might not be safe. There were five active
volcanoes in the Democratic Republic of the Congo (DRC).

Even the tiniest animals could prove deadly. "Mosquitos are the UAVs of
Africa," Matherne said, "delivering biological warfare agents as the vanguard
of the continent's attack on humanity." The class laughed nervously, and
Matherne smiled. "Seriously," he said, his smile vanishing, "if you feel like
you have the flu in Africa, you probably have malaria."

Insects were not the only disease vectors. Dogs often had rabies. Bats and
monkeys transmitted Ebola. And humans didn't just carry the obviously
deadly things such as guns and machetes; the UN's own staff, according to
Matherne, had a high rate of HIV infection. The numbers bore him out;
Africa *was* dangerous. Of the thirty U.S. embassies around the world that
were designated as "high risk" in 2019, half of them were located in Africa,
and twenty-nine peacekeepers had been killed in combat on the continent
in 2019. However, during the same period, disease had killed more of them,
with the UN estimating that one peacekeeper died every month from malaria
in its sub-Saharan missions.

Matherne concluded his briefings with the recommendation to look out not only for our own mental health but also for that of our comrades. "The most stressful part of being a UN peacekeeper in Africa," he warned, "is being a UN peacekeeper in Africa." I assumed Matherne knew what he was talking about since he had served with the UN's mission to Mali in 2015, but personally I had never seen the point of worrying about stress before I actually experienced it.

* *

A dozen of us were in the class. Several army and air force officers were headed to Mali and the Central African Republic (CAR), and one navy officer was deploying to the DRC. Two other Marines were deploying with me to South Sudan: Maj. Emmanuel Carper, who went by "Emm," and Maj. Christopher McAllister, who made it emphatically clear that he did *not* go by "Chris."

But despite the radically different operational environments and jobs to which each of us was headed, our training with USMOG was all the same, and it continued with an overview of the UN as a whole and with a deeper look at the organization of its Peace Operations and Operational Support Departments, both of which we would be dealing with in the year ahead. The UN had been sending its blue-helmeted troops to keep the peace since 1948, when it authorized its first mission to Palestine. Since that time, the UN had organized sixty missions to thirty countries, twelve of which were still active.

Six of those missions currently had American peacekeepers assigned to them, and four of those six were in Africa: Mali, the DRC, South Sudan, and the CAR. These "Big Four" multidimensional operations consumed 70 percent of the total budget for peacekeeping. Each of these missions faced unique challenges. The situation in Mali was characterized by a state of war between an Islamic insurgency and a weak central government supported by external military forces. Both the CAR and the DRC sat on trillions of dollars' worth of diamonds, oil, gold, and other minerals, but they had weak governments, had widespread corruption, and lacked the infrastructure to capitalize on their natural resources. They were also plagued by numerous local and foreign armed groups.

South Sudan, where I was headed, was quite different. While its central government was strong, often brutally so, it had significant opposition military forces, and a large part of the civilian population was armed. Although the country was enjoying a period of relative calm due to a ceasefire that had begun in September 2018, dozens of people still died violently every week in what were described somewhat dismissively as "cattle raids."

The Big Four missions often faced similar challenges but for different reasons. On the African continent, no UN forces were able to move freely and easily on the ground. Those in Mali faced the threat of IEDs and insurgent ambushes. In the CAR and the DRC, the road conditions were terrible, and bandits abounded. In South Sudan, the roads were as bad or worse, and UN vehicles were often stopped at government checkpoints and forbidden to pass because "it was too dangerous ahead," which generally meant that human rights were being violated in the area just past the checkpoint.

Despite their differences, the standard structure of all these missions was similar. The largest and most visible component of each mission was its military personnel, those ubiquitous blue-helmeted peacekeepers who made up around 80 percent of the total number of UN personnel working in peace operations. The peacekeepers deployed in battalions of two hundred to five hundred troops from a wide range of countries: India, Bangladesh, China, Rwanda, and Ethiopia, among others. They were colloquially referred to as "the force," and they worked in their assigned conflict zones to create security and stability under the guidance of a headquarters commanded by a high-ranking military officer, usually a general with previous experience in peacekeeping.

That general, in turn, worked for the mission's civilian leader, a senior diplomat appointed by the UN secretary-general who also held sway over the remaining 20 percent of the mission, including the UN Police (UNPOL) and the civilians who specialized in human rights, political affairs, development, and other fields relevant to the mission's mandate. While each of the Big Four had a unique mandate from the UN Security Council, all those mandates shared three common themes: protect civilians, promote human rights, and facilitate the delivery of humanitarian aid.

We were introduced to the challenges we would face in carrying out our mandates during a staff exercise in which we assumed our assigned roles in an imaginary UN mission. The exercise subjected us to rising pressures from a series of compounding crises, any one of which might have been challenging on its own. Fighting between government and militia forces, flooding, and a cholera outbreak were complicated by the vague and some-times contradictory information and orders we received from our civilian and military leaders, who were role-played by the USMOG staff. It seemed like overkill at the time, but in the months to come, I would learn how simple that exercise had been compared to what actually was in store for us.

6   The Land That *TIME* Forgot

> To tell the stories that matter most, to spark conversations that
> drive global change, and to provide context and understanding
> to the issues and events that define our times.
> —*TIME* MAGAZINE'S MISSION STATEMENT

15 March 2019. I was in the second week of training when I heard the first
reports that in Christchurch, New Zealand, a young man with assault weapons
had walked into first a mosque and then an Islamic center, and killed fifty-
one people. This horrifying act made headline news around the world. In
the month that followed, *TIME* magazine alone ran forty-four stories about
the tragedy; it was the cover story of its international edition on 1 April.
But in that same month, young men with assault weapons in South Sudan
had killed 182 people—including women and infants—in eight separate
attacks. The worst single massacre took the lives of eighty-eight people.
And in that whole period, *TIME* published nothing on these killings. Only
two articles referenced the country of South Sudan at all; both highlighted
that Anna Nimiriano, the editor of the *Juba Monitor,* was persevering in
spite of threats and censorship. To judge from what a person could read
or hear or see in the U.S. media, it felt as if the lives of civilians in South
Sudan didn't really matter.

* *

Meanwhile, the U.S. government felt our own lives mattered very much and
spared no expense to ensure that we knew how to preserve our lives in all
situations. Our most likely problem set as peacekeepers was getting isolated
in an urban area and either having to evade capture or, if we were caught,
resisting interrogation and hopefully engineering an escape.

Training for these unique skills was known as "evasion and conduct after
capture" (ECAC). As with *Fight Club*, the first rule of ECAC was "Don't talk
about ECAC." So I will not, besides noting that the training was incredi-

bly valuable. It taught me a great deal about the psychology of survival, particularly the importance both of controlling one's natural emotional responses to stressful and traumatic situations, and of being able to create a human connection with the "bad guys" holding the guns. That element of the course would prove a lifesaver before the year was out, though I had no way of knowing that at the time.

7   Through American Eyes

> The U.S. in particular appears to have abdicated its leading role in South
> Sudan diplomacy; outside of other Horn of Africa states, no country
> has stepped up to assume the mantle. The absence of diplomatic
> leadership is baffling. A more proactive posture is urgently needed.
> —INTERNATIONAL CRISIS GROUP REPORT, 13 MARCH 2019

21 March 2019. British journalist Peter Martel had noted that "the first time
the Stars and Stripes fluttered in South Sudan was in the 1860s, on the back
of a slave ship," and it marked the beginning of a long and sad entanglement
between the peoples of the two countries. As part of my preparations for
deployment, I had made a point to research the current U.S. policy on Africa
and had found—to my surprise and disappointment—that the official policy
of the Donald Trump administration for the entire continent was simply
the transcript of a speech that National Security Adviser John Bolton made
in December 2018.

"This strategy . . . ," said the mustachioed Bolton, "reflects the core tenets
of President Trump's foreign policy doctrine. . . . Under our new approach,
every decision we make, every policy we pursue, and every dollar of aid we
spend will further U.S. priorities in the region." It had been odd to hear him
say that "we understand that lasting stability, prosperity, independence, and
security on the African continent are in the national security interest of the
United States," and then find little in my further research to indicate that the
United States planned to support any of those things. The strategy would
focus instead, Bolton had said, on "three core US interests on the continent:

"First, advancing U.S. trade and commercial ties with nations across the
region to the benefit of both the United States and Africa. . . .

"Second, countering the threat from Radical Islamic Terrorism and violent conflict. . . .

"And third, . . . [to] ensure that U.S. taxpayer dollars for aid are used efficiently and effectively." Pointedly, Bolton had stated, "We will no longer support unproductive, unsuccessful, and unaccountable U.N. peacekeeping missions. We want something more to show for Americans' hard-earned taxpayer dollars."

Quite a few of those dollars had gone where I was headed. "In South Sudan," Bolton said, "an ongoing civil war has ravaged a young nation, displaced millions, and led to the deaths of hundreds of thousands of people. . . . Between 2014 and 2018, the United States provided approximately $3.76 billion in humanitarian aid to South Sudan and refugees in neighboring countries."[1] But his reference to the state of the civil war hinted that maybe American policymakers hadn't really been paying that much attention to South Sudan, where the peace treaty ending the war had been signed three months before Bolton made his speech.

With national-level policy guidance seeming so vague, I was happy that our pre-deployment training included a panel at the Pentagon with senior leaders from several organizations focused on peacekeeping: Maj. Gen. Hugh Van Roosen, the UN deputy military adviser; Joseph Manso from the State Department; and Patrick Antonietti, the director of stabilization and peace operations in the Office of the Secretary of Defense.

Van Roosen noted that the UN fielded the largest deployed military force in the world—eighty thousand soldiers—and that in terms of U.S. national interests, this meant "there are twenty-two places in the world where we don't have to send US troops."[2] Pat Antonietti built on that point. "The military creates the space for a political solution," he said, "and from a cost perspective, a U.S. brigade deployed to Africa would cost eight times what a UN brigade does." He described our upcoming deployments as "an opportunity to be a part of history" and added that UN peacekeeping operations were a key tool for policymakers.

Joseph Manso agreed. "You cannot overstate the importance of peacekeepers," he said. "We want to make peacekeeping better because it is an incredibly valuable tool."

The panelists encouraged us to write and share our experiences and to engage through the team at USMOG if we ran into any problems. Along with my fellow peacekeepers, I nodded my affirmation before we adjourned for coffee.

* *

My only problem at the time was one that the USMOG staff was already working on: with less than two weeks remaining until my deployment date, I still hadn't received the official visa from South Sudan that would allow me to enter the country. I was assured that it would arrive any day now. Meanwhile, I was going to have plenty of other things to worry about as the final and most rigorous week of our pre-deployment training was about to kick off.

8   Shoot, Move, and Resuscitate

Amateurs do it till they get it right; professionals
do it till they can't get it wrong.

—LUKE DOAK, O'GARA INSTRUCTOR

3 April 2019. In the Marine Corps, we summed up the fundamentals of tactical operations with three simple principles: you had to shoot, move, and communicate. But as UN peacekeepers, the first person to render trauma care would often be yourself, and you might have to treat another person as well. So shoot, move, and *resuscitate* was the order of the day.

We learned that 28 percent of combat deaths are preventable and that most result from three things: bleeding out, a blocked airway, or pressure in the chest cavity. Ninety percent of those preventable deaths occur before the victim can be transported to a hospital, so it was critical that we learned how to help ourselves and our fellow peacekeepers.

Tourniquets are the key to preventing blood loss. Properly used, they could save lives 67 percent of the time, but most people don't know the basics of how to use them.

After arterial bleeds, blocked airways and collapsed lungs are the leading killers, so we practiced threading nasopharyngeal airways—that is, running green rubber tubes first into the nostrils of a training dummy and then into the noses and down the throats of our fellow peacekeepers. And we rehearsed putting a deliberate hole into the chest cavity with a fourteen-gauge needle to decompress the area and allow the lungs to re-expand and do their job, but thankfully, we only had to do this on the training dummies. We practiced splinting, triage, moving injured people, and a handful of other useful skills.

We also learned that the most important things to increase an injured person's chance of survival, once the bleeding stopped and the victim was breathing properly, were powerful painkillers and antibiotics. Shockingly, they were not part of the combat lifesaver bags that we would deploy with.

It turned out that the U.S. government trusted us with deadly weapons and ammunition but not with life-saving drugs. I made a mental note to visit a pharmacy once in-country and see if I could pick up some codeine and amoxicillin over the counter to augment our medical kits since someone's life might well depend on it.

I found the medical skills training challenging, although our instructor, a lanky ex-special forces medic, said it was just due to the pressure. "Tactical stuff is easy," he said. "Medical stuff is easy. Combine them and it gets hard."

Shooting felt easier to me in comparison. My shot groups were consistently tight and centered in the black center of the target. Throughout the course of the week, we put over a thousand rounds downrange, mostly using our pistols, but we also practiced with weapons that we might pick up in the middle of a fight, such as the ubiquitous AK-47.

The final phase of our training was driving, which was statistically the most dangerous thing anyone in the U.S. military did whether they were at home or deployed. There were tens of thousands of deaths due to vehicular accidents every year in the United States alone. Such accidents had killed as many U.S. military members over the years of the "Long Wars" as hostile fire had. Our driving instructors referred to driving a car as "riding the bullet" and said that we should think of roads as war zones. People could and did die there every day. I knew this to be true, having once had a woman die in my arms after being hit by a vehicle in which I was a passenger. My mother had also died in a car crash, and I'd already survived both a car wreck in a winter storm and a vehicle that flipped in the Saudi desert when the driver lost control. So I took every opportunity to improve my skills behind the wheel.

We practiced recovering from skids and ramming through checkpoints. We also learned to use our vehicles as weapons in maneuvers where we forced an aggressor's vehicle to spin out by pulling up alongside them, lining our bumper up just behind the other vehicle's rear tires, and then steering into them.

This training emphasized being able to drive fast, to drive safely, and to recover from bad situations, and it was all based on a simple tactical truth: "A rolled vehicle is a bad place to fight from." So we practiced escaping from rolled vehicles, bailing out of them while under fire, and taking control of a speeding car from the passenger seat if the driver was shot or otherwise rendered unconscious. The capstone exercise was the "worst day," which included all aspects of our training: defensive and offensive driving, shooting, and trauma care.

The day before our scheduled departure, my visa still had not arrived. But rather than worry about something I could not control, I continued to pack and study, expecting that the paperwork would show up at the last minute. And it did. Koz hand delivered it to me at Dulles International Airport just in time so I could check in for my transatlantic flight.

* *

At about the same time that I was going through the security line at Dulles, Pope Francis was kissing the feet of South Sudan's president Salva Kiir and of the opposition leader Riek Machar at the Vatican, imploring both leaders to "stay in peace . . . let us go forward . . . resolve your problems." The pontiff was doing what he could to stabilize the region, which had been shaken by the news from neighboring Sudan, where longtime president Omar al-Bashir had just been overthrown in a military coup.

As I listened to the news, a familiar feeling began to take hold somewhere deep in the pit of my stomach, and I thought of the ancient Chinese curse, "May you live in interesting times." It was hard to describe the physical sensation, that brink-of-something feeling. I'd had it before—on the ground in Afghanistan as rockets hit our airfield and at twenty-five thousand feet over the Gulf of Mexico as my T-34 aircraft stalled and began to spin. Now, I felt it once again, that first instance of facing the unknown. Given time, the extraordinary would become ordinary. Enemy artillery would become a nuisance, simply spinning toward the waves below, as if just another training event. But at that moment, I savored the sensation, shouldered my bag, stepped onto the plane, and headed into what was destined to be one of the most transformative years of my life.

9 Into Africa

Now, being in Africa, I was hungry for more of it, the
changes of the seasons, the rains with no need to travel,
the discomforts that you paid to make it real.

—ERNEST HEMINGWAY

13 April 2019. Emm, Christopher, and I spent the whole day in transit. The
UN maintained a Regional Service Center in Uganda that handled much of
the administration and logistics for its various missions throughout Africa,
so we would be spending a week there en route to South Sudan itself. Landing at night, I was struck by the darkness of the countryside surrounding
Uganda's international airport at Entebbe. The illuminated network of roads
and suburban neighborhoods that I was used to seeing on nighttime flights
into American and European airports simply did not exist here.

We were greeted as we came off the plane by Maj. Dave Smith, who had
flown from Juba to ensure our arrival went smoothly. Dave was a U.S. Army
officer who had been in UNMISS for six months already and had six more
to go; compared to us, he was an old hand here in East Africa. He met us
with a cadre of drivers who took our baggage and a local fixer who helped
finesse our weapons and ammunition through customs. We took them to
the local police station in a Toyota 4x4, escorted by two policemen armed
with AK-47s who rode in the truck's open bed. Our arms and ammunition
would remain in the police armory until the following Monday when Dave
would ferry them quietly into South Sudan on his return flight on a UN-
chartered aircraft.

As we drove with the windows down, I was struck by how peaceful it
felt, how dark the night, how cool, and how quiet. This familiar feeling
evoked memories of other nighttime arrivals in African cities—Accra and
Windhoek. Another short drive from the police station brought us to our
hotel, where we slept in late and spent a long, lazy Sunday recovering

before starting the check-in process at the UN's Regional Service Center Entebbe on Monday.

That check-in process, as Lt. Col. Brent Quin wryly observed, consisted of four hours' worth of paperwork crammed into three days. Brent was from New Zealand, or a "Kiwi" in the vernacular, and he—along with a Norwegian major named Marius Undlein—became one of our closest acquaintances in the group of officers who were in-processing for UNMISS duty.

We all tried to relax as the waiting dragged on, reminding each other not to "fight the process," and by Friday, everyone was ready to board the flight to Juba—everyone except Emm, Christopher, and me. It turned out that in addition to our visas, we were required to have a special letter from South Sudan's Ministry of Foreign Affairs. Ours had been overlooked. So we bade farewell to Quin and Marius and prepared to wait out a two-week delay.

The ministry's letter appeared exactly two weeks later. Emm's and Christopher's names were on it, along with those of several officers from other countries, but mine was not. Not to worry, I was told, my name would appear on the next letter, which had not yet received its final stamp of approval but surely would within a week or perhaps a little longer. So while my fellow Marines prepared their bags for shipment on a UN cargo flight and worked on their final predeparture paperwork, I found myself with lots of time on my hands and no particular direction for how to use it.

10 A Short History of Peacekeeping

> Peacekeeping is a job not suited to soldiers,
> but a job only soldiers can do.
> —DAG HAMMARSKJÖLD

21 April 2019. Although organized peacekeeping was comparatively short lived in contrast with the institutions of war that it opposed, its history could fill the pages of many books. I turned to some of those volumes during my downtime in Uganda, trying to learn more about the challenges that I might face in the year to come. I familiarized myself with the earliest UN interventions in the 1940s, where unarmed volunteers went to monitor the ceasefires after the first Arab-Israeli war and after the first Indo-Pakistani war. Those missions remained active, a testimony to both the utility of a UN presence and the difficulty in resolving some militarized political standoffs.

Throughout the Cold War years, from the 1950s to the early 1990s, the UN sent peacekeepers to various locations, mainly in the Middle East, but it remained notably absent from those arenas where the superpowers carried out their proxy wars in Korea, Vietnam, Laos, and Afghanistan. After the Cold War ended, renewed international enthusiasm for the idea of peacekeeping was buoyed by the apparent success of a major UN operation in Southeast Asia, where a combined force of 15,900 military personnel, 3,600 police, and 2,450 civilians deployed as part of the UN Transitional Authority in Cambodia temporarily took over the administration of that nation, organizing and running elections to create a democratic government. Its apparent success caused some to call it a "shining example" of what the UN could do to end conflicts and bring peace and liberal democracy to war-weary people. But then came Somalia, Rwanda, and Bosnia.

In 1994, just a year after the successful elections in Cambodia, a Canadian general named Roméo Dallaire, serving as the force commander of the UN assistance mission in Rwanda, tried in vain to prevent the wave of genocide that swept the country and claimed over a half a million Tutsi lives in only a hundred days. Dallaire not only lost twenty-seven of his own people but also was prevented from intervening to save others' lives because he lacked the necessary troops, and his political superiors had ordered him first not to intervene, then to actually withdraw. General Dallaire refused to obey and did what he could with the 400-odd troops who remained after Belgium and other countries unilaterally withdrew their remaining 2,171 troops from the UN force in Rwanda.[1] Some believed the UN member countries were reluctant to take action after the disastrous example of peacekeeping-gone-wrong in Somalia, where eighty-six peacekeepers—including twenty-six Americans—had been killed the previous year.[2]

A year after the Rwandan genocide and halfway around the world, UN peacekeepers deployed to Bosnia and Herzegovina. Over the next three years, 110 of them would be killed, 831 would be wounded, and hundreds more would be taken hostage. While their presence allowed humanitarian organizations to distribute aid to the impoverished population, they failed to prevent the ethnic cleansing that claimed thousands of innocent lives. A Human Rights Watch report on the massacre of Bosnian civilians at Srebrenica documented cases where peacekeepers had simply watched as Bosnian Serb soldiers killed unarmed men and raped civilian women. Further, it attributed the carnage to "the mishandling of the crisis by the U.N.'s Bosnia peacekeeping force . . . from the craven decisions of its field commanders prior to the fall of Srebrenica, to its apparent suppression and destruction of evidence of massive human rights abuses immediately after."[3]

I had a personal link to Srebrenica. I traveled to the region on a field trip during the 2007 conference of the International Association of Genocide Scholars in Sarajevo. There I visited the site of a mass grave that had recently been discovered beneath a soccer field. I saw the tangled bones, the rotting clothing, the skulls with their empty eye sockets staring reproachfully up at me. I had told myself then that *this* was why I was a Marine and pledged that if I ever had a chance to prevent this from happening again, I'd do better than the UN troops stationed in Srebrenica had.

After those two disastrous missions, the UN had passed the second half of the 1990s in a series of smaller operations with lower stakes and less probability of failure. That it often returned to the same places over and over again—UN forces went to East Timor twice, to Haiti four times—raised questions about the effectiveness of its interventions. The operations had a worldwide focus. Missions were deployed to countries in Africa, Asia, Europe, and the Americas. But after the new millennium, the peacekeeping efforts seemed to shift very much to the African continent: Ethiopia and Eritrea, Chad and Côte d'Ivoire, Liberia and Sudan. Africa was where the UN's biggest missions remained in 2019 as I prepared to join the largest of them all—UNMISS.

* *

The UN Mission in South Sudan had started out as a relatively small organization back in 2011, when South Sudan had first gained its independence. Its mandate was focused on supporting the new government to develop its capacity for security and justice—that is, to help them prevent conflict, to protect civilians, and to aid in the economic development needed for long-term peace. UNMISS was challenged by a wave of ethnic violence in the eastern state of Jonglei in late 2011 and early 2012, and found it had too few blue helmets to satisfy the "protection of civilians" component of its mandate.

The situation worsened in 2013 with the outbreak of the civil war. Again, the mission struggled to protect civilians in many parts of the country, though it sheltered near its bases around 240,000 people in ad hoc refugee camps, which were referred to as protection of civilians (POC) sites.[4] The military component grew from 7,000 to 12,500 peacekeepers, who were deployed into four military sectors. Its mandate now focused on protecting civilians, monitoring human rights, and supporting the delivery of humanitarian assistance.

But when the second round of the civil war began in July 2016, sparked by Riek Machar's return to Juba that April, the mission again failed to carry out its mandate. UN property was looted, aid workers were sexually assaulted, and hundreds of civilians were killed in Juba alone. In August the UN Security Council again increased the size of the force, authorizing an additional 4,000 peacekeepers, but only 2,226 arrived. These troops helped to form a new Sector Juba that was intended to maintain peace in the capital and prevent a *third* repeat of the poor performances of 2013 and 2016.

The latest peace agreement, the Revitalized Agreement on the Resolution of the Conflict in the Republic of South Sudan, had been signed in September 2018, and it called for Machar's return to the capital on 12 November 2019 to assume once again the position of vice president. My job would be to help ensure that if the worst happened—if his arrival triggered a third phase of the civil war—that UNMISS would be prepared to respond effectively. If our military component was prepared to do that, we would also be capable of handling any other crisis that might emerge in the course of the year. Or at least, so I believed.

11   Disastrous Passions

Aid makes itself out to be a practical enterprise, but in Africa at least, it's romantics who do most of the work—incongruously, because Africa outside of books and movies is hard and unromantic.
—DEBORAH SCROGGINS

29 April 2019. All work and no play makes Jack a dull boy, so while I was stuck in Entebbe, I logged on to the most ubiquitous of the contemporary dating apps and quickly connected with Jennifer, a smart, charming, and attractive aid worker in an open relationship with a Nairobi businessman. She was quite frank about what she wanted, and the possibility of a no-strings encounter represented a much-needed opportunity for human contact. Physical touch was definitely at the top of my "love languages." Besides, I reasoned, even if we didn't have good chemistry, it would still be a great chance to get a firsthand perspective on humanitarian efforts in the region, so I agreed to meet her for coffee and a screening of *Avengers: Endgame.*

Uber drivers were quite happy to offer their cell phone numbers and better rates if you called them directly, which was how I'd met Davis. He was an amiable man of my age who said working as a driver gave him both flexibility and a good income. I called and asked if he was available to give me a ride to Kampala that evening.

When he asked if I would need a ride back, I said, "I don't know."

He laughed. "Just call me if you do."

Davis dropped me off at the Acacia Mall early enough to buy a pair of tickets for the nine o'clock show. Then I wandered to the coffee shop where Jennifer and I had agreed to meet. She had scored a table for two on the patio, and as we greeted each other, she jokingly intimated that she'd been doing a little cyberstalking. "You seem safe enough," she said, "but I've got friends that will come looking for me if I don't check in with them." We shared a laugh, ordered some coffee, and chatted about what had brought us to Uganda.

It turned out that Jennifer had quite a background in South Sudan, having been there through some of the worst violence in 2016. She was still working for a humanitarian nongovernmental organization (NGO) but now in Uganda, where almost a million South Sudanese were living as refugees. We had some time before the show, so we caught a ride to a local restaurant and indulged ourselves with a cheese platter and a bottle of wine. We never did make it to the movie.

Deborah Scroggins, in her book *Emma's War*, said of the eponymous Emma McCune that "she was more honest than the rest of us, that she wasn't afraid to admit she was here because she wanted to be here."[1] That rang true for me—I was definitely here by choice—and was something I also had in common with Jennifer. I liked that she freely admitted to being an "adrenaline mercenary" who did humanitarian work in large part for the experience, the rush, the excitement of never knowing what fresh thrill the near future held. And at a certain level, she said, the money was actually pretty good.

I had to agree. Working for the UN had already led me to new adventures and new friends, given me a way to clear an administrative hurdle on my road to retirement, and qualified me for extra pay every month. Finally having a chance to use military force in a peacemaking capacity was icing on the cake. Jennifer told me to lower my expectations on that final score. In her experience, UNMISS hadn't done much to make the country safer for locals or aid workers.

I began to wax philosophic about how I planned to change that—one patrol base at a time—but saw in her body language that hearing a newcomer to the region mansplain security and humanitarian development was not exactly having an aphrodisiac effect, so I steered the conversation back to safer and more stimulating topics. Jennifer was kind enough to forgive my uninformed enthusiasm on the topic of peacekeeping, perhaps in consideration of my somewhat better-informed enthusiasm in other areas. I thought she might see me as a naïf with a savior complex, but I hoped that her opinion would change over time. For my part, I found her to possess a certain je ne sais quoi. In my journal, I later wrote: "I am becoming quite attached to the idea of her, although it is difficult to say just what that idea is."

We enjoyed each other's company so much that we made plans to meet again the following evening. I spent a lazy afternoon recovering from the wine, whiskey, and cigarettes of the previous evening before I returned to Kampala, where our second date was much like the first—dinner, drinks, and conversation late into the night; a few passionate hours in her apartment; and then an early morning return trip to Entebbe so that I could make my daily appearance at the Regional Support Center. Jennifer was flying to Nairobi the following day, so we made plans to meet in Entebbe upon her return.

In the meantime, I followed up on the status of the missing letter from the Ministry of Foreign Affairs. There was still no word, but "any day now," I was told.

* *

Emm and Christopher departed on Sunday, leaving me alone in Entebbe, where I spent my time working out and reading—mostly books about peacekeeping and South Sudan. Mostly. One of the books I read was titled *Disastrous Passion*. Jennifer had recommended it to me, laughingly observing that if I could get past the title, there was actually a lot of truth about the human side of humanitarian operations in it. The book had been published anonymously by one of her friends and set out to satirize the Harlequin romance genre while also gently mocking certain aspects of the humanitarian aid community.

Jennifer was right. While it was a fun read, the book highlighted serious problems with the institutions and individuals that the scholar and practitioner Séverine Autesserre had dubbed "Peaceland" in her 2014 treatise on the unintended consequences of traditional approaches to peacebuilding. *Disastrous Passion* was chock-full of acronyms and stereotypical characters, and I thought it was a bit overdone—not knowing that I'd encounter nearly all those words and all those kinds of people in the year ahead.

12   Louder Than Words

> The Terrain incident and the unwillingness to extract humanitarian
> staff more generally was deeply concerning. . . . The humanitarian
> community probably had too much reliance on [UNMISS], but
> it was shocking that . . . they couldn't go—they wouldn't go.
> —HUMANITARIAN OFFICIAL SPEAKING
> ABOUT THE 2016 VIOLENCE IN JUBA

15 May 2019. My liaison with Jennifer made the weeks spent in Uganda
significantly more enjoyable. We met when our schedules aligned, usually
in Kampala but occasionally in Entebbe, enjoying pizza and beers by the
lakeside before finally watching the movie that we'd skipped on our first
date. "What an interesting woman and a curious situation," I wrote in my
journal. "I am looking forward to seeing what becomes of us. She is exactly
the sort of woman I could become deeply involved with." When she was out
of town, I found myself missing her more than I'd expected, so I was happy
to discover something significant to take my mind off her.

A major peacekeeping convention being held at the Regional Support
Center the following week would bring together leaders from all the UN
missions in Africa. Since I was already in Entebbe, I easily got myself registered as a member of the UNMISS contingent and started studying the
topic of the conference—a UN program called "Action for Peacekeeping."

* *

Like the U.S. government, the UN rightly saw peacekeeping as one of its most
effective tools to promote and maintain international peace and security, and
it realized that its very diverse missions all faced some similar challenges
that undermined their ability to deliver results. Political solutions were often
absent, and the security council's mandates—which were supposed to guide
the missions' leadership—tended to lack both focus and clear priorities.[1]
Sometimes the behavior of the peacekeepers themselves was an issue. All

these factors made it increasingly difficult to provide protection to civilians and achieve the long-term, sustainable peace that the UN hoped to attain in countries where it had voted to deploy its forces.

This conference had brought together former and current military officers who had worked in peacekeeping, as well as representatives of the various missions and from UN headquarters. Some faces were familiar to me. I had seen Major General Van Roosen a few weeks before when he briefed me and my fellow officers at the Pentagon. Others, such as Brig. Gen. Bjørn Gaute Herlyng, the Norwegian officer who served as the force chief of staff for UNMISS, were new to me. Herlyng's first name was derived from the Old Norse word for "bear," and like his namesake, he was big, strong, and smart. In his early fifties, he had a boyish face, tousled blond hair, and an easy smile. His ability to navigate difficult conversations came as little surprise; he'd served in several diplomatic roles before, most recently as the Norwegian defense attaché in Germany. I could tell right away that he'd be a great person to work for and with.

* *

A UN report titled "Improving Security of United Nations Peacekeepers" had been released two years previously, and the conference focused most on this topic. I thought it was odd that no one seemed to be worrying about improving protection of civilians. Indeed, that core mandate task appeared in the report only twice—once in the caption for the cover's photo and then in its abbreviated form as a recommendation that all UN agencies should spend 20 percent of their budgets improving infrastructure because bad roads and washed-out bridges were a major impediment to providing security and humanitarian aid to distant villages. My biggest takeaway from the briefings was that UN Headquarters wanted us to do more for our peacekeepers but with less money. This resonated with me because I would be serving as the chief of the policy and plans (U5) branch for the UNMISS Force, and both the strategic deployment of the mission's 14,946 peacekeepers along with budgeting for the costs of doing so would be part of my future portfolio.

The second day of the conference ended with a bittersweet piece of news. Deng Kuethpiny Mayar, the undersecretary for South Sudan's Ministry of Foreign Affairs, had signed the approval for my entry into the country. I was cleared to depart for South Sudan.[2] All I had to do was to finish the conference, check out from the UN base in Entebbe, and catch the next flight to Juba. The process took four very busy days and a couple of pleasantly sleepless nights.

＊ ＊

Jennifer was back in Kampala and invited me to join her on Friday for dinner with a group of her friends. Unsurprisingly, we ended the night back at her apartment, where I stayed until I left the country. Our last long weekend together was one of those perfect bits of time. As the apocryphal revolutionary philosopher Quellcrist Falconer would observe in a distant and fictional future, "Take what is offered, and that must sometimes be enough."

I told Jennifer that I looked forward to seeing her on my first leave period and that she was always welcome to visit me in Juba, but she replied that she had no intention of ever returning to South Sudan. She'd been shaken by the 2016 attack on the Terrain Compound, a humanitarian residential complex in Juba that South Sudanese security forces had overrun during the violence that marked the return to war. Women had been raped, and a man had been shot point-blank in front of his horrified colleagues.

UNMISS had not acted on their pleas for help, even though the Terrain Compound was less than a mile from the UN base and even though the UN mandate obligated its forces to prevent such attacks or to respond to them. While I felt shame that my organization had failed, I knew I couldn't really comprehend how it must have felt to have been a civilian in Juba, to see firsthand how easily people very much like oneself were abandoned in extremis by the very organization that was meant to protect them. So I apologized and changed the topic, not wanting to spoil the weekend. I also wondered again why the UN seemed more interested in talking about improving security for its own troops than in taking decisive action to secure the lives and dignity of civilians. But answering that would be a matter for another time. Just then, I had other, more pleasurable issues to focus on.

Then it was time to go. Early Sunday morning, I kissed Jennifer goodbye. In the cool predawn darkness of the Kampala night, I slipped out of her apartment and into Davis's minivan and headed back to Entebbe to catch my long-awaited flight to Juba.

PART 2

Crossing the Threshold

13   Boots on the Ground

The journey of a thousand miles begins with a single step.

—LAO TZU

26 May 2019. Pleasantly exhausted from my last night in Uganda, I slept through most of my flight to South Sudan, waking as the pilot began to make a slow, banking approach to our destination. Juba sprawled across an area of flat and unappealing land; from above, its thirteen thousand acres with its 385,000 inhabitants looked like an upraised fist. The international airport defined the city's northeastern edge, and on my map, it resembled a pair of brass knuckles. Its single runway had been built on a right angle to the Nile River, which bounded Juba to the east and whose dark waters were bisected by the span of a lone bridge. The capital's southwest edge was marked by a singular geographical feature—Jebel Kujur, a solitary mountain rising 2,200 feet from the plain. At the southern foot of the Jebel, where its steep face gave way again to the flatlands, lay my new home—the base known as UN House.

      * *

The UN had its own terminal at the airport that facilitated the movement of both humanitarian supplies and UN personnel into and throughout the country. It also simplified the process of arriving with weapons, ammunition, and body armor. The UN's air terminal was also a key part of the mission's original base, Tomping, which still handled the bulk of UNMISS logistics and where about a third of the forces based in Juba resided. Dave Smith and Emm were waiting for me outside when I cleared customs and helped me wrestle my bulky bags into the back of the white SUV with its black-stenciled UN markings. Then we headed across town to the exclusive gated community where I would be living for the year to come.

     "There's a couple of ways to get there," Emm said, as I glanced at a colorful laminated map of the city. "This one's the fastest."

2. Map of Juba used by UN personnel, circa 2019. Based on United Nations map.

"Fast" seemed to be a relative term. In some places the road was worn asphalt, crumbling and potholed, but much of it was rough red dirt. Dogs lounged in the streets, and goats wandered across them. We drove west on Airport Road and turned left at an intersection where white-clad police waved us on. Dodging traffic through the larger and busier roundabout at Doctor John Garang's Memorial Park, we then slowed to a crawl through a tightly packed street market. Vendors hawked clothing, stalks of sugarcane, and bottles of water and gasoline. After another turn onto Jebel Road, we passed the infamous "Blue House" of the National Security Service, where so many South Sudanese had been detained, tortured, and killed, and then we made a final turn onto the deeply rutted dirt road that led to UN House.

Once on the base, I dropped my kit off at my new home—an airy three-room bungalow that consisted of a studio living room/dining room/kitchen and a bedroom with an en suite bathroom containing a toilet, shower, and my own washer-dryer. The roads in South Sudan might be rough, but it looked as if life here would be significantly more comfortable than my last posting to a conflict zone—a deployment to Afghanistan in 2013.

I didn't have time to unpack, though; we were expected at the U.S. Embassy for a Memorial Day barbecue. I changed into civilian clothes before making the trip back "downtown," which was our shorthand for the part Juba that lay generally in the northeast. Most of the foreign embassies were based there, along with the local headquarters for big UN and humanitarian agencies that worked in South Sudan. Not surprisingly, it was also where one could find many of the other standard elements of expatriate existence: hotels, restaurants, and Western-style grocery stores.

Outside my bungalow, Dave introduced me to the other "old boys": Ethan, Chris, and Drew. They rode in Dave's vehicle, while Christopher and I rode with Emm in a white Nissan Patrol with the UN black stencils that he said was mine. "It belongs to the chief U5," he said, "and that's you."

Our small convoy took the slower route this time. It curved around the base of the Jebel along "Rock City Road," so called because adjacent to the route were the homes and businesses of the many small artisan operators who were slowly dismantling the mountain for building materials and leaving their piles of gravel and neatly chiseled slabs of granite on display along the road. Twenty minutes later, we passed through the multilayered

3. The author's bungalow on UN House, the largest of the UN bases in Juba. Author photo.

security systems of the U.S. Embassy and then onward into its social hub—a tiki bar and restaurant that fronted a small swimming pool.

The barbecue was hosted by U.S. ambassador Thomas Hushek. He greeted me warmly, but I knew that I unlikely would have many future interactions with the tall, balding career diplomat. Instead, my main point of contact with the embassy staff would be with his defense attaché, Lt. Col. Kyle Walton of the U.S. Army.

Kyle and I chatted about the current situation in-country while enjoying a classic American holiday meal. It occurred to me that there was a certain incongruity to gorging ourselves on meat and fresh vegetables in a country where 61 percent of the population—almost 7 million people—were in what the World Food Programme (WFP) deemed as a "crisis" level of food insecurity, meaning they suffered from high levels of malnutrition. Of that shocking number, over twenty thousand South Sudanese civilians were actually in a state of famine: destitute, starving, and dying. But no one went hungry at the U.S. Embassy, even those of us who left early. The six other American peacekeepers and I left a little after six o'clock, just as the party was really starting to get going, because the UN maintained a seven o'clock curfew in Juba, and we had a twenty-minute drive back to our base. Besides, Monday was fast approaching, and I wanted to be well rested for my first real day on the job.

* *

I got into the office and quickly found myself consumed with assimilating the issues that I'd be working on and getting the American contingent squared away. This small group of officers for whom I was now responsible drove too fast, didn't do vehicle inspections, and were some of the few people who carried weapons in uniform. This longtime policy wasn't really appropriate for the current operational environment, and I'd heard that the special representative of the secretary-general (SRSG) didn't like seeing armed staff officers on base, so I gave the order that we would leave our weapons locked in our bungalows unless the security situation deteriorated. *No sense needlessly irritating the mission's top civilian*, I thought, *since I'll probably need his approval for something in the year to come.*

I also had another round of induction training to complete, and as I was driving to Tomping, where these classes were held, I heard a bizarre story on the radio. Two Ugandan teachers had been pulled from their car and shot dead near Rumbek, while the mob spared their driver, the South Sudanese headmaster of their school. It seemed a senseless act of violence, and I wondered what had motivated it.

Outside of random roadside killings, the major driver for conflict in the country was intercommunal violence. Cattle raids between groups of pastoralists were a regular occurrence in the eastern and central regions of the country; in the west, incursions of cattle into the fields of farmers led to more fighting. In the southeast, hit-and-run battles between government forces and the insurgent National Salvation Front (NAS) predominated, and bandits took advantage of the instability to carry out armed robberies on the single paved road that led from Juba to the border with Uganda.[1] The banditry and guerrilla warfare made sense, as did the idea that violence might occur where nomadic herders intersected with settled farmers. But what were cattle raids?

The shorthand explanation that I got was that cows were currency, particularly when it came to buying a bride or paying off a blood debt. So, if you didn't have cattle, you had to steal them from someone who did. But if someone else stole *your* cows, you had to get them back at all costs, and woe betide the man, woman, or child who got in the way.

I suspected that these attacks were more complicated than that but accepted the explanation at face value. I also made a note to learn more about these kinds of raids after I was fully functional in my dual roles as the chief U5 and the U.S. senior national representative.[2]

14 Colleagues, Caveats, and Contingency Plans

> We, Member States of the United Nations . . . stress the importance
> of avoiding all caveats which have a detrimental impact on mandate
> implementation and performance. We as Member States commit to
> redouble all efforts to identify and clearly communicate any caveats.
> —DECLARATION OF SHARED COMMITMENTS ON
> UN PEACEKEEPING OPERATIONS, 2018

30 May 2019. When I was young, I thought of the military in terms of
its hardware—its assault rifles and armored vehicles, its helicopters and
fighter jets. But two decades of service had taught me that it was really a
"people business"; the quality of the individuals defined the organizations
in which I had served. My colleagues in UNMISS only reinforced this belief.
That group of women and men truly exemplified the expression "strength
through diversity." Some of them worked for me, others were peers, and a
few were my bosses. Still others were mainly social connections—people
with whom I shared hot coffee and cold Tusker beer—but all of us considered each other colleagues.

First, there was "Team America," or the seven officers who made up the
U.S. contingent in UNMISS. Emm, Christopher, and I—all of us Marines—
were the "new guys." We joined the four other Americans who were already
in the mission: two U.S. Army officers—Maj. Dave Smith, a logistician
who worked with the Mission Support Center, and Capt. Drew Ziccardi, a
civil affairs officer who worked in the Civil Military Coordination (CIMIC)
Branch—and U.S. Air Force officers Capt. Chris Wong, who worked as an
engineering staff officer, and Capt. Ethan Thorpe, who served in the Joint
Operations Center. Although most of us worked in different locations, we
all lived in the same neighborhood of UN House, and we met formally on a
weekly basis to coordinate and informally to represent our country at social,
athletic, and charity events. As the senior U.S. officer, I was responsible

for their quality of life, safety, training, and administrative oversight. This meant I would always stand a little outside the circle as not just "one of the guys" but always, on some level, as "the boss."

In addition to Team America were the officers of the U5. My deputy, Lt. Col. Murray Brown, was from New Zealand, and six staff officers from a diverse range of other countries worked for us. Besides Emm, there was Maj. Stig Rogne from Norway, Maj. Himadri Roy from Bangladesh, Maj. Hugh McKeown from Australia, and Maj. Bin Cao from China. We also had a Danish naval officer, Martin Borgwardt Schmidt, whose rank of lieutenant commander was equivalent to that of the majors and who looked very much like a modern Viking, with his neatly trimmed beard complemented by long hair worn in a tight braid.

Along the walls of the open floor in which our cubicle farm sat were a pair of private offices belonging to two of my several bosses. One was reserved for my direct superior, Col. Theodomir Bahizi, a Rwandan officer who served as the deputy chief of staff for operations and was nominally in charge of policy and plans. Most of my orders came from the other office, where the force chief of staff, Brigadier General Herlyng, worked tirelessly at a desk piled high with papers.

I didn't yet know many people beyond my immediate group of military colleagues with one key exception. Lt. Col. Brent Quin, whom I'd met in April during our initial induction training in Entebbe, had been in-country for over a month before I arrived and worked as the military adviser to the highest-ranking member of the mission—the SRSG. Since 2017 that position had been filled by David Shearer, a career politician from New Zealand who had previously worked with UN missions in Iraq, Lebanon, and Afghanistan.

Brent was a source of annoyance to some in the force because he never wore his uniform. The SRSG preferred not to have uniformed personnel in his front office, and I didn't care what someone wore as long as that person was good at the job. Personally, I thought it was great to know another officer of equal rank who had a direct line to the head of the mission. Brent and I got along very well—he'd tipped me off to the SRSG's perceptions of staff officers wearing weapons on base—and we both felt strongly that the mission needed to improve the effectiveness of its patrols. This topic arose frequently in our discussions and correspondence, and we began to work our ideas into a "patrolling framework" that we could pitch to our respective bosses.

Outside of the mission and the country, my personal connections were even more tenuous. Jennifer had stopped responding to my notes soon after I'd arrived in South Sudan, but I wasn't entirely surprised by that. Though I hoped she might reach out in the future, I wasn't holding my breath, and I did have other prospects. I'd recently connected with another aid worker, a blonde Canadian named Ashley who was also based in Uganda. Our paths had crossed in the airport; on the morning that I flew to South Sudan, she had arrived for a temporary assignment in Kampala. I thought that perhaps in time something would come of that serendipitous connection. For now, it was much too soon to tell.

* *

Two issues—caveats and contingency plans—both consumed my attention and helped me to expand my networks in UNMISS and across town at the U.S. Embassy. Caveats were restrictions that troop-contributing countries put on what their peacekeepers could do and where they could go. In theory, there shouldn't have been any caveats. Every officer and soldier should have been ready and willing to follow any lawful order from the force commander or the generals who worked for him. In reality, different countries were believed to put certain constraints on their troops loaned to the UN, and they were commonly cited as reasons when peacekeepers failed to protect civilians. One of my tasks was to get to the bottom of caveats in UNMISS.

Regarding the contingency plans, the mission and the force developed them for emergency situations—including mass violence and outbreaks of Ebola virus—and I had been tasked to update our Ebola plan given an outbreak in the neighboring Democratic Republic of the Congo. More problematically, the U.S. government also had its own contingency plans for Team America in a crisis—in short, what we would do if UN House was in danger of being overrun. I didn't care for the general idea, which was for us to make a run for the embassy or the airport; my own opinion was that if the bullets started flying, my place was with the UN. But that was what caveats did: they allowed senior U.S. military leaders on another continent to pull my strings if they really wanted to. Unfortunately, even if I took my own emotions out of it, the plan as it had existed for the last three years was full of holes.

Unlike most of the other country contingents, we Americans didn't have our own vehicles, radios capable of contacting our embassy, and a backup internet connection. If the situation got so bad that we *were* ordered to pull out, we had no way to communicate and coordinate with the embassy's security personnel when the cell towers were taken offline and no way to get to the airport. We *did* have a lot of extra ammunition—evidently no one had been going to the firing range for practice—but we didn't have enough prepackaged rations even to meet the minimal requirements of the force's own crisis procedures. That was not acceptable, so I took action to obtain all these items along with bicycles so that we could do our part in the UN's "Greening the Blue" initiative.[1] As a former supply officer, I felt duty bound to in ensure that I'd leave the American contingent in better shape—logistically speaking—than I'd found it.

My free time was spent reading books or working out alone. Early morning runs within the perimeter of the UN camp were a pleasure. The air was cool, the base was quiet, and I would occasionally encounter one of the tiny, shy deer known as dik-diks, whose diminutive hoofprints could often be seen in the soft mud at the roadsides. This time alone helped balance out the very social nature of the UN workplace and the new experience of dealing with our counterparts in the South Sudanese military.

15 Freedom of Movement

> Frequent government violations of the status of forces agreement,
> including the restriction of movement of UNMISS personnel,
> constrained UNMISS's ability to carry out its mandate, which
> included human rights monitoring and investigations.
> —U.S. STATE DEPARTMENT REPORT, MARCH 2019

11 June 2019. The Juba Crown Hotel was not the most luxurious building
in South Sudan, but it was "Juba good"—an expression that officers in the
force wryly used to describe things that weren't really that great but were
so much better than anything that could be found elsewhere in the country. Inside were plush red carpets and marble floors, but from the outside,
with its industrial beige styling and boxy lines, the six-story building could
easily have been a low-rise apartment complex in Tulsa or Wichita. But the
presence of a camouflaged truck with a machine gun mounted in the rear
was proof that I was not in Kansas anymore.

The Joint Verification and Monitoring Mechanism Workshop was meant
to allow for candid discussions between UNMISS and the South Sudanese
defense community, and I was eager to begin working toward improving
relations with our host nation. Our focus was on restoring the mission's
freedom of movement, which had been severely curtailed for several years
due to a practice known as sharing of information (SOI). While originally
been intended to ensure that UN patrols would pass unmolested by South
Sudanese military units, it had slowly become a bureaucratic burden, mor-
phing into a system of preclearances that government and opposition forces
used to prevent peacekeepers from going anywhere that they weren't wanted.[1]
Our South Sudanese counterparts had their own agenda: they wanted to
see some positive results from our patrols and wanted the UN to grant them
office space in four of our outlying bases.

4. Participants at the Joint Verification and Monitoring Mechanism Workshop included the SRSG, David Shearer (*in suit, middle row*); the author (*far left, front row*); and general officers and staff from UNMISS and the South Sudanese security forces. Author photo.

The workshop began with an address by the mission's senior leader. The SRSG, David Shearer, highlighted our freedom of movement issues with a recent example: an UNMISS patrol escorting a WFP convoy had been held up for six days. "People were waiting for the food," he said. "They couldn't get it because the peacekeepers couldn't get clearance."

The response from Maj. Gen. Gabriel Jok Riak was conciliatory. "Let us open a new page," he said. "Let us agree. There should be no conflict between us." Jok Riak, the chief of defense forces (CDF) for the government, went on to assure Shearer that his troops would try their best to fully cooperate with the UN, as they hoped to be a part of future peacekeeping missions.

I thought that last point would be the best "carrot" to encourage cooperation. Nearby Rwanda and neighboring Ethiopia had both successfully transitioned from having UN peacekeeping missions on their own soil to sending their soldiers to serve as peacekeepers elsewhere, including here in UNMISS.[2] Becoming a source of military manpower for the UN offered a boost in prestige and a way to offset the costs of maintaining a defense force, and South Sudan was certainly in need of both.

But after the SRSG left, General Jok Riak attempted to justify the restrictions to our freedom of movement, telling us that without these clearances, the government "could not guarantee your safety." In principle, our patrols were quite capable of ensuring their own safety. In practice, they were rarely allowed to do so because they were frequently stopped at checkpoints consisting of nothing more than a handful of soldiers and a rope thrown across the road.

The current policy was for patrols to go out with forty-eight hours' worth of supplies so they could spend two full days trying to negotiate their passage. If they failed to do so, then they were inevitably ordered to return to base. Even if they were eventually allowed to pass, many very bad things could happen in forty-eight hours, as a report by the UNMISS Human Rights Division (HRD) made clear:

> Between September 2018 and April 2019, HRD documented violations and abuses resulting in the unlawful killing of 104 civilians and the wounding of 35 others, as well as the abduction of at least 187 civilians for forced recruitment, forced labour and sexual slavery.... At least 99 women and girls, including girls as young as 12, were raped and subjected to other forms of sexual violence during the reporting period.... Due to access issues, including access denial by Government forces, HRD has reason to believe that these numbers are likely under-representative of the full scale of the crisis.[3]

These attacks had occurred in the southern state of Central Equatoria, the area with the highest density of peacekeepers in the country. Despite the presence of three UN bases and attempts by peacekeepers to patrol the area, government forces routinely prevented the blue helmets from going where they were needed most.

It was one of the many quiet, dirty truths of South Sudan, but it wasn't a dirty secret. The UN knew about it, and the U.S. government knew about it too. At least until now, no one had done anything substantive to resolve the matter. But I was new and genuinely believed that this forum could make a difference.

* *

In the end, the workshop was one of those mainly performative events that I would come to know well in South Sudan. Two sides would come to the table at a richly appointed conference venue with their positions and their talking points. After everyone had spoken their piece, we'd all enjoy our afternoon tea, shake hands, and ultimately return to our respective offices, leaving the reality on the ground completely and utterly unchanged.

Maintaining this broken status quo did not sit well with some people, particularly Lt. Col. Ronald Gilissen, the force's chief legal officer. Ronald pulled no punches. He stated emphatically that extensive research into the soi issue had led him to conclude there was no freedom of movement in unmiss. He went on to say that our failure to go where civilians were being killed, tortured, and raped might amount to criminal negligence. Ronald asked rhetorically, "What was known in the wider un community, and what did unmiss do about it?"

* *

The answer was that the wider un community, as well as the U.S. government, knew exactly what was happening. Meanwhile, the mission itself consistently did nothing. Our own reports had documented the killings of 531 civilians in the three months between February and May 2019, representing a 192 percent increase compared with the same period the previous year. Most of those attacks took place in areas where unmiss had thousands of peace-keepers stationed; however, unmiss patrols were repeatedly denied access to those areas where the killings were occurring, and the mission refused to exercise the freedom of movement to which it was entitled.

One of the challenges seemed to be that the global media didn't devote many headlines to human rights violations in South Sudan, so no one demanded accountability. I couldn't help mentally comparing the nonexistent coverage of an official report of the killings of more than five hundred South Sudanese civilians with the media's reaction to the Christchurch massacre in the same period, and I wondered if the Kiwis, such as Brent, Murray, and the srsg, noticed this disparity as well. The atrocities here in South Sudan were well documented in dry, bureaucratic language in the un's own reports, but who read those things, anyway? I never had. Like most Americans, I previously hadn't even known they existed.

But ignorance could no longer excuse inaction. I remembered standing at the edge of that mass grave in Bosnia. *Not on my watch*, I thought to myself.

Then I told Ronald that I would lend him my voice and influence. As staff officers, the two of us would have to work through our colonels and generals to make any substantive changes to the way things were done, but together, and with our colleagues, I was certain that we could change the status quo.

Meanwhile, I felt that I needed to get a better understanding of what the situation was on the ground—outside the comfort and safety of UN House—so I volunteered to accompany General Herlyng on a visit to Sector West.

16 The Lay of the Land

Peacekeeping operations "behave" like developed
countries in developing countries.
—UN ENVIRONMENT PROGRAMME REPORT, 2012

17 June 2019. Traveling on UN aircraft required a lot of paperwork, most
of which was made considerably simpler when one was accompanying a
general. Herlyng's assistant, Rob Williams, had taken care of the details; all
I had to do was pack two days' worth of kit—including my body armor and
pistol—and wait for the bus to arrive. While we did, I chatted with Rob, an
Australian warrant officer who had been in the mission only slightly longer
than I had. The Australians' policy was to rotate their officers every six
months. That had both pros and cons: it meant that more of their military
personnel had the opportunity to serve as peacekeepers, but almost as soon
as officers felt as if they'd figured it all out, they were headed home, and
another Aussie was taking their place.

When the bus finally arrived—half an hour late—we were driven at a
breakneck speed from UN House to the air terminal at Tomping. Hurtling
through Juba in the predawn darkness, the driver wove around ruts and
potholes and the occasional goat or pedestrian.

The plane was an Antonov 26B-100, and the flight to the northwestern city
of Wau took about two hours. South Sudan was a large country, and as an
American, I thought of it as being the size of Texas. It was also comparable
in area to France or Ukraine, and that meant that our 310-mile flight from
Juba to Wau was roughly the same as flying from Dallas to San Antonio,
Paris to Zurich, or New Delhi to Lahore.

West of Juba, the terrain consisted of tropical forests, swamps, and grass-
land intersected with seasonal rivers like the Jur and Sopo. Patrols that
could easily cross parched riverbeds during the dry season found the same
routes impassable in the rainy season due to a lack of suitable bridges. The

population comprised largely the Dinka, Jur Chol, Luo, Fertit, and Balanda ethnic groups. The Dinka fought the other tribes, and Dinka clans fought each other.

Wau was home to the headquarters of Sector West, which was headed by a Chinese brigadier general named Chaunjing Wang, a canny leader with a cheerful face, ready smile, and excellent English. The forces at his disposal included two infantry battalions from Nepal and Bangladesh, an independent infantry company from Ghana, engineering companies from China and Thailand, and an assortment of support troops: doctors, military police, and communications experts. With these troops, he was responsible for a massive expanse of land with four different UN bases, each the site of a separate field office.

It was a matter of pride for the far-flung battalions of UNMISS peacekeepers to show great hospitality to visiting generals from Juba, and we had a lavish lunch of delicious curries at the Bangladeshi officer's mess while listening to General Wang's thoughts and concerns. For the peace process to succeed, the general believed that a UN-led program of disarmament, demobilization, and reintegration (DDR)—that is, taking former soldiers and helping them transition to civilian life—was extremely important. Unfortunately, this task was not in the UNMISS mandate.

After lunch, we left for a tour of the POC camp. Wau was the newest of these sites and, despite housing fourteen thousand people, one of the smallest. The inhabitants were mostly ethnic minorities, forced to flee their homes during three years of fighting between government and rebel forces in the area, and 20 percent of them were children.

As we passed through the camp, it was apparent that while few people were openly suffering, most were merely surviving, not thriving. They lived in huts made of woven reeds covered with white and blue tarps that gave them an average living area of forty-three square feet per person—a space more confined than the smallest U.S. prison cells. These shelters sat behind a wall made of HESCO barriers—wire mesh containers filled with rubble and topped with rusting razor wire—that was reinforced at intervals with guard towers manned by UNMISS peacekeepers.

The food ration consisted of just a handful of ingredients: some sort of grain, usually sorghum or maize; lentils or chickpeas; vegetable oil; salt; and sugar. Thinking back to my own filling and healthy lunch of chapati

5. Map of UNMISS locations and forces in South Sudan, June 2019. Based on United Nations map.

6. Children in the Wau protection of civilians (POC) site. Author photo.

bread, vegetable curry, rice, and salad, I couldn't help but think of what a difference it made to be on one side of a fence than another.

We ended the day with a short drive through Wau itself. As we left the base, we found ourselves sharing the road with more goats than cars. The road was paved at the beginning—a rarity here in South Sudan—but it soon turned to packed red earth, rutted from the passage of vehicles. We passed buildings of redbrick, many of them unroofed and partially demolished. The people who once lived there had been displaced by three years of violence that had started in 2016; they now lived in the POC camp. The few structures still livable were more recent constructions of mud brick with thatched roofs. In the city center, solidly constructed buildings of white-painted brick with rusted roofs of corrugated iron that dated to the colonial era still stood. Fresh fruit and vegetables were sold on the side of the road. It seemed quite peaceful, quite ordinary in the middle of this state capital. Its infrastructure appeared on par with some of the smaller villages I'd passed through during my limited travels in neighboring Uganda.

Returning to the base as twilight painted the sky in brilliant pinks and purples, we dined again with the Bangladeshi battalion before retiring to our accommodations for the night. The containerized housing units were tiny, prefab apartments consisting of a single room with a self-contained shower and toilet set in one corner. They featured a bed draped in mosquito netting, a writing desk and chair, a refrigerator, and a small wardrobe. Luxurious by South Sudanese standards, these dwellings were the norm for staff officers at most bases outside of UN House, whose comfortable little bungalows with their kitchens, living rooms, and washer/dryer setups were quite the exception.

* *

In the morning, we headed to a military base run by the government's forces—namely, the Fifth Division's headquarters of the South Sudan People's Defense Force (SSPDF). Most South Sudanese divisions were named for one of the large, iconic, and dangerous animals inhabiting the country, and we would visit the "Elephant Division" that day. The armed forces had traditionally been known as the SPLA, but in October 2018 the government had rebranded its military forces as the SSPDF. While the new moniker suggested they existed to defend the people, the organization consisted of the same impoverished troops, led by the same wealthy generals, and retained, as far as I could tell, the same penchant for war crimes.[1]

En route, we passed a mosque set back from the road at the end of a large, open field of red clay, and its green-capped dome and elegant minaret made a lovely contrast with the cloudy sky. While only 8 percent of the country identified as Muslim, Wau had long been strongly connected with the mainly Islamic regions to the north given its location at the terminus of the country's only railroad line, which ran to Sudan's capital of Khartoum. No trains had run along the track since the outbreak of civil war in 2013, but there was talk of reopening the line. The existence of such mosques highlighted that religious freedom and tolerance had generally prevailed after South Sudan obtained its independence in 2011. Here, people fought and died for many reasons, but religion wasn't usually one of them.

Past the mosque lay the local military base known as Girinty Barracks. We entered the base through a massive double-arched gateway. In the distance, I noted three T-72 tanks parked in the shade of a low building, and wondered if they were operable. Within the perimeter of the installation, the single-story masonry buildings painted a light blue were of a better construction than we'd seen elsewhere. Our little convoy of white suvs pulled up in front of the largest building, and we piled out to meet our hosts.

The courtyard was full of government soldiers, and they showed signs of consternation as we began to enter the building. I was about to learn an interesting lesson about power in South Sudan. The soldiers were adamant that those of us with weapons should not bring them into the conference room. It just was not done. We discovered that in this society, the people with real power—governors, generals, and their staff officers—did not carry weapons. That was what common soldiers were for. I unstrapped my holster and handed my pistol to Rob. The German officers did the same. In the force, we were extremely collegial, and rank didn't usually count for much unless you were a colonel or a general. Most of the time the staff referred to each other by first names, nicknames, or call signs. I went by "Carp"—the abbreviated version of my last name—which had been my call sign for years. But Rob was technically the lowest-ranking among the officers present, so it fell to him to hang out with the South Sudanese soldiers outside the conference room while the rest of us filed in to meet with the commander of the Fifth Division, Gen. Keer Kiir Keer.

General Kiir was a big man, easily a foot taller and twenty pounds heavier than General Herlyng, who was one of the biggest men in the force head-quarters (fhq). But for big men, the talk was relatively small. Kiir said that the beginning of the year, his relationship with the local Sudan People's Liberation Army-in-Operation (spla-io) troops had been good: their men now came to his camp to shop in the small commissary, and if they misbehaved, he called one of the generals on the opposition side and turned the offender over to them for discipline. There was a remarkable lack of rancor shown considering these forces had been in conflict less than eight months before.[2] Nothing was said about the eleven civilians killed two days earlier only thirteen miles away, although General Herlyng did ask about the availability of weapons in the local area. General Kiir said guns and ammunition were brought in from Sudan and Libya, and added that he was ready to disarm the civilian population if called upon to do so. But, he declared, "we won't act without guidance from the governor." This was a nod to the liberal democratic principle demanding civilian control of the military, but that concept was a bit of a sham in South Sudan since most of the state governors were former military officers themselves.

The meeting was short, just a courtesy call between two generals. Even so, this itself was a form of diplomacy, or a Track 1.5 engagement.[3] And it might actually have been a meaningful one if we had gone into the meeting knowing what other UN elements in South Sudan already knew: General Kiir's men had been rounding up boys in Wau and neighboring villages for months and taking them to this very base for induction into military servitude as child soldiers.[4] But the UN's own Commission on Human Rights in South Sudan hadn't shared this information with the force, so it was all smiles as we waved a cheery goodbye to the local "big man" and headed north.

* *

The red dirt road to Kuajok was in good condition. The air was pleasantly warm, and the sky was overcast, with the sort of humidity that hints of rain not too far away; we were in the middle of the wet season, after all.[5] About halfway to our destination, we crossed a new bridge on a tributary of the Jur River that the European Union (EU) and the WFP had recently constructed at a cost of $6.5 million. The project seemed just what the country needed more of, because it had employed about eighty local workers for about eighteen months under the leadership of WFP engineers, and its 393-foot span now connected thousands of people to markets in Kuajok. This sign of progress inspired more hope than our meeting with the UN team at our destination did.

The head of the field office was away, so we met with her deputy, who believed that the force's presence was highly beneficial and who had only good things to say about the Bangladeshi battalion. Of the most recent violence, he observed that "fighting used to stop in May because you had to farm, but this year, it has continued because the government and the opposition are backing the fighters." He told us that the Dinka—the dominant ethnic group in the region—believed that any wrong, even murder, could be redressed by a payment of cattle.[6] "Fifty-one cows for a life," he said. "Can you believe it?"

The scale of the violence that he briefed us on was worrying. He told us of a recent three-hour raid in which uniformed men armed with AK-47s and machine guns attacked six villages. Twenty-two civilians were killed, twenty-one were wounded, and 3,900 cattle were stolen. The attackers were believed to have been Nuer from the bordering Unity State, and our host noted that "more UNMISS military presence had been requested in the conflict sector." But although almost a month had passed, that request had not been acted upon.

On the drive from Wau to Kuajok and back again, I saw nothing that I would recognize as a checkpoint, at least nothing with the ability in terms of obstacles or firepower to block military vehicles. Just past the bridge, a lean man wearing a tank top, camouflage trousers, and flip-flops drew back a knotted string stretched across the road for us. *Was that it?* I wondered.

What did strike me as we drove across the countryside was the lack of agriculture. The ground appeared fertile, but I didn't see a single plow or even the simple implements that I used as a boy on my family farm: hoes, rakes, shovels, or picks. In the few fields where I did see people tending crops, their cultivation tools seemed limited to digging sticks. We saw no vehicles on the road besides our own, passing a few people walking and one man riding a bicycle. A young girl in a pink dress waved from the door of a mud-brick building.

That girl was, it seemed to me, very much the reason we were here. If we could only act on our mandate of peace, she would have a chance to grow up with a degree of security and prosperity that no previous generation of children in this part of the country had enjoyed. If we failed, she was likely to soon become an anonymous data point in one of the many reports of violence against women and children in South Sudan.

* *

We got back to the base at Wau just before sunset, and the Chinese engineering company on behalf of General Wang treated us to dinner at the "best Chinese restaurant in Wau." There was plenty of fresh and delicious food, as well as copious quantities of *baiju*, a clear, distilled liquor with a 60 percent alcohol content. When it was my turn to raise a toast, I acknowledged General Wang as the senior representative of the People's Liberation Army, saying I was happy to represent the second generation of my family to work in cooperation with members of the Chinese military. I noted my father's service as a Hump pilot in World War II and expressed the hope that our countries would chart a course focused on cooperation vice competition in the years to come. That toast was met with pleased surprise from our hosts and was reciprocated by the Sector West commander, who thanked me for my family's military service and echoed my desire for our nations to let peacekeeping set the example for what could be achieved when China and America worked together. After dinner, our visiting delegation was invited to a less formal gathering at General Wang's accommodations, where we sat in his garden and talked long into the night, drinking beer and eating peanuts.

This was the social aspect of being a senior officer in a peacekeeping mission: you hosted some gatherings that highlighted the culture and the generosity of your own country, and in turn, you attended the gatherings hosted by others. It was a good way to build connections within the mission and beyond, and through such relationships, I began to discover that a lot more was always going on than met the eye.

17 Easy Buttons and Hard Truths

> Local humanitarian professionals, while taking on a significant
> bulk of operational tasks of aid programs, are also much less
> compensated compared to their international counterparts. . . . They
> also receive less training, livelihood benefits, security provisions, and
> psycho-social support compared to their expatriate colleagues.
> —JUNRU BIAN

19 June 2019. I couldn't believe what I was hearing. "One thousand dollars?
Per truck?" I was at dinner with an aid worker from the Danish Refugee
Council and his girlfriend, and he'd just told me that to move aid shipments
around the country cost humanitarians about $1,000 per vehicle.

"Yes, per truck," Krishnan said, and Courtney nodded her agreement
around a mouth of noodles. In the Tomping district of Juba, we were eating
dinner at Lily's Café, a cozy little French-Asian fusion restaurant whose
interior would have felt comfortably familiar to any denizen of Paris or New
York. But the presence of a bored-looking security guard with an AK-47
hanging across his chest was a reminder that we were still in a conflict area.

I'd met my dinner companions through a mutual acquaintance. One
of the best practices I'd picked up from my years abroad was to leverage
recommendations for local contacts from fellow expatriates: aid workers,
military personnel, and itinerant travelers. My friend Trisha, whom I'd met
while studying at the Naval Postgraduate School in Monterey, California, had
spent her whole adult life in the humanitarian sector, working everywhere
from Myanmar to the DRC. I figured that if anyone in my network knew
someone in Juba, it would be Trisha, and she had obligingly connected me
with Krishnan.

"That would mean there's a whole line item somewhere on the World
Food Programme's budget for paying bribes in South Sudan," I said.

Krishnan laughed. "Don't think too much about it. You'll go mad."

Or get mad, I thought, shaking my head and making a mental note to raise the issue with more senior leaders. Surely, this was happening below the radar.

"Okay, another question," I said.

"Shoot."

"What do you make of the security situation here in Juba? I mean, we are supposedly in a hardship duty area, but . . ." I gestured at the room around us. "This doesn't seem like hardship to me."

Krishnan laughed again. "Okay, man. What you have to understand is the real motivation behind things. You're in the military, so you guys don't get it. But for all your civilian friends in the UN? As long as Juba is considered 'hardship,' their R&R package is so much better."

I knew he meant "rest and recuperation"—a benefit that the UN gave its civilian employees to protect their health and well-being—but I didn't get the context. "Why's that?"

"Talk to Human Resources. You'll find out that because this is considered 'Hardship Class E,' the civilians—well, not the local hires but the expats— they get five days of R&R every six weeks. Which includes a round-trip flight out of the country. That's in addition to their regular leave."

"Hardship Class E" meant the most dangerous and difficult living conditions, and this post just did not feel to me as if it met that threshold.[1] I shook my head. I'd just found out about the institutionalized bribery on the roads, and now I'd been given an example of the UN's unfair treatment of local employees. They were assumed not to need R&R, as if living in South Sudan somehow gave them a superpower that civilian employees hired from abroad did not have. To me, it appeared a way to scrimp on costs and devalue the expertise, experience, and labor value of local staff. That seemed to go against the UN's own core principles of equality and nondiscrimination.

These hard truths about corruption and discrimination were not only infuriating but also well beyond my power to do much about, at least immediately. I'd long attempted to follow the advice of Stephen Covey on where to focus my efforts. In his book *The Seven Habits of Highly Effective People*, Covey suggested that leaders consider where a particular problem fell in relation to a pair of concentric circles, which he called one's "Circle of Concern" and "Circle of Influence." Not surprisingly, for most people, their circle of concern—the things that they could and often did worry about—was much bigger than their circle of influence, which represented those things that they could actually *do* something about.

Effective leaders paid attention to what popped up in their sphere of concern but focused their time and energy mainly either on addressing matters inside their circle of influence or on expanding it. So I added Krishnan's intel to the growing list of concerns I planned to raise with my leadership in UNMISS. It was up to them to address those issues; I had plenty of work to do within my current circle of influence, and some of it I'd brought upon myself.

In my first one-on-one with General Herlyng, I'd told him that the U5 would be his "easy button"; that is, anything that didn't fall in a specific bucket but needed doing could be given to us, and we'd make it happen. It wasn't long before he took me up on the offer, asking me to serve as the force's coordinator for an upcoming visit by a high-level consultant, a retired general who would be assessing our performance and offering recommendations on what should be done to improve our support of the mandate. To learn from an acknowledged expert in the field of peacekeeping seemed like a great idea, so when I said yes to General Herlyng's request, it wasn't just military protocol but also self-interest that motivated me.

18 An Outsider Looks In

> You don't find yourself in a Board of Inquiry for what
> you've done wrong, but for what you've failed to do.
> —MAJ. GEN. PATRICK CAMMAERT

24 June 2019. The visit of Maj. Gen. Patrick Cammaert came, in my opinion, a little too early and a lot too late—not in time for his advice to save the hundreds of South Sudanese civilians who'd already in been killed in 2019 but too soon for him to meet directly with the incoming force commander. Only a handful of more junior leaders in the force would get to hear the general's commentary on our situation straight from the source.

Cammaert was a Dutch officer who had retired in 2007 and was well known in Peaceland. During his years of active service with the Royal Netherlands Marine Corps, he had served several tours with the UN in Asia, Europe, and Africa, most notably in the volatile DRC. There, he had cemented a reputation for strong leadership, enforcing the principle that "UN forces are impartial and not neutral." Cammaert explained that being neutral meant standing by and saying, "Well, I have nothing to do with it," while being impartial meant judging each situation on its merits and taking the action that was needed. His actions in the eastern DRC had been aggressive: his troops had engaged rebel forces in firefights, disarmed the fifteen thousand combatants who were willing to commit to a DDR program, and used helicopters to rout the ones who refused to surrender and then burned their camps. He had been in the fortunate position of having both an SRSG who encouraged his bold action and subordinate commanders who were keen to take the fight to the militias. That was not entirely the case here in UNMISS, as far as I could tell.

The UN had asked Cammaert to conduct several inquiries into the 2016 violence in South Sudan and discover why the peacekeepers had been unable to deter the attacks or respond effectively to aid civilians. Now he had returned to assess how well UNMISS was doing at implementing the recommendations from a review of the mission that the Office of Peace-keeping Strategic Partnership had conducted in early 2019.[1] I was happy to see his name appear in my email because Cammaert was one of the few investigators to ever give UNMISS recommendations on what it should do to improve. Other so-called experts highlighted problems that were often the results of our own actions—or inactions—but made recommendations only to other parties, never to the mission itself.

＊ ＊

Cammaert was frank about the problems he saw. Some improvements had been made since his previous visits, but he thought that more could and should be done, and that this work started at the top. The anticipated arrival of Lt. Gen. Shailesh Tinaikar, he observed, was "a golden opportunity to put things in a new direction" and to enhance the working relationship between the incoming force commander and the SRSG, David Shearer.

The retired general was also refreshing in that he didn't just talk; he also listened. When members of the staff and I shared our concerns regarding command relationships and community engagement, he took notes. He was also supportive of creating a new military sector in Unity State—a concept that the SRSG and the acting force commander did not favor due to concerns about the potential expense. I had sketched out a cost-neutral option that would allow us to stand up the new sector without incurring additional costs, and I hoped Cammaert's final report would endorse the plan. I genuinely liked the man and his no-nonsense approach, but I did find some of his opinions troubling.

"There are places you should go," he said, "because nasty things are hap-pening there . . . but you cannot start a war by forcing your way through a checkpoint. Peacekeeping has limitations, and one of those limitations is the consent of the host government."

That sort of talk—and the inaction it encouraged—was part of the prob-lem, as far as I was concerned. I hated hearing euphemisms such as "nasty things" used to describe torture, gang rape, and summary executions. In my opinion, using soft words to mask the brutality of the crimes that we should have prevented made it easier for decision-makers to justify taking the easy way out. Besides, according to South Sudan's own laws, we weren't supposed to be stopped at checkpoints. I didn't think that Salva Kiir's government wanted a fight with the UN, nor could it afford our leaving. After all, we brought a great deal of money into the country and were the only security guarantor that ensured aid agencies stayed.

But I didn't try to argue the point. I wanted to work through General Cammaert to influence the SRSG's thinking on a few issues, so I figured that it was best to hold my tongue and save my words for where they could do the most good. "Never miss an opportunity to keep your mouth shut in front of a general" was a piece of advice I'd been given long ago and had ignored pretty much ever since, but I figured this might be a good time to see how it worked.

I recorded my misgivings during one of our meetings, writing in my notebook: "Listening to General Cammaert, I get the feeling that as long as things don't cross into a full-on genocide, Force and Mission won't push the issue." I didn't realize just how prescient that note would prove to be in some ways and how optimistic it was in others.

* *

I already knew that Cammaert and I were aligned on the value of Sector Unity, and I was happy to discover that we also agreed on the importance of hiring more language assistants and of giving battalion commanders money to do quick impact projects (QIPs)—that is, small, labor-intensive engagements that took problems identified by a community and ideally employed some local workers to solve them. As a foreign area officer, I knew well the value of being able to communicate in the local language, and as someone who'd grown up poor in rural Arkansas, I also knew firsthand how valuable any opportunity to make money through meaningful work could be for young people who lacked employment.

"Success in peacekeeping relies on community engagement," Cammaert observed during one of our meetings. When I replied that it was hard to engage without funding, he looked quizzically down the table. "Who manages your QIP funds?"

I explained that they were all held at the mission level, with the Relief, Reintegration, and Protection Section.

"And the projects that they do, is the local population involved in construction?"

I shrugged and said that I didn't know; the force was never consulted. The general made a note, and while he said nothing further, I expected that he might do so later and hopefully to someone with the power to do something about the issue.

The UNMISS implementation of the concept of "early warning" was another concern of mine that Cammaert evidently shared. "It's usually there," he said, "but no action is taken. Malakal, Semuliki, Kamanyola . . ." He ticked off on his fingers a list of places where missions—including UNMISS—had known in advance that trouble was coming and failed to take strong measures to prepare and prevent disasters. Malakal was here in South Sudan. In February 2016 attackers had killed thirty civilians and burned large parts of the UNMISS POC site there. Semuliki and Kamanyola were in the neighboring DRC. The former saw an attack on a UN base that had killed fifteen peacekeepers in 2017; the latter experienced an incident that same year in which thirty-seven civilians were killed while peacekeepers watched and did nothing. I knew other examples in UNMISS that he could have referenced—Akobo in 2013, Bor in 2014—and I wanted to look back on my year in the mission without seeing more villages or bases added to that ignominious list.

So when I read a draft copy of Cammaert's report, I was happy to see that the issues I felt were most important had been briefed to David Shearer and that we would be able to use "the Cammaert Report" as a reference in developing our plans for the year to come. All of the recommendations he made were in line with the many discussions I'd been a part of, and all of them seemed like common sense. Unfortunately, many were simply restatements of what he and others had been putting in public reports since 2016.[2]

Why were outsiders still having to tell mission leadership to improve command and control (C2) relationships and early warning protocols—particularly to prioritize patrols that lasted three days or longer and to address freedom of movement restrictions? To actually listen to what community leaders told us they needed and then use our QIP funds to make it happen? I suspected the answers would include bureaucracy and risk aversion, but rather than worrying why these things hadn't been implemented before, I chose simply to focus on how they could be put into effect now.

19 International Relations

We all become great explorers during our first few
days in a new city, or a new love affair.
—MIGNON MCLAUGHLIN

1 July 2019. Until our new force commander arrived, I couldn't do all that
much to address the issues General Cammaert had identified, so I decided
to take the opportunity to return to Uganda and meet Ashley in person.
We'd been chatting via WhatsApp for over a month, and although our
conversation hadn't quite crossed the line of friendly flirtation, clearly we
had a good connection. Jennifer had never replied to my last message, so
I was pretty sure that ship had sailed. Given the open nature of her mind
and our relationship, I suspected she wouldn't have disapproved.

Ashley and I had matched as we—or at least the GPS settings in our
dating apps—had crossed paths at the end of May. The vivacious blonde aid
worker was in Kampala doing a three-month consultancy, and we had a few
things in common, including long work hours and a love for the outdoors.
I was a bit jealous that she'd already been whitewater rafting on the Nile
and walking with rhinos. Adventures on the rivers and in the bush were
serious work in South Sudan but weekend fun in Uganda.

Ashley had previously worked full-time as a humanitarian but had dealt
with the burnout by opting to spend significant time living as an expat in
places such as Thailand, where a little money went a long way. She'd pick
up short-term contracts whenever her funds started to run low and thus
established an enviable work-life balance that sounded pretty awesome to me.

I knew that once the new force commander arrived, I'd almost certainly be
hard-pressed to take any leave for a while, so I suggested that we take a long
weekend to explore one of Uganda's national parks. Lake Mburo National
Park was only a couple hours' drive from Kampala and was supposed to
be one of the better chances to see leopards, which I'd never spotted in the

wild. Ashley was up for the adventure and suggested that we start the trip as "travel buddies" and go from there. That suited me just fine. I thought that we had potential, but for what, I wasn't sure. There was only one way to find out, though, and that we both had the same block of time free in a pair of busy schedules seemed serendipitous.

I booked a cheap flight on Ethiopian Airlines and discovered that it was much easier to get out of South Sudan than it had been to get in. Soon I was back in the familiar environs of Kampala, with its streets packed full of motorcycle taxis known as *boda bodas* and hawkers selling their wares. My destination was the Skyz Hotel, where I had a booking that I hoped I wouldn't have to use and a date for après work drinks with Ashley on the rooftop bar.

We hit it off at once. She was fit and curvaceous with gray-green eyes and a great smile, but more importantly, she was smart, well traveled, and fun to talk with. As I'd suspected, I never did see the inside of my hotel room. She took me home, took me to bed, and took me in pretty much every way imaginable. The weekend was off to a very good start, and it only got better.

Davis, my go-to Uber driver in Uganda, arrived early the next morning to drive us to the park. Employing him for the trip wasn't terribly expensive and, for a weekend safari, was easier than trying to rent a car and navigate ourselves. I enjoyed self-drive adventures and had spent a couple of weeks navigating to and through the big national parks in Namibia, Botswana, and Zimbabwe in 2015 with a German friend, but such trips required preparation. On that particular adventure I had discovered my own personal "Laws of Driving in Africa": The first law was "Never miss an opportunity to fill your fuel tank." The second law was "Don't drive at night." Hiring Davis had meant that I could leave the refueling and driving to him while I just enjoyed the scenery and Ashley's companionship.

Both were awesome. We didn't see any leopards, but we did see zebras, giraffes, Cape buffalo, and antelopes. We hired a guide to walk through the bush on our first morning and hired her again to take us driving through the park that night.

We spent one night in a rustic cottage at the lakeside and another in a luxurious chalet on the ridgeline overlooking the park. The food, conversation, and sex were all great. Long weeks of hard work in the service of a good cause punctuated by the occasional long weekend in good company? *If this is life in Peaceland*, I thought, *I could probably get used to it.*

So what if I was leaving the military in a year? This weekend with Ashley had proven that there were not only opportunities in the humanitarian sector for the kind of work and lifestyle that I'd become accustomed to in the military but also travel buddies who shared my proclivities for off-the-job adventures. I felt rejuvenated, ready for whatever challenges the new force commander might bring, and was already looking forward to my next block of leave.

* *

I arrived back in Juba just in time to oversee another one of my easy button tasks: the U5 had been asked to run an exercise of our Ebola preparedness plan for the mission's senior staff. A few cases had recently been reported in the DRC, and there was a real concern that the disease might cross the border. Were we prepared to respond if it did?

The answer, unfortunately, was not really.

All the mission's key personnel, from the SRSG on down, gathered in his conference room the morning of the exercise. External organizations were on hand as well with representatives from the World Health Organization (WHO) and the WFP. I briefed the scenario and gave them the first critical input: a hypothetical UN staff member had checked into the clinic at our Yambio base complaining of Ebola-like symptoms after attending a funeral in a neighboring country. I started my stopwatch and waited. Everyone was supposed to go through the steps that they would take, and I would score their "response" and give them another complication: the patient would test positive, the government would demand action, and so on. It didn't take long for the game to break down, devolving into convoluted conversations between the SRSG and some of the other high-ranking staff.

In my postexercise assessment, I noted that communications had been poor, and few people had consulted our existing contingency plan to guide their actions. The WHO rep and the mission's chief medical officer disagreed on how and where to test samples, and who was in charge of contact tracing. We didn't have good isolation facilities or a plan to transport infectious patients, and how an Ebola outbreak would affect ongoing operations was unclear. The bottom line was that very little had changed since the mission had run its last Ebola exercise eight months earlier, in December 2018, so I had little confidence that the recommendations that came out of this exercise would be implemented either.

But that wasn't really my problem to solve; it was a matter for the chief medical officer and the SRSG's special assistant. I was going to have my hands full with the military-specific planning that I'd been sent here to do. It was time to focus on helping to make our robust mandate more than mere words on paper.

20   A Disturbance in the Force

> What is needed most for a successful peacekeeping operation, is
> not just the best equipment, nor the best-trained soldiers, not even
> modern fighting units like artillery and tanks, what is needed,
> above everything else, are remarkable field commanders.
> —PRINCE ZEID RA'AD AL HUSSEIN

6 July 2019. The new force commander, Lt. Gen. Shailesh Tinaikar, met with all the branch chiefs on Saturday and conducted a quick review of the staff before starting the presentations. The Australians were horrified by how my beret looked. Marines never wear berets in our regular assignments, and even in the UN mission, we wore them only on special occasions, donning UN blue ball caps at all other times. This time was the first I'd had a reason to wear my beret, and Rob Williams promised that after the day's work was done, he'd show me how to shape it "properly"—by boiling the bloody thing and molding it to fit my head while it was still damp and pliable. The next step, he said, would be to shave it with a razor, but that was further than I had any desire to go.

General Tinaikar was a compact, wiry man who radiated a strange sort of energy, as if simultaneously channeling a kindly family man and a battle-hardened commando. He was, in fact, both of those things. The general sat impatiently through our prepared briefs. His body language suggested that he wanted to be done with the PowerPoint presentations and quickly. When it was my turn, I explained that we were short of our authorized troop strength by 2,054 troops, or about two and a half battalions; showed where they should have been located; and touched briefly on the concept of Sector Unity. Then I noted the recurrent issues with freedom of movement and addressed the problems with our current operations, using a recent patrol report as an example.

The patrol leader had noted in his written report that the road to the village was overgrown with bushes and should be cleared to improve access, and that the local people needed immediate humanitarian assistance in the fields of health, education, and sanitation. "So," I asked rhetorically, "what action resulted? Did we succeed in clearing the road? Did we contact the right agencies to arrange for the humanitarian assistance?"

The force commander's expression suggested that he already knew the answer.

"The truth is, sir, that right now we have no idea. But we have the power to change that." I closed my brief with the observation that to build trust and confidence, actions would speak louder than words. "Every time a patrol visits an area and identifies a problem, some positive action should quickly be the result," I said and was happy to see the general nod in agreement.

After the last of the chiefs had given a status update on their contribution to the force, General Tinaikar shared his own thoughts and gave some preliminary guidance. He said while he appreciated the effort that had gone into making our presentations, he wanted us to answer one simple question for him: "Are we, as a force, deployed and doing our job in accordance with the mandate?" But he didn't want us to voice our responses here in the conference room; instead, he requested that the staff prepare a coordinated assessment and give it to him within four days.

* *

During his morning brief the following Monday, General Tinaikar again impressed me with his leadership style. The intelligence chief reported that a civilian vehicle had been attacked on the Juba–Nimule Road, resulting in the death of two civilians, and the operations chief noted that a patrol was planned in five days.

"Why this delay?" asked the force commander. "I want them dispatched immediately."

The operations chief tried to explain that we were waiting for SOI, but General Tinaikar waved the notion away. He was fine with SOI in principle, he said, "but if there is a need for us to go, we must go!" He wasn't afraid to lead by example, either; he would go anywhere, talk to anyone. The force commander met people—military officer or civilian, high ranking or not—on their own turf, looked them in the eyes, shook their hands, and listened to them. *This is the sort of leadership we've been missing*, I thought,

7. Lieutenant General Tinaikar (*left*) talking with a counterpart in the opposition. Author photo.

confident that our performance as a military organization was about to take a turn for the better.

The force commander was talking with people by day and reading by night, and as Wednesday's deadline for the coordinated assessment approached, he added more items to be addressed. General Tinaikar wanted updates on our progress in addressing the concerns raised by both the Office of Peacekeeping Strategic Partnership and the Cammaert Reports, and he wanted details on the South Sudanese forces. What was the state of the cantonment areas? Did we have maps of the government and opposition bases, and biographies of their commanders? Attempting to answer that last question quickly provided one of my first insights into one of the fundamental problems with the way the mission operated.

21 The Agony of JMAC

Complex peacekeeping missions involving multiple organizations have
tended to rely on informal networks and personal relations to enable
the sharing and exchange of non-public and sensitive information.
—LAUREN HUTTON

10 July 2019. Five years earlier, Lauren Hutton had been working as a research
fellow in the Conflict Research Unit at the Clingendael Institute, a think
tank based in the Netherlands. She had ten years' experience working in
sub-Saharan Africa with development and humanitarian organizations
including the Institute for Security Studies in South Africa, Saferworld,
and the Danish Refugee Council.

That year, she authored "Prolonging the Agony of UNMISS: The Implementation Challenges of a New Mandate during a Civil War," a twenty-
seven-page report that focused in large part on the shortcomings of the
UNMISS "early warning system"—in layman's terms, how the mission collected information about the security situation in the country and used it
to prevent violence. She had written that the failure of UN peacekeepers to
get off their bases and into the countryside was a big part of the problem,
observing they couldn't build relationships or collect information if they
didn't get into the villages.

Lauren also had pointed out that peacekeepers were rarely sent where
they were most needed. She noted that during the violence in Jonglei State
in 2012, UNMISS had deployed 550 peacekeepers equipped with armored
personnel carriers to the outlying UN base in Pibor, but there was "little
evidence to suggest that there were any attempts to protect outlying communities."[1] Her 2014 report had ended with the grim assessment that "the
Security Council has chosen to prolong the agony of UNMISS [by] mandat-
ing them to protect civilians without the capacity to deter attacks against

population centers; to monitor a seemingly farcical ceasefire agreement, while still keeping the door open for future state building interventions."[2]

In 2016 she had seen how little improvement her report had made when she was in Juba during the worst of the violence. Now, three years later and as the chief of the Joint Mission Analysis Center (JMAC), she was a key leader in UNMISS with a great deal of potential to address the very issues that she had so clearly identified as a researcher. Although we both held the title of "chief," her rank in the UN's civilian personnel structure made her the equivalent of a brigadier general, a distinction that I was well aware of when I was summoned to her office.

Lauren was South African, tall, and with brunette hair in a messy bob and a relaxed air about her. She was easy to talk to, which was a good trait for someone in the business of collecting and analyzing information to have. "I heard the force was looking for this," she said with a conspiratorial smile as she handed me a folder, "and it's close-hold, so please don't share it. But it will probably help you find what General Tinaikar wants to know about the South Sudanese armed forces."

I thanked her for the information, and she said that I was always welcome to come to her directly if I needed anything. For my part, I told her that I'd bring the folder back as soon as I had a chance to absorb the key details and left her office feeling a bit conflicted. On the one hand, I'd made a good connection and obtained the information I needed. On the other hand, this was a perfect example of a massive problem.

There was no reason that I should have had to go directly to the chief JMAC for an intel product that had existed in the mission for five months but had not been made available to the force's key staff officers. The process was ineffective and inefficient—I'd already gotten the exact same report "sideways" from a fellow lieutenant colonel who was assigned to JMAC—but more concerningly, I suspected a lot of information wasn't flowing at all.

For now, I didn't have the luxury of putting too much thought into an issue that was beyond my power to solve directly. I'd raise the issue with my generals and let them work with their peers in JMAC, the Joint Operations Center, and the rest of the SRSG's leadership team to resolve this big-picture problem. Meanwhile, I focused on those issues that I *was* empowered to solve, such as how to better position our forces to protect civilians and humanitarians alike.

22 Coordinated Assessment

> The Security Council . . . decides that the mandate of UNMISS shall
> be as follows, and authorizes UNMISS to use all necessary means to
> perform the following tasks: . . . to protect civilians under threat of
> physical violence, irrespective of the source of such violence . . . ; to
> implement a mission-wide early warning strategy . . . ; to deter and
> prevent sexual and gender-based violence . . . ; to ensure the security
> and freedom of movement of United Nations and associated personnel.
> —UN SECURITY COUNCIL RESOLUTION 2459, MARCH 2019

12 July 2019. With the documents from JMAC in hand, I easily finished my
part of the assessment for General Tinaikar. It began with a quick review
of the current uneasy peace. When the current agreement between South
Sudan's government and the opposition was signed on 12 September 2018,
it had started an eight-month "pre-transition period" after which a transitional government of national unity was supposed to be formed. That
caretaker government would lay the groundwork for a general election to
be held within three years.

Unfortunately, the parties had missed the eight-month deadline to form
the transitional government in May, but Salva Kiir and Riek Machar had
agreed to give their political-military teams a six-month extension to complete the key pre-transitional tasks. The government was now supposed to
form on 12 November.

The first task was to bring together eighty-three thousand soldiers—half
from the government forces, half from the opposition—to create the Necessary
Unified Forces (NUF) to provide security until the elections were held. The
second was to settle the issue of how many states would be acknowledged
once the current government was dissolved and the new government formed.

Since the beginning of 2019, there had been no significant military clashes
between the SSPDF and SPLA-IO, but government forces continued to wage

a scorched-earth campaign against NAS, the separatist guerrilla movement in Central Equatoria led by the renegade general Thomas Cirillo.

It was against this backdrop that we had to consider our answer to the force commander's original question: "Are we doing our job in accordance with the mandate?"

The answer, unfortunately, was not really.

Deliveries of humanitarian assistance had fallen by 5 percent from the same period in 2018, so it was hard to say that we were doing well at "creating conditions conducive to the delivery of humanitarian assistance."[1] In terms of facilitating the return of internally displaced persons (IDPs), the numbers were also moving in the wrong direction: more people were coming to UN protection of civilian sites than were leaving them, and in Sector West, people attempting to return to their homelands from the camps had been killed.

It remained shockingly dangerous across South Sudan, and the presence of peacekeepers hadn't resulted in peace. Approximately 150 civilians were killed every month in violent attacks, with hundreds more injured, abducted, and raped.

Their stories were heartbreaking, if anyone had bothered to look for them. Survivors of the attack on Rocrocdong in June recalled how their elderly chief had been shot in the back of the head with a Kalashnikov as the attackers taunted him with ethnic slurs.[2] His killers had set his body on fire as they left. All this had happened less than thirteen miles from the UN base in Wau.

Thus, we acknowledged that the force was not currently fulfilling the "protection of civilians" pillar of the mandate. We *were* maintaining safety and security within the POC sites—no major incidents in or around them had occurred lately—but those sites only housed 15 percent of the 1.5 million IDPs in South Sudan. The rest lived in dozens of other camps scattered around the countryside, where their support came from humanitarians and their little security from UNMISS.

One thing holding us back was the lack of local translators. When government troops stopped you at a checkpoint, you might be able to talk your way past them—but only if you could communicate with them. If the checkpoint guards spoke only Juba Arabic or a local dialect, and you spoke only English and Hindi, then you had no way to attempt even simple negotiations. And there were far fewer language assistants in-country than there were patrols that needed their aid.

In terms of contingency planning, I noted that while the force had a plan in case of a third wave of violence in Juba, that plan depended on the two subordinate commanders in Sector Juba and Sector South, respectively, to carry it out. Those officers each had their own plans, which hadn't been coordinated, and it was unclear whether UN forces in the capital were any better situated to protect civilians if fighting broke out again than they had been in 2016.[3]

Information-sharing within the force itself was not great, and between the force, JMAC, and the Joint Operations Center, it was worse. Several agencies were duplicating their efforts, and no common operating picture existed.[4] My fellow branch chiefs reinforced the message that information sharing structures were neither streamlined nor formalized: the force's Intelligence and CIMIC Branches didn't even have access to JMAC's early warning matrix and were told that a memorandum of understanding was required to put them on the distribution list.

The CIMIC chief also raised other problems that were common knowledge among the staff: The force was not allotted any budget to conduct its own QIPs, and the current UNMISS approach did not lend itself to rapid implementation of small-scale activities since the mission favored high-profile, large-scale projects. We asked General Tinaikar to advocate for $20,000 per sector—just 5 percent of the mission's $1.5 million QIP budget—to be allocated to the peacekeeping battalions so they could respond to requests from the community leaders with whom they interacted on their patrols.

Throughout the hour-long brief, I'd been watching General Tinaikar to see what I could learn from his body language. I'd never seen anyone manage to look simultaneously impatient and impassive before, yet the force commander seemed to do so. When the brief concluded, he told us that he appreciated the assessment and would give us verbal guidance shortly and written orders to follow.

23 Orders in Work

> In preparing for battle, I have always found that plans
> are useless, but planning is indispensable.
> —PRESIDENT DWIGHT D. EISENHOWER

14 July 2019. The verbal guidance that I received was to create the detailed
written orders that General Tinaikar had alluded to; that was the key function of the Policy and Plans Branch. Our new operations order would be a
cornerstone document, representing the way that a military organization
such as the force translated ideas into action. The order under which we
operated was over a year old and lacked specific provisions for addressing
the challenges presented by the transition in South Sudan's governance that
was scheduled for November. It glossed over many important issues such
as the role of women, the employment of language assistants, the use of
QIPs, and our approach to patrolling.

The document I was tasked to draft would describe the situation in which
we found ourselves, clarify our mission vis-à-vis the mandate, and contain
the force commander's guidance on how each of the many elements of the
UNMISS military component was intended to operate to achieve that mission.
That guidance would take the form of a short paragraph summing up the
"commander's intent" followed by longer descriptions of the overarching
concepts that drove our operations. Finally, it would include detailed lists
of specific tasks for every element of the organization: the sectors, the individual battalions, and the various divisions of the FHQ itself.

The thirty pages that made up the order were just the tip of the iceberg;
much of the specifics were contained in eleven appendixes that spanned
another seventy-one pages. Fortunately, I wasn't doing it alone. Assisted
by Emm, Hugh took charge of actually writing the massive document. My
deputy, Murray Brown, had returned to New Zealand and been replaced
by Lt. Col. Tracey Tibbs. She took on oversight of the budgeting and the

day-to-day minutiae of running U5, which freed me up to focus on deep thinking, research, and discussions with my fellow branch chiefs and other stakeholders. The process of developing the massive document helped me gain a much deeper understanding of the country, the conflict, and many of the key players involved.

* *

The draft operations order described the situation in the early summer of 2019 as characterized by political tension at the national level of government, uncertainty and unrest at the state level, and a constant threat of flood, famine, disease, and violent death at the individual level—that of civilians in the villages.

At the national level, the major issue was that the 2018 peace agreement had not been implemented. The preconditions required the unification of the armed forces, an agreement on the number and the borders of the states, and the arrangements for a VIP protection force in Juba to ensure the safety of both Salva Kiir and Riek Machar. The six-month extension that had been granted in May was now nearly half gone, and almost no progress had been made on these preconditions.

The number of states could be solved with spoken words between politicians and the scribble of a pen on paper, but unifying the fractured military forces would take time and money. Neither the government nor the opposition was making any real progress in the planned two-part process of mustering troops in cantonment sites for medical screenings and then sending those who were fit and willing to serve to other sites for the training that was meant to forge the former opponents into a unified force.

The document's situation section also contained a brief on the neighboring states, each of which was of interest for a different reason. Kenya supported South Sudan diplomatically and economically, and until recently, it had provided many of the peacekeepers in UNMISS. But Kenya pulled out those troops after Secretary-General Ban Ki-moon sacked the Kenyan general Johnson Ondieki from his role as force commander following the violence in Juba in 2016. General Cammaert's report found the "chaotic and ineffective response" of UNMISS was due "to an overall lack of leadership, preparedness and integration among the various components of the mission."[1] Kenyans believed, with good reason, that General Ondieki had been made a scapegoat for the failings of others. The force was only one of the various components that had failed, and the person responsible for all of them—the SRSG, a Danish diplomat named Ellen Margrethe Løj—was not held accountable. Instead, she was allowed to extend her assignment in South Sudan by four months and exit gracefully on her own terms and time line, with Ban Ki-moon praising her "dedication, commitment and important contributions" to UNMISS.[2]

Uganda's president had long supported Salva Kiir's government, irritating Machar and his generals. The country also anchored one end of the only paved road into Juba—a vital pipeline for imports that included most of the nation's food.

While Ethiopia provided many peacekeepers and supported the diplomatic solution, it was also a source of tension. The territory of the Nuer people transcended national boundaries, and a large population lived in the Gambella, a border region of Ethiopia that abuts the eastern edge of South Sudan. Given that Riek Machar and the majority of the opposition military forces were Nuer as well, the South Sudanese government looked upon Ethiopia with a degree of suspicion.

To the north and west, the neighborhood was even more problematic. Sudan was politically unstable after the fall of its longtime dictator, Omar al-Bashir, but it still made a claim to the Abyei Administrative Area. The UN maintained its own Interim Security Force for Abyei (UNISFA) in this politically contested area while the governments of Sudan and South Sudan negotiated to see how the small area of land and the large oil reserves on which it sat would be divided. To the west were the DRC and the CAR, each wracked with violence and hosting major UN peacekeeping missions. The border regions where the DRC, the CAR, and South Sudan met represented vectors for many problems: guns, illegally extracted resources, slaves, cattle, and diseases such as Ebola.

But in the operations order, those issues and areas—as large and problematic as they were—received only a summary review. Our main focus was on our own area of responsibility, which was one of the most politically and militarily disorganized environments I had ever seen.

* *

When UNMISS arrived in South Sudan in 2011, it established field offices in each of the ten states, whose areas varied wildly in size and population. In each state, the field office was collocated with the state capital, and the senior civilian leaders of these UN outposts held the title "head of field office" (HOFO). They wore many hats while directing and coordinating the activities specialists working in political and civil affairs, human rights, the rule of law, and so on. Also, they traditionally served as the area security coordinators for their respective states. Our peacekeepers were deployed in sectors that did not always align with the areas allocated to the existing field offices. That meant our sector commanders might find themselves answering to more than one field office, and some HOFOs might find themselves with multiple sector commanders under their nominal control.

The situation was worse in Juba, which was the site of two sector head-quarters on separate bases. Sector Juba was stuck on the outskirts of town at UN House, as Sector South still occupied the key terrain at the airport and downtown. Airmobile units, which needed access to fixed-wing aircraft for rapid deployment, were assigned to Sector Juba and based far from the airport. During a crisis, it was unclear who was in charge of what, and that had been one of the major problems in 2016. A realignment of these tangled command structures would be, I was certain, a key measure to undertake before Riek Machar returned to Juba in November.

* *

The operations order also laid out what we considered to be the "most dangerous" course of action (COA) and the "most likely" COA. They represented what we believed were the greatest threats that the force might be expected to face in its defense of the mandate and those threats that, while less potent, were more probable. The most dangerous threats included a return to civil war, which could be triggered in November by Riek Machar's planned return to Juba to form the transitional government or if the transition failed to happen. Another possibility was for a large Nuer force to attack the Murle tribe in the eastern state of Jonglei as had happened in 2011. The most likely threats included increasing intercommunal violence resulting in dead and displaced civilians, stolen livestock, and a continuous cycle of revenge attacks.

My job in creating the operations order was to prepare and position the force to deal with the most dangerous possibilities at any time while enabling us to maintain a day-to-day focus both on suppressing the most likely threats to the safety of civilians and on ensuring the free movement of humanitarian supplies. I took this job very seriously. For the first time in a long time, I felt I was doing something that really mattered, something that could really make a positive change—at least in this small and overlooked corner of the world.

24 Unity!

> One of the deadliest attacks was launched by Dinka from
> [Warrap] on a cattle camp in [Unity State] in mid-January
> 2019, which killed and injured hundreds of civilians
> including dozens of women, children and infants.
> —REPORT OF THE COMMISSION ON HUMAN
> RIGHTS IN SOUTH SUDAN

15 July 2019. Cynics often quip that few things ever go according to plan,
and military logistics officers tend to be very cynical people. Alexander the
Great had once observed that "my logisticians are a humorless lot. They
know they are the first ones I will slay if my campaign fails." My own military
background was logistics, and I'd spent twelve years of my career working in
that field, with occasional forays into advisory assignments, strategic think
tanks, and teaching to break the monotony. Although I wasn't particularly
worried that General Tinaikar would slay me if his campaign to create
a more secure environment in South Sudan failed, two other proverbial
quotes about military planning were never far from my mind: The first was
that "no plan survives first contact with the enemy"; the second was that
"a vision without resources is a hallucination." Thus, I worked to create an
order that was as resilient, flexible, and cost-neutral as possible and used
all the levers at my disposal to ensure that the resources we would need to
implement it—people, money, and equipment—would be available to the
force when the order was ready.

Fortunately, my other roles as the chief U5 positioned me extremely well
to pull those levers. I was responsible for overseeing the force's input on the
results-based budgeting process, managing the flow of new units into the
mission as old ones rotated out, and overseeing the updating of the documents that specified what equipment was brought in by those units. I was
also assigned to draft the force's input to the secretary-general's recurring

reports to the Security Council. That meant I'd have a chance to use the power of the pen both to highlight where we were currently falling short of fulfilling the mandate and to suggest ways to do better.

UNMISS already had a base in Unity's state capital of Bentiu, which was also the location of the UN's biggest POC site, but the peacekeepers there currently fell under the command of Sector North, which was located 124 miles northeast in Malakal. History had repeatedly shown the problem of trying to manage the security situation in Unity from afar, and while the idea to stand up a new sector headquarters there had been circulating since 2017, it had always been deemed too expensive.

But I had seen something interesting in our budgeting protocols. One unique detail about the UN's method of reimbursing the troop-contributing countries was that every soldier in a headquarters staff—whether a sergeant or a general—cost the same on paper. Our current budget allowed for a total of 431 staff officers in the force, but we only had about 420 assigned. After discussions with General Herlyng and General Cammaert, both of whom agreed that it was a logical way to improve command and control in this key region, I'd put together a plan that would allow us to stand up a sector headquarters at Bentiu so that it wouldn't cost us anything extra, and I had it ready to brief the force commander as soon as he arrived.

Without expanding the budget, we could bring in nine more officers plus a brigadier general to command them and a colonel to serve as the deputy, and we could supplement those numbers with the dozen officers who were currently working in Bentiu but taking their orders from Malakal. The new sector would have slightly fewer officers than some of the others, but as General Cammaert had acerbically observed one month before, "I get the impression that these headquarters are not understaffed."

The force commander endorsed the plan, and I was asked to brief it to the SRSG at his principals' management meeting. At this weekly forum, the mission's senior leadership convened to decide issues of policy, operations, and resources as they pertained to the implementation of the mandate, the welfare and safety of the UN staff, and the perceived risks to the mission's reputation. Each "principal" headed a major component of the mission. Besides the SRSG and his chief of staff, there were a pair of deputy SRSGs, one focused on political issues, the other on humanitarian concerns; the force commander and the UNPOL police commissioner; and the director

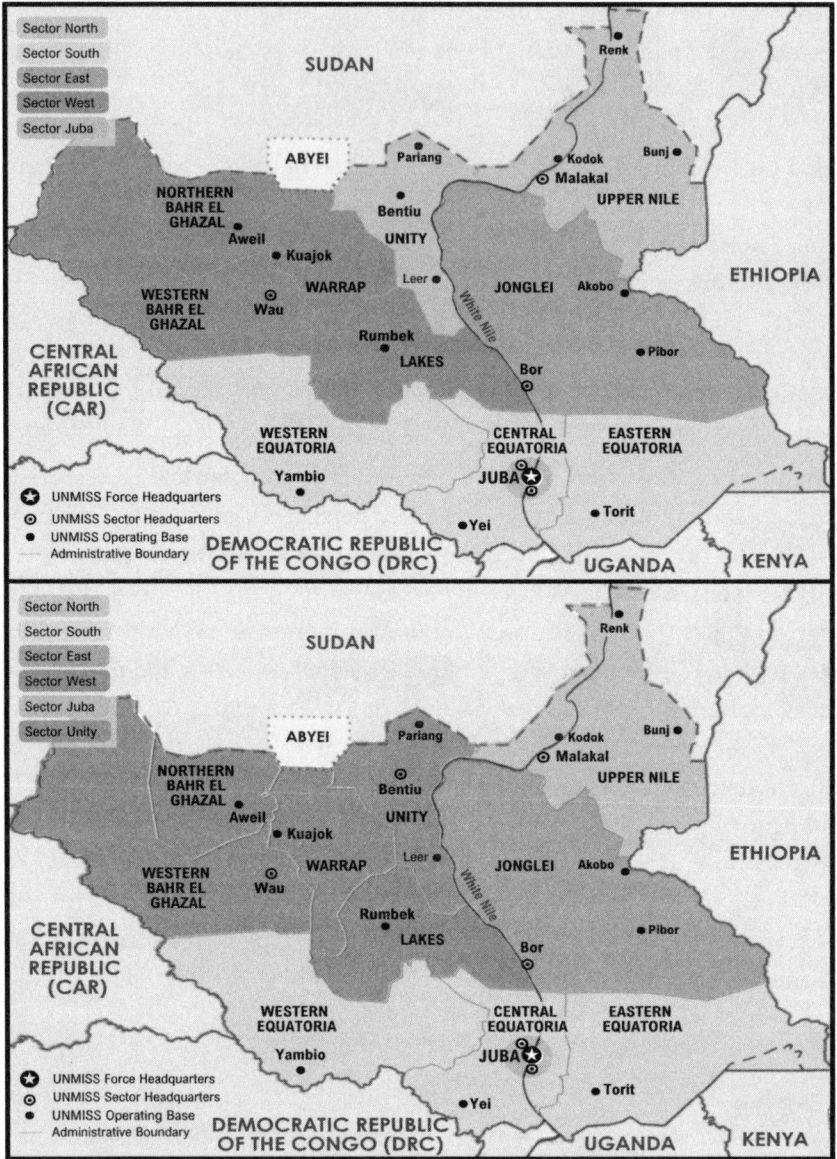

8. Maps of UNMISS military sectors before and after the creation of Sector Unity. Created by author based on United Nations maps.

of mission services. It was my first time pitching to the SRSG, but I wasn't nervous. I'd already met him informally during the security workshop at the Crown Hotel in June and at various social events around base. A big, tall, balding man in his early sixties, David Shearer evinced the athleticism of an aging sportsman. He preferred open collars to ties, and his default expression was a genial smile, although I'd seen his face harden when talking about serious matters.

As expected, the SRSG approved the initiative in principle, but it wasn't lost on me that in spite of small victories such as this one, much was still to be done. Sector East had reported that three hundred "armed youths" were on the move south of our outpost in Akobo. But were they three hundred young men under one leader? Ten groups of thirty men? What were their intentions? What were they armed with? Did we have a plan to send a patrol out to engage with them? That no one had answers to any of those questions highlighted the gaps in information gathering that continued to challenge the force even when neither the government nor the opposition was actively interfering with our operations.

Nevertheless, my confidence was buoyed by this early win. There was a still a lot to do, but I had a great team working for me, and all of my senior leaders seemed willing to support initiatives that made sense. I felt that we should build on this momentum and use the new operations order to deliver on the implicit promises that the mandate made to the people of South Sudan and the humanitarian community that served them.

25 Women, Peace, and Security

> It's crucial that women participate in the peace process and peacebuilding,
> because they are affected by conflict. . . . But when you bring together
> the parties of the conflict, women are not on their minds. . . . And
> when the issues of women are brought up, it's always older women who
> occupy the space. [But] young women . . . were the first to think and
> understand the context of the current conflict; they were innovative. . . .
> I believe young women's inclusion in peacebuilding will create
> sustainable peace, because they know how to address these issues.
> —NYUON SUSAN SEBIT

19 July 2019. Almost two decades before, the UN Security Council had unanimously adopted a resolution on women, peace, and security, acknowledging the disproportionate impact that conflict and war had on women and girls, as well as the critical role that women could and already were playing in peacebuilding efforts. The four pillars of the resolution were aimed at increasing the participation of women in decision-making at all levels, protecting the rights of women and girls in conflict zones and emergency sites such as refugee camps, preventing violence against women, and ensuring that relief and recovery efforts both addressed women's needs and gave them agency in the process.

As a military officer, I'd been pushing for elements of this agenda for years, promoting the idea of gender equality in the Marine Corps and military forces writ large while doing what I could to stamp out the insidious specter of sexual harassment, discrimination, and assault that still haunted the U.S. military. I knew the value of women in the armed forces; many of the most competent officers and enlisted personnel I'd worked with were women. Now in UNMISS, I had new opportunities to help level the playing field.

The commitment to "women, peace, and security" was a priority of the secretary-general's 2018 "Action for Peacekeeping" initiative, and the

Security Council mandated the UN peacekeeping operations to implement its eight pillars into our plans and operations. Thus, I was also making sure that our evolving operations order expanded and codified our approach to employing women peacekeepers and increasing their numbers in our battalions.

Additionally, I had contacts at the Sea Services Leadership Association, an organization focused on networking, education, and mentorship of women serving in the U.S. Navy, Marine Corps, and Coast Guard. They were holding a Joint Women's Leadership Symposium in Washington DC that was open to servicewomen from around the world, and I had suggested to Kyle Walton that we should sponsor a senior female officer from the South Sudanese military to attend. I believed it would be very beneficial for such a leader to attend the event and to get a sense of the level of professionalism and diversity seen elsewhere in the world's militaries. I also thought it would help increase the prestige of women in the South Sudanese armed forces. Kyle agreed with my assessment and said he would raise the issue with the right people in the embassy.

* *

Although my approach to dealing with women in my professional capacity was deliberate and methodical, the same could hardly be said of my personal life. Ashley and I had stayed in touch, and I managed to squeeze in a brief but passionate visit with her the next time I was in Uganda.

I was there on leave for a ten-day safari with another woman, a friend who was visiting from the States. She was a brilliant polymath, a great travel companion and conversationalist, and a woman who wanted our relationship to be something more than I was willing to make it. Despite a degree of awkwardness and some early miscommunication, it ended up being a very lovely trip. We walked with rhinos, visited Murchison Falls, and saw the famous tree-climbing lions of Ishasha. We blew out tires and burned out alternators, but we got through every tight spot via the kind of hospitality and get-it-sorted practicality that would be—for me—one of the enduring hallmarks of East African culture.

* *

I returned to South Sudan feeling refreshed. The brief vacation had been nice, but it felt genuinely good to be back in the mission, working in service of something that I believed in. Now I understood the importance of taking regular short breaks to sustain my mental health, and I wondered again why our local staff members weren't given similar opportunities.

My return coincided with the celebration held at the Chinese Embassy of the ninety-second anniversary of the foundation of the Chinese People's Liberation Army. As I shared food, drinks, and conversation with my Chinese colleagues, members of their embassy staff, and the other foreign guests, I reflected that one of the great strengths of UN peacekeeping was the way it brought national military forces together in a cooperative environment; this was especially valuable in cases when the forces in question generally viewed each other as strategic competitors. Again, it gave me hope that our countries might someday adopt a more cooperative approach in general, and I regularly shared that sentiment with my colleagues. Now I also had another cause for hope but one that I kept to myself, because it involved a woman on whom I'd had a crush for many years.

* *

Jayde and I had first met in 2011 in Jakarta, where I had been attending the Indonesian Naval Command and Staff College and she had been running her own English school whose profits funded charitable work throughout Indonesia. Since then, she'd moved to New York to run a marketing firm focused on science communications, while I'd continued to bounce from place to place: the Carolinas, Afghanistan, Hawaii, Washington DC, and now South Sudan. Through it all, we'd maintained a friendship that consisted of long periods where we were focused on our own lives, punctuated with occasional meetings to catch up in person.

Those meetings were usually linked to interesting events—TED Talks, visits to tech conferences, science awards presentations, and the like—but now she'd sent me a note out of the blue saying that she wanted to visit me somewhere in Africa.

I'd been attracted to Jayde—who was tall and curvaceous with a platinum blonde bob, blue eyes, and a brilliant smile—since I'd first laid eyes on her. I suspected that if she saw any romantic potential in me, it would probably be complicated as I'd been dating one of her friends when we first met. But that was a very long time ago, and for the first time in a while, both of us were single. So I told myself that if we met up as planned, I'd do something that I'd been putting off for almost a decade and ask if she wanted to take a chance on finding out if friends really did make the best lovers.

* *

Back in the office, I started the final editing of the operations order, which included some significant changes from previous orders. One was a two-page appendix titled "On Gender" and required us to assess the implications of our actions for women, men, girls, and boys, and to include gender as a consideration in planning, intelligence, and operations.

It also demanded that we work toward gender equality in the area of operations—that is, use the valuable differences in the understanding, experiences, and capabilities of women in peace operations—and engage with the Office of Military Affairs at UN Headquarters to formulate and implement a plan to advance the UN's goals for achieving gender parity in our peacekeeping forces. That plan was meant to create achievable, structured goals and incentives to increase the number of women in peacekeeping contingents and leadership positions throughout the force. It was not lost on me that the United States had made no particular effort to ensure women were selected for its handful of peacekeeping billets, but when they were assigned such roles, their performance was outstanding.

I knew I had much to learn about what role gender—and culture more generally—played in South Sudan and rued again that most of my training with USMOG had been focused so much on contingencies and so little on the country itself. But I rationalized that as with so many things in my military career, I would figure it out as I went along.

26 Rhythm and the Rains

The devastation that we're witnessing there is unprecedented. The people in these areas are used to flooding—they're telling us that these are the worst floods they've ever seen. The impact that rain can create is massive, because there is no infrastructure, no roads.
—KIM COLLINS, MSF LOGISTICS COORDINATOR, AND
ADHAM EFFENDI, WFP HEAD OF LOGISTICS

1 August 2019. Every three months, the mission had to draft a report on the situation in South Sudan and what we were doing to improve it. In turn, the secretary-general would submit it to the UN Security Council for its consideration. Writing the force's input brought it home to me that fully a quarter of my year as a UN peacekeeper had already passed. What had I accomplished so far? Not much, judging from what I was reviewing, and my thoughts were as gloomy as the skies outside.

Although the force was the largest element in the mission, we provided very little in the way of data or metrics to the report; mostly we supplied some very questionable numbers that supposedly represented the extent of the patrols we'd sent. We weren't required to document any concrete results from those patrols—just the numbers—and clearly no one was even looking at those, as they fluctuated wildly and were never questioned. Other pillars of the mission—the Human Rights Division, the Civil Affairs Division, the Political Affairs Division, and the Child Protection Unit—*did* submit metrics, but no one seemed to pay much attention to those numbers either. Total deaths were down from the previous period, but it wasn't due to our patrols, which were being stopped even more frequently than before the conference in June. Instead, South Sudan, which had suffered a drought the previous year, was now experiencing its heaviest rains since 2015, and much of the country was flooded. Attacks were down because the high waters and terrible road conditions hampered movement. The number of people

9. Rainy season road conditions in South Sudan. Courtesy of UN World Food Programme.

seeking refuge in the POC camps was still going up, not down, and the WFP had adjusted its estimates of how many South Sudanese citizens would need food aid just to survive upward by an astounding 1.5 million people.

Yet the amount of money budgeted to feed them did not increase, and in fact, only 45 percent of the required funds had been provided by August. Worst of all, the terrible conditions of the roads made distributing aid even more difficult.

The passing months also meant time was ticking down toward the 12 November deadline for the transitional government's formation, but no progress was being made to satisfy the prerequisites. Also, the process of getting our own operations order approved was taking longer than I'd hoped. The order called for a reorganization of some of our forces and an emphasis on longer patrols that used a hub-and-spoke principle.[1] But it was a new approach for which consensus building was key.

   * *

My grim mood didn't last long. While I still had concerns, I was well trained at suppressing negative emotions and presenting a cheerful face to the world. Psychologists define "compartmentalization" as a defense mechanism or a

coping strategy, and they often consider it to be maladaptive if used unconsciously. But in the U.S. military, I'd learned it was a useful skill to block
out distracting or problematic thoughts and focus on the tasks at hand.

I had also found my social circle—being a token American among the
"Auswegians," a loose association whose nickname derived from the nation-
alities of its majority members—which was held together by common
interests in hard workouts, good food, and great parties.[2] My entrée into the
group was a natural extension of the people I worked with. Hugh McKeown,
the undisputed champion of the "best sideburns" award in the FHQ, had
dubbed our team the "Fantastic Five" because we got along so well. Our
only vacant desk had recently been filled by Sgt. Devendra Prasad, who
made our lives infinitely easier with his ability to obtain any hard-to-get
item or service through his network of fellow noncommissioned officers.
"The most important thing to have in this Mission," I wrote in my journal,
"is a good Admin Sergeant."

I had fallen into an easy battle rhythm by now. Up early for a hike or
a run around the base, shower, breakfast, and a walk to the office. A scan
of the news, then off to the force commander's morning meeting. Coffee,
work, lunch, meetings. Afternoon tea, work, CrossFit, dinner. Every day
of the work week was much the same until Friday.

When the weekend arrived, almost always some sort of social event or a
string of them would help the leisure hours fly by. The rowdy rooftop bar of
the Tulip Inn, a popular hotel near the airport, had happy hours. If we left the
office right at 4:30 p.m. on Friday, we could be there by 5:00 p.m. and have
an hour and a half of socializing with the expat community before piling
into our vehicles and dashing back to UN House before the gates closed for
curfew. The SRSG could frequently be seen holding court in the Tulip's more
genteel downstairs lounge, and the running joke was that you couldn't be
late if you got back before he did. One of my friends, Sonia Hamid, was our
usual designated driver. As a Muslim, she was always sober, but she loved to
socialize and never complained about taking the wheel. "You can pay me with
songs," she'd say and would laugh as we belted out various national anthems
and Broadway hits while our vehicle bounced its way along Juba's dirt roads.

There were also birthday parties for fellow Americans, going-away parties
for colleagues leaving the mission, and events such as the "culture weekend" hosted by the Chinese peacekeeping battalion where all the other

10. The shipwreck in the Nile near the AFEX compound. Author photo.

battalions showcased elements of their national traditions. Many of these gatherings were held on UN House, where a large *tukul* (round traditional hut) sited between the buildings of the force headquarters and the mission headquarters formed the nexus of on-base social life.

Saturdays offered us a chance to leave the base for a day and go shopping, have lunch, or lie by the pool at one of the luxury hotels or residential compounds that catered to foreigners and wealthy locals. Our go-to spot was the picturesque AFEX river camp, one of the oldest of the secure compounds in Juba and where visiting expats often made their home.[3] It provided residential and office spaces, a swimming pool, a gym, and, most importantly from the perspective of us day visitors, a bar and restaurant set on the bank of the Nile. The AFEX cantina was one of the most iconic expat watering holes in Juba, mainly because its riverside bar overlooked a large, double-decker passenger ship whose stern lay submerged in the riverbed. About three-quarters of the vessel angled up out of the swirling waters at a thirty-degree angle.

There were various stories about the provenance of this wreck. Some accounts said it had been sunk by rockets fired during one of the many rounds of fighting in Juba, but the truth was more prosaic. The ship's engine had failed, and it had drifted to its current location in 2015. The stern slowly sank, and by 2017 it had attained its current appearance.

Sundays I usually spent doing some sort of volunteer activity with local schools, church groups, or similar organizations. One weekend featured the inauguration of an athletic field that our Thai engineering battalion had built for the Exodus Academy, a school near UN House where Emm often helped out. The field was simply hard-packed dirt but suitable for sports such as soccer and touch rugby, with the latter being the first game played on it.

A tent was erected, and various local dignitaries, including the SRSG, came out to watch two teams of local kids play a spirited game of touch rugby. The game was refereed by Gemma Robson, a British aid worker who, in her spare time, had put together the "Touch Rugby Trust" to help local children learn to play a game that had the potential to open doors for them in the future. I'd played rugby in college, and since then it had proven a great way of getting connected into the expat community almost everywhere I went: Japan, Indonesia, and now again in South Sudan. Gemma told me a group of rugby aficionados played touch rugby at one of the parks in Juba's midtown, and it soon became another part of my weekend battle rhythm—volunteer coaching touch rugby at the Exodus Academy on some days, playing touch rugby with the local aficionados at Doctor Biar Park in downtown Juba on others.

Despite the rainy weather, life for the UN staff in Juba was pretty good, and it was easy to forget that this wasn't the case for most people in most parts of the country. It was also easy to get lulled into believing that our routine would remain the same. I'd soon learn the dangers of that sort of thinking.

27 The Tigers of South Sudan

In a country plagued by horrific violence and rampant corruption, South Sudan's National Security Service (NSS) stands out as particularly ruthless, secretive, and well-funded. Fear of the NSS is pervasive in South Sudan. . . . Its personnel have been involved in widespread, grave human rights abuses, including kidnapping, torture, and illegal detention, and the organization operates without regard for basic human rights.
—REPORT BY THE SENTRY

16 August 2019. "I could have you all killed!" were not words I thought I'd hear when I joined the peacekeepers from one of our Rwandan battalions for a Wednesday night patrol in Juba. Our vehicles were pulled up at the side of the Gudele Road as a plainclothes officer from the National Security Service shouted at our patrol leader, Lt. Aimable Nteziryayo, who listened impassively to the tall South Sudanese man's tirade.

The imposing man claimed to be a colonel, and although he wore no distinguishing identification, I figured the best way to defuse the situation was to take him at his word. I'd been standing by, watching the scene play out, but I didn't want to see it escalate. We had sixteen armed Rwandan peacekeepers in our pair of vehicles, and the NSS officer was backed up by a half dozen men with assault rifles.

I recalled from my ECAC training that making aggressors feel respected and establishing some sort of common connection with them were often the best ways to dial back a tense situation, so I saluted the colonel and identified myself as a lieutenant colonel and the senior UN representative in the group. The salute seemed to take him aback, and he waved his hand half-heartedly in return. Then he asked why an American was out with a Rwandan patrol.

"Just an observer," I replied.

"What are you doing out past curfew?"

"Just making sure all is peaceful, in accordance with our mandate."

"Of course, things are peaceful. Have you seen any troubles in the street?"

"Not so far."

The colonel was adamant that Juba's own police and security forces were capable of keeping the peace. I nodded acknowledgement, saying that we were just following the orders from our general and that I'd report on how calm things appeared. "Perhaps if the chief of the NSS could talk to General Tinaikar . . ."

My interlocutor seemed a little mollified. I got him to agree, reluctantly, that even colonels and lieutenant colonels had to follow orders. But then, whereas moments before he'd been trying to convince me there was no need for our night patrols, he pivoted the conversation 180 degrees, saying that the streets weren't safe for us.

I said we appreciated his concern and that we would drive slowly and safely. I added that we were already on the return leg of our patrol, headed back toward UN House, which was technically correct.

He nodded. "Very well. You can go on your way, but call me if you have any problems." He gave me a number scribbled on a piece of paper. "Look out for the tigers," he said, as Lieutenant Nteziryayo got back into our vehicle. Tigers are not found in Africa—they are an Asian species—but I knew what he meant.

We continued down Gudele Road and turned left onto Rock City Road, which took us south around the Jebel toward UN House. About ten minutes down the road, we were stopped at a checkpoint manned by members of the SSPDF's Tiger Division. They were members of the Presidential Guard's forces, whose reputation in Juba wasn't much better than that of the NSS.

Their leader said we couldn't continue and that he would escort us to their base for questioning. When I told him that we had clearance from the NSS, he replied, "They don't grant clearances."

I dialed the number on the piece of paper and handed him the phone. "Please explain this to my friend," I said.

The officer took my phone and began talking into the handset in a language I could not understand but presumed to be Dinka. His tone was harsh at first, but then he fell silent. After listening, when he spoke again, his tone was much more deferential. He handed the phone back to me.

"You are cleared. Go ahead."

I thanked him, and we continued on our way back to the base. I'd just experienced my first taste of the casual harassment that our peacekeepers saw on a regular basis, but I had a final surprise waiting for me the next day.

I'd sent a note to the Rwandan battalion's operations officer, Major Munana, thanking him for the opportunity to go on patrol with his men and asking for a copy of the patrol report. When I read it, I was surprised to see that the section of the patrol report titled "Incidents" contained a single word— "none." The activities of the South Sudanese security forces in the city were also listed as "normal." Of the previous night's misadventures, the report only said that the patrol had encountered checkpoints that "were asking why the patrol was still in the city at that time. However, they were not aggressive."

I shook my head. If the peacekeepers who went on these missions daily didn't consider death threats and attempts to take them in for questioning as aggressive or even unusual, then there was definitely a disconnect between what actually happened on our patrols and what got reported on paper. It was one thing to read about these things but very different to experience them for oneself.[1] *What must such situations be like*, I wondered, *for civilians who lacked the symbolic blue helmet and didn't have a dozen well-armed peacekeepers to back them up?*

28 Inconceivable

You keep using that word. I do not think it
means what you think it means.
—INIGO MONTOYA

18 August 2019. General Tinaikar was holding his first commander's conference in Juba, and I had been tasked to brief the draft operations order
to the sector commanders. In it, we proposed three "lines of effort": The
first was to improve our internal knowledge base and early warning mechanisms, the second was to expand our patrol and outreach strategies, and
the third was to upgrade our infrastructure. Underlying all three would be
a realignment of our sector boundaries and a consolidation of the units
assigned to each sector.

We would measure effects instead of numbers and would focus our
efforts on securing those areas that we had reason to think would be the
most dangerous for civilians. We would start implementing longer patrols
using a hub-and-spoke approach—that is, moving to a problematic area and
setting up a temporary base that would remain in place for two weeks as we
launched shorter foot patrols from that site to neighboring villages. We would
stand up Sector Unity, move our High Readiness Company to Tomping, and
consolidate our Nepalese reserve battalion so that we could reinforce any
sector on short notice. That would mean swapping out the two companies
of Nepalese peacekeepers in Yei with an equivalent number of Rwandan
peacekeepers from Juba. This brief wasn't particularly controversial. All the
sector commanders had their own planning sections, and since July they
had all been working with the Fantastic Five to come up with this very plan.

For their part, when given a chance to address the force commander, the
sector commanders brought up a set of legitimate and interlinked concerns.
General Alam from Sector East noted that during a recent operation to take
medicine to a village, the mission's air operations cell would not extend the

pickup by an hour until he—a general—had gotten involved. "Why," he asked, "does everyone seem to work against us?"

Sector Juba's General Nkubito noted that the UN's own Department for Safety and Security had tried to prevent his night patrols from leaving the base at Tomping on the grounds that it was too dangerous.

General Wang from Sector West reiterated the point that he'd brought up when we'd visited Wau in June: the missions in Mali and the DRC had DDR programs, so why didn't we?

When he spoke later in the afternoon, SRSG David Shearer answered that last question. He informed us that the mission would not support a DDR process logistically for political reasons, explaining, "We would be blamed for it not working." He added that the failed attempt at disarmament in 2011 had been a disaster. Maybe there could be some sort of reintegration program for ex-combatants, but he didn't believe in taking weapons or buying them back.

This was certainly surprising. Only a few months previously, Shearer's home nation of New Zealand had banned almost all small arms following the Christchurch massacre and had planned, approved, and implemented a $131 million gun buyback program in just four weeks. The country's prime minister, Jacinda Ardern, had shown how quickly a nation could disarm when the political will was there. I thought to myself, *UNMISS could use a leader like Ardern—someone who was not afraid to make an unpopular decision and do what was right to reduce violence.*[1]

The SRSG ended his session by asking us to be "robust" in our approach, warning, "The South Sudanese won't respect us if we appear weak." While "robust" was a word that Shearer threw around liberally, whenever I'd heard the term used in UNMISS lately, I'd begun to think of the iconic scene from *The Princess Bride* where the swordsman Inigo Montoya questioned whether his Sicilian compatriot really understood the words he was saying.

Shearer bade us a good day and left the conference room. At that point, the force commander concluded the day with a speech that was part pep talk and part scolding.

"The military is the pride of any nation," General Tinaikar said, "and we must be the pride of UNMISS. We have the most people, so we must set the pace." He paused. "We are not here to fight, we're here to bring peace. But we must be prepared to use our weapons. If you say that civilians are preventing you from doing the right thing, why are you letting them? Pick up the phone! Call me. Call General Herlyng."

* *

In the "most dangerous threats" section of the operations order, our Intelligence Branch had noted the potential for an attack by a large Nuer force against the Murle people in eastern Jonglei. It had been one thing to read that simple statement yet another still to see what such an attack would be. A German officer on his second deployment with UNMISS had recently sent me a brief and a report from 2012, during his first time in the mission, and I'd found them deeply unsettling.

The PowerPoint slides contained images of the White Army—thousands of young Nuer men carrying rifles and machetes—marching in a column through the grasslands east of the Nile.[2] From the air, they looked small, ant-like, incapable of hurting anything, but other pictures taken from the ground showed what had happened when they reached the villages of the neighboring Murle tribe. Undefended settlements had been burned, and bodies stretched their charred limbs in mute appeal from the wreckage of smoking houses. No one was spared. In one image, a woman's body lay sprawled in the grass, her colorful dress stained dark with dried blood. Within reach of her outflung arm was the body of her child, perhaps six years old. Their meager belongings spilled from the faded blue plastic laundry basket that she must have been carrying as she ran south toward the UN base at Pibor.

The attackers only withdrew when confronted by that superior force. At Pibor, the UN had armored personnel carriers (APCS), and the government forces stood with them against the Nuer militia, which retreated to Akobo. The images were a grim reminder of why we were here, and I promised myself to do everything I could to prevent any repeat of the 2012 attacks in Jonglei and of the violence that had rocked Juba in 2013 and 2016.

The force was far from perfect, and despite our shortfall of 2,054 troops, we still had twice as many peacekeepers as in 2013 and 30 percent more than in 2016.[3] I was confident that General Tinaikar was not a leader to shy away from direct action, and now during the wet season, we had time to prepare—time to redeploy as necessary, to rehearse our plans, and to improve our intelligence networks. The people of South Sudan had been repeatedly failed by their own leaders and by those of UNMISS. I meant to ensure that they would not be failed again.

29 UNMISS Inaction

> Our lives begin to end the day we become
> silent about things that matter.
> —DR. MARTIN LUTHER KING JR.

23 August 2019. As the weeks passed, the news began to fill with disturbing reports. At a bridge northwest of Aweil, government forces ambushed a group of Paul Malong's soldiers.[1] When the shooting stopped, ten of the rebels—including two generals—lay dead. Eighty-seven of Malong's troops were captured, and a quarter of them were found to be child soldiers. It made me wonder how many of the dead were just boys carrying guns. But we wouldn't find out, because—once again—the same government troops who had carried out the ambush were preventing our peacekeepers from patrolling in that area.

In the North, our base at Bunj was flooded; our soldiers there were in the same situation as thousands of civilians throughout the country. Fighting also had broken out in Maiwut between a renegade general named James Ochan Puot and the local Sudan People's Liberation Army-in-Opposition forces. Again, UNMISS did not intervene, despite reports that the combatants killed and raped civilians and that the violence had displaced twenty thousand people. Closer to home, UNPOL arrested some of the local leaders in POC 3, because those elders had been helping wanted criminals escape capture. This resulted in a massive protest, which was only defused when Angelina Teny arrived to mediate. Madam Angelina, Riek Machar's first wife and the minister of defense for the SPLA-iO, was now living much of the time in Juba—although it was not yet considered a safe place for her husband. Women in South Sudan were very often more vulnerable than the men were, but under certain circumstances, they could perform an intermediary role and safely go where a man from their clan, tribe, or political group could not. The inhabitants of the POC sites were mainly Nuer, and

Madam Angelina held great sway with her people. The mediation succeeded, and the protests ceased.

* *

Once a week the mission's Public Affairs Office published a glossy newssheet of six to eight "good news" stories titled "UNMISS in Action," but more and more it felt as though the headlines should read "UNMISS Inaction." All around the country, civilians continued to die in small tranches: nine killed in a Buya-Toposa revenge cycle in the Equatorias, seven killed by General Ochan in Maiwut, and twenty-two killed in cattle raids in Tonj.[2] And we never did anything to prevent or respond to any of it.

This made me recall the note that I'd made during General Cammaert's visit: "As long as things don't cross into a full-on genocide, Force and Mission won't push the issue." So I started to push it myself.

Every weekday morning, the force commander convened his key staff officers to review the news and intelligence from the last twenty-four hours, to discuss the result of the previous day's patrols, and to give guidance on emergent issues. In these meetings, I began to advocate more vociferously for us to take action—that is, to insert a significant force into Maiwut via helicopter and to deploy company-size hub-and-spoke patrols to the parts of Tonj where we knew violence occurred with regularity. Although my recommendations were noted, nothing meaningful happened.

Rather than being deterred, I vowed to keep verbally highlighting the problems as I saw them until the generals told me to knock it off. To their credit, they never did.

* *

To be fair, the news wasn't *all* bad. Every pillar in the mission had good intentions. For example, the mission's Relief, Reintegration, and Protection Section had refurbished a Women's Center in Wau at a cost of $45,000. Labeled as a quick improvement project, it was intended to "provide a safe space where women can meet to promote their participation in conversations that can and should promote their agency in governance and economic empowerment."[3] But what did it do to help the thousands of women who lived in the Wau POC camp and were unable to return to their homes for fear of violence? When asked what they wanted, those displaced women said security, housing, and simple tools that would enable them to earn a living, not a community center.

"Most of the houses have been destroyed," said one displaced woman in Wau. "It's not easy for you to go at once and resettle. You need some reconstruction."

Another woman said, "If there is security, we will not depend on the NGOs."

Around the country, displaced women said similar things. Various aid agencies came and asked the women what they wanted, but then the agencies often ignored their answers. Mary, a woman in Juba, politely expressed the frustration felt by many: "International NGOs, thank you for the work you do, but sometimes you come with solutions that you don't get from the people."

Those solutions, if anyone was listening, were often extraordinarily simple. "If I had my sewing machine now," lamented another displaced woman, "I could generate income. I could even train others on how to use the machine here. But I don't have it."[4]

How much housing could have been built, I wondered, *and how many sewing machines could have been purchased with $45,000?*

* *

Some women did have it better. Awut Deng Achuil had been named to serve as South Sudan's first female foreign minister, and the few thousand women who served in the uniformed forces seemed likely to benefit from the $1.8 million that the African Union (AU) had delivered to kickstart the cantonment process. This important element of the peace deal was meant to bring government and opposition soldiers into "cantonment sites," where they would be screened for their suitability as soldiers. They would be transitioned to civilian life if they were not eligible for the NUF, but if chosen to continue a life of military service, they would be trained and reintegrated into a single, new military organization.[5]

On the surface, the cantonment process sounded as if it would be the start of what South Sudan needed most. With all of its disparate government and opposition armies integrated into a single smaller force, trained to a common standard, and deployed to defend the nation's people, it would serve as a new army for a new nation. But I would soon discover that it was not at all what either Salva Kiir or Riek Machar had in mind.

30 Fraying at the Edges

Humanitarian aid is designed to keep desperate people alive from one day to the next, whereas development assistance is meant to take the country towards a state where people can look after themselves.
—NICHOLAS COGHLAN

5 September 2019. It was easy to get complacent in Juba and to let yourself believe that South Sudan, despite its lack of paved roads, its overzealous security forces, and its general decrepitude, wasn't such a bad place to be. If you knew where to find them, the city had much to offer: baguettes warm from the oven, fresh vegetables, riverside cafés, and hotels with pools by which one could bask while awaiting a massage on a lazy weekend afternoon. That's why it was important to get out of Juba, so I did whenever possible.

The center held—the government and opposition officials, the UN staff, and the humanitarians in their own headquarters all enjoyed clean water, fresh food, cold air-conditioning—but the edges were fraying. I'd expected to see evidence in the towns and villages, but it came as a surprise to see that the UN's most far-flung outposts were themselves falling slowly apart.

I first discovered this in Sector East while traveling with General Herlyng to visit our "austere operating base" at Akobo, which sat near the Ethiopian border. The base was manned by soldiers from India, and the hospitality they displayed was outstanding. Our briefing room was a small tent filled with plastic chairs, and the detachment's commander made his presentation using a whiteboard propped up in front. We'd walked past the kitchen facilities, which had looked sparse and primitive, yet as the brief proceeded, a sergeant brought us a parade of small items: glasses of water and chai, nuts, samosas, and some delicious balls of a sweet coconut confection. As we savored these unexpected delicacies, the commander started in on the final part of his presentation, highlighting what he needed from the FHQ. "The language barrier is a major challenge," he said, giving examples of the difficulties that his patrols had in communicating with the local population before requesting a dedicated translator. He also asked that a section of engineers be sent to improve the conditions his men were living in, which he proceeded to demonstrate with a tour of his small base.

I was appalled at the conditions of their base. To call it "austere" was to engage in the same sort of disingenuous wordplay that had allowed General Cammaert to describe brutal killings as "nasty things." The HESCO walls were in sad repair, the troops were living in tents, and their bathroom facilities were squalid and accessible only by walking on shaky boards laid above a morass of mud, but despite these poor conditions, the Indian soldiers were cheerful and kind.

I had good reason to think that things would get better for these peace-keepers. The operations order, which had just been signed, called for an expansion of the base at Akobo. Soon they would be getting new, hard-sided prefab buildings; a wastewater treatment plant; and a new toilet and shower system. As with many issues, getting senior leaders to approve the plans seemed to have been the hardest part; the rest was just a matter of waiting for the rainy season to end so that we could move matériel and engineers to Akobo and build it.

* *

After the briefing and the tour, we were served a lunch of rice and curry; then we made the short walk into the village of Akobo to meet with the local leadership. On our way, we passed an old man sitting under a tree who wore a distinctive cloak of animal hide draped over his shoulders. The garment appeared worn and faded, and I wondered if the creatures still existed in this area. I'd neither heard of them here nor seen them anywhere else in my travels throughout the country. "A leopard-skin chief," I noted at the time, though I would later find that I was incorrect.

That colloquialism was just one of the many mistranslations that plagued South Sudan. Anthropologist Deng Nhial Chioh noted in 2017 that the Nuer title *kuaar muon* actually meant "earthly custodian," but he confirmed that earlier anthropologists had gotten the nature of the role correct if not the title. The position was one of mediator, particularly for serious crimes such as murder. The *kuaar muon*'s home was a sanctuary where a killer could remain in safety while the mediator attempted to arrange a compensation payment of cattle to settle the blood debt. The wearer of the leopard skin, however, had no official powers beyond that of persuasion and the respect of the people for his position. He could not coerce, only convince.

We didn't stop to talk with him, as his influence did not extend to the secular realms in which we operated. Instead, we met with Lt. Gen. John Gai, the local inspector general of police for the opposition forces and the senior official figure in the area. Gai greeted General Herlyng warmly and voiced a particular sort of gratitude that I would come to expect whenever we met opposition leaders.

"I'm happy that UNMISS saved the lives of the Nuer in Juba," he said, adding poetically, "because my soul is the same as those of the displaced people in the camps."

We met inside an old building in the center of the town. Other local leaders were also in the room, which had a tin roof, plaster walls, and a concrete floor. There was no electricity; the only light streamed in through a single window.

Outside were many armed men carrying AK-47s, M-16s, and a few belt-fed machine guns. Inside, the dignitaries sat on faded, overstuffed couches, and we visitors arranged ourselves on the ubiquitous plastic chairs that had been set up for the occasion. Most of the people in the room didn't speak English, and none of us spoke Arabic or Nuer. We lacked a translator, so Gai did the talking for his people, stressing that the population of Jonglei supported the opposition and were ready for peace. "The delays are not from our side," he added, "but the side of the government."

When General Herlyng asked how the local citizens felt about the UNMISS base outside town, Gai smiled. "The presence of UNMISS is very much appreciated by the people of Akobo," he replied, but everyone in the room knew that it had not always been the case.

Our little base, which now sat near the airport, used to be in the town itself, but in 2013, at the start of the civil war, forty-six Dinka families had taken refuge inside the base, where a platoon of peacekeepers from India—about thirty men in total—had sought to protect them. Thousands of Nuer had attacked the base, killing two peacekeepers and slaughtering the refugees: pregnant women, children, elderly men, and several young couples. The remainder of the peacekeepers, along with an assortment of UNPOL officers and humanitarian aid workers, had been taken hostage and were later evacuated by helicopter. The base was abandoned and gradually looted of the equipment left behind. Thereafter, no permanent UNMISS presence existed in Akobo until early 2019, when the new base had been established on David Shearer's orders.

No one mentioned this grim history. When General Herlyng wondered aloud about the large number of armed men outside, General Gai said that it was just a few, really, and that most opposition fighters had gone to the nearest cantonment site at Pieri.

Herlyng then said that he had heard that the site in Pieri lacked water, shelter, and medicine for the soldiers, eliciting a surprising response from his fellow general.

"No one should complain that a site lacks water and medicine," retorted Gai, "because everyone in South Sudan is lacking these things. Everyone drinks what water they can find." Returning to the matter of the armed men outside, Gai stressed that they were here for local protection only, because it was a dangerous area. Recently, he said, a gunman from the neighboring Murle tribe had killed a Nuer subchief in his home.

General Herlyng nodded, and Gai pivoted to his big ask, which he linked to his professional capacity as a law enforcement official: he wanted a shipping container to use as a jail so that apprehended criminals couldn't be seen. "Because if the family of the victim can see the perpetrator, you know . . ." He made a throat-cutting gesture. We got the point. It seemed to be very much an eye for an eye out here. But sitting in a locked shipping container in the heat of the dry season seemed a sort of cruel and unusual punishment—maybe even a death sentence—and I was not the only one who saw the deadly potential. General Herlyng wouldn't commit to providing a shipping container, saying that would be police business; he was a military man.

"You should bring the police commissioner on these trips," countered Gai. It was a good point. The UNPOL commissioner, Unaisi Bolatolu-Vuniwaqa, was an imposing and effective leader, but she'd never accompanied us to the field. Despite the recommendation of General Cammaert, neither had the SRSG.

* *

We returned to Juba by way of Bor, a small port city on the eastern edge of the Nile and the western edge of Jonglei. Its population of twenty-six thousand belied its significance as the capital of Jonglei State and a historical hub of economic and administrative activity. Under the British, it had been an ivory trading depot and a place where steamers on the Nile could replenish wood for their boilers. This was where the 1983 Bor mutiny launched the two decades of civil war that ultimately led to South Sudan's independence. It was here, too, that Riek Machar's Nuer fighters massacred over two thousand Dinka civilians in 1991 and where Dinka fighters had attacked the POC site at the UN base in 2014, killing fifty Nuer civilians.

The UN base in Bor was the headquarters for Sector East, and our short visit gave me a chance to see a completely different view of what could and was being done in Jonglei. A company of South Korean engineers was among the UN forces based here, and their compound could not have been more different than that of the infantry assigned to Akobo. The engineers' site was neat and dry, and its many hard-sided buildings housed a library, a gym, a computer center, and a very high-tech operations center. It felt as if we had stepped into a little piece of South Korea. But most remarkable was what they had done outside their camp—in fact, just a little outside of the base itself.

The Korean engineers had constructed a vocational training center for teaching South Sudanese women and men valuable skills: baking, sewing, agricultural techniques, electrical wiring, masonry, and woodworking. Their Hanbit School graduates received assistance in job placement in addition to learning valuable trades. *This is a model for what we should be doing everywhere*, I thought. It represented what many military units probably would have been doing with QIP funds if we had been able to get them. South Korea was among the richest of the troop-contributing countries sending units to South Sudan, so it could afford to give its contingents money for projects such as the Hanbit School even when the mission did not. The same was not true for many of the other countries that assigned peacekeepers to UNMISS.

As we flew back to Juba, I thought about what more I could do to get QIP funds into the hands of the local commanders, especially for programs such as the Hanbit School that had proved they could do the most good. I talked to General Herlyng, who had also been impressed by what the Korean engineers had accomplished, and we agreed that the most effective way to improve the QIP program was make it a formal task in the operations order and assign it to him. He would personally lead the effort to transform and optimize the process with the goal of allocating a substantial portion of funding directly to the force so the sector and battalion commanders could execute truly quick impact projects. For my part, I said that I would request specific funding from the U.S. government to allow our Team America to do some developmental work of our own.

31 Things Fall Apart

Many of those who deploy on UNMISS end up frustrated and
demoralized, unable to bring about change. . . . [The mission]
has lost the initiative in South Sudan and, as an organization, has
embraced a reactive, non-proactive approach to peacemaking.
—MAJ. CHRIS YOUNG, FORMER UNMISS MILITARY OBSERVER

23 September 2019. The operations order had finally been signed, so the
job of the Fantastic Five was largely done—at least as far as that order was
concerned. Now the onus had shifted to the Operations Branch and to
the various sector commanders to actually carry out the orders, while my
team members and I turned our attention to updating the force's standard
operating procedures and to working toward developing a common operating picture. At least, that's the way it would normally have worked, but
this month was where the best-laid plans kept going off the rails—both
personally and professionally.

The standup of Sector Unity was being held up by the facilities staff at
Bentiu who now claimed that there weren't enough accommodations for
the seven new officers. My attempt to send a senior woman in the South
Sudanese armed forces—Brig. Gen. Aboach Bak Bal—to Washington DC to
participate in the Joint Women's Leadership Symposium had failed. The plan
had the backing of Kyle Walton and the U.S. Embassy's Public Relations and
Gender Affairs Office, but in the end, we weren't able to get a visa approved
and the funding for her attendance. Finally, I'd sent Jayde a proposed plan
for a trip through Kenya at the end of August but had heard . . . nothing.
But the worst was yet to come.

* *

I was in Nairobi attending a workshop on security sector reform (SSR), and
during a break between classes, I saw that I was copied on an email from
the force commander to the SRSG. The note said that he'd discussed our

planned troop movements with the CDF and that General Jok Riak was opposed to the idea. As a result, he wrote, our plans were temporarily on hold. Attached was a draft memo, meant to be signed by both the CDF and the force commander, that set the new terms for how SOI would be dealt with in the future.

I scanned the document and couldn't believe what I was reading. *If this memo is signed*, I thought, *we'll lose what little freedom of movement we currently have.* Adding to my concern was that both the SRSG and General Herlyng were out of the country and—unlike me—out of our time zone. Shearer was in New York briefing the Security Council; Herlyng was on leave in Norway. If the force commander signed the memo before they replied . . .

Knowing the potential repercussions of allowing the government to tighten restrictions on our patrols and of giving it veto power over the locations of our battalions, I could not just watch them happen without trying to do something. I drafted a reply to the force commander—one in which I knew that I was walking a fine line.

Gentlemen, I must highlight in the most respectful and yet strongest manner my concerns regarding this message.

"*. . . UNMISS must share information of movement of its patrols in advance, as a recognition of sovereignty of the Government of South Sudan . . .*"

"Must" is extremely strong language in legal terms and we are in danger of losing what little Freedom of Movement we now possess if we sign documents containing it. UNMISS is not required to do anything that prevents us from carrying out our mandate, regardless of the desires of the SSPDF. . . . It is to be remembered that the SSPDF is only one of several military actors in the country at this time and that we are meant to be impartial.

If this becomes the "new normal" we will have taken a large step backwards in terms of Freedom of Movement—we will give the SSPDF grounds to completely halt our ability to move quickly to respond to humanitarian access issues, human rights violations, threats to civilians, and literally *every* . . . aspect of our Mandate. And they will be able to hold up this piece of paper and say "well, you agreed to it . . ."

. . . Additionally, the idea that the CDF is being given the "deciding vote" on where UNMISS positions its military forces is very concerning. . . . The very troop movements that are even now being put on hold because the CDF does not like them are the same ones that the SRSG clearly stated as being his intent and priority.

I apologize if anyone takes offense at my plain language, but I would be failing in my duties as a Staff Officer if I did not raise these concerns regarding actions which have the potential to significantly impact the Mission's ability to carry out the mandate and prepare for the Most Dangerous COAs associated with the November timeframe.

I closed the letter with the words "respectfully submitted" and sent it to the force commander and to the other key leaders who had been copied on the original email from General Tinaikar.

My reply was the first, but it was neither the last nor the weightiest. The UNMISS deputy SRSG (political) Moustapha Soumaré responded next with a shorter letter that said essentially the same thing: we should not agree in writing to terms that would further limit our freedom of movement. A few hours later, the SRSG himself weighed in against agreeing to the CDF's proposed terms. That all appeared to settle matters in favor of proceeding with our plans as written—or so I thought. Nonetheless, the whole situation put something of a damper on my mood for the remainder of the SSR course, but after graduation, I returned to South Sudan with more knowledge than I had when I left and an eagerness to put it to use.

      * *

Back in Juba, there was some good news on the professional front: we had resolved the logistics issues for Sector Unity and were already moving people and equipment into Bentiu to prepare for the arrival of the new sector commander in November. The child soldiers captured in the fighting near Aweil had been released to the International Committee of the Red Cross (ICRC) for reintegration into their home villages, and the African Development Bank had just approved $17.7 million to improve basic education for children—money meant to provide water and facilities along with furniture and learning materials.

I still had no word from Jayde. That did not entirely surprise me. She doubtless had no shortage of candidates for her affection. Anyway, plenty of other things demanded my attention. I didn't really need the distraction of another period of leave when so much was going on in the mission.

✳ ✳

It had become clear that the CDF didn't want Rwandan troops in Yei, but no one seemed to know exactly why. The CDF's intransigence didn't seem to make much sense, as the major peacekeeping force in Torit, Eastern Equatoria, consisted of Rwandan infantry. Like Yei, Torit was also close to the border with Uganda, and the Rwandans' presence there didn't seem to be controversial.[1]

During the first week that I was back in Juba, the staff had initiated the necessary steps to realign our forces for better C2, a more responsible airmobile posture, and a functional reserve force that could be surged to places where violence threatened civilian lives. There was equipment to be packed, transportation manifests to be filled out, and many other minutiae involved in moving large units of peacekeepers from one location to another. Fortunately, for every aspect of such a complex endeavor, an officer specialized in making it happen, and so far, all was proceeding according to plan. But on Saturday, I received a note from the force commander saying that due to political considerations, the movement of Rwandan troops to Yei would not take place.

That was not a problem. My team had been working on alternate options, and we had a solution that would allow us to consolidate the Nepalese battalion in Juba by moving Ethiopian troops from Tomping to Yei instead of the Rwandans. But during a hastily arranged planning conference, a very different decision was made: there would be no realignment of forces at all.

I was asked to rewrite the operations order and to reissue it immediately. I tactfully refused to do so, noting that this major order represented the culmination of a deliberate planning process that had taken several months. Changing a single element—such as the movement of particular units—was supposed to be done by issuing a short fragmentary order that addressed only that single aspect of the overarching plan. General Herlyng concurred with my assessment and directed that the Operations Branch, which normally handled those types of orders, should draft the document for review.

The outcome was disappointing, but that was the nature of being a staff officer. We could give advice and prepare the paperwork, but in the end, the commander gave the orders. There was no point losing any sleep over it, and there was nothing personal in General Tinaikar's decision. At least that was my perspective, but not everyone felt the same way.

32 No Country for Young Men

There is no road that leads to nowhere.
—NUER PROVERB

11 October 2019. Morale within the Fantastic Five had taken a hit when our carefully crafted plans had been suddenly put on hold, and it deteriorated further when the Operations Branch began rewriting the entire operations order—all without the required deliberate planning framework and despite the clear guidance from the force chief of staff that it was simply to write a fragmentary order halting the realignment of troops between Juba and Yei.

I was headed to Yei—in fact, already seated in the back of an Mi-8—when I got the news from Emm, so I fired off a note to General Herlyng, asking him to help defuse what was becoming an increasingly tense situation in the headquarters. Then I tried to relax as the engine coughed to life, the rotors began to spin, and the helicopter lifted into the dawn sky. We flew at a low altitude, which made it possible to appreciate that the terrain here—low rocky hills, many small valleys, riverbeds and gullies, no roads—would make for rough fighting. The land was beautiful and seemed relatively untouched by the hand of man.

My mind wandered from the scenery to my general situation as I had neared the halfway point in my deployment here. My role as the senior national representative was demanding more from me than it had from my predecessors. The rotation of new officers in and old officers out would have increased my workload at any time, but the mission had started a "direct-to-Juba" induction protocol. It was cheaper and more efficient. Instead of transiting through Entebbe as my cohort had done, newly assigned UNMISS officers flew directly into Juba from their home countries and completed all their in-processing at Tomping. This process had been tested and refined with staff officers from other nations since September, but unlike those officers, the Americans were bringing weapons and ammunition in and out of the country. These required special clearance letters from the government security apparatus, and I'd had to ask my generals to intervene personally with their South Sudanese counterparts to get our weapons' letters signed and stamped.

On the plus side, I felt as if I was making progress on improving the security for the U.S. contingent and reducing our environmental impact. Bikes were being purchased in the United States and shipped to us, and $14,000 had been transferred to the U.S. Embassy to pay for our WiFi setup. Now I just needed to figure out a solution to our lack of vehicles and to avoid dwelling on how it seemed much easier to get money and matériel to improve life for my fellow Americans than to do so for the people of South Sudan. My musings were cut short as the chopper descended to the airfield at Yei, its rotors beating red dust from the ground and causing the blue-helmeted force protection troops stationed around the runway to turn their backs against the momentary storm.

We loaded in suvs and made the journey to Lasu with a heavy escort of APCs. The Yei–Lasu Road was one of the most dangerous in the country for civilians. Several were in our group, with the most notable being the Indian ambassador, His Excellency Shri S. D. Moorthy. We didn't have any women in our patrol. While our orders called for gender-integrated patrols, the reality on the ground often didn't match up. I scrawled a note to myself to encourage us to do more to close that gap.

I looked for signs of trouble on the road and found them quickly. The few checkpoints were the first I'd seen that resembled actual fighting positions, with dug-out foxholes reinforced with sandbags. A damaged T-55 tank rusting along the roadside showed that whenever fighting erupted in South Sudan, this was a contested area. To the left and right of the road were occasional clusters of houses, even villages with storefronts facing the road, but everything was empty, abandoned.

We were in Lasu to assess the security situation and to talk to the local leaders about what they needed from UNMISS. The meeting's venue was a small metal shed, and the leadership included the local SSPDF commander and several elderly chiefs, ancient men with skin like worn leather. Other people drifted in and took seats in vacant plastic chairs.

The force commander asked the assembled chiefs why the villages were empty and when the people would return. The oldest man spoke for the

11. A visit to the village of Lasu in Central Equatoria. Author photo.

group through our translator, and his companions nodded their concurrence with his replies.

"Outside Lasu, there is no security. People stay close to the IDP camp because they want their children to attend school, and they feel secure near this base because the local SSPDF commander patrols the area."

"Why is security bad, and what do the people want from UNMISS?"

The chief waved toward the small crowd of about fifty civilians and a handful of soldiers that had gathered. In the background, I heard the shouts and laughter of children who, like children everywhere, were making joy from nothing. "For them, all they are asking for is peace."

"Have they heard about the current peace process?"

"Yes, and they have heard about the 12 November deadline too."

"Do they think the new government will form?"

The chief shook his head. "That's their responsibility." He claimed that he didn't know who was responsible for attacks in the area but said that if UNMISS can "bring the rebel groups to join the peace," that would be helpful. The opposition forces here, he went on, were not "those of Riek Machar" but those of NAS.[1] Thomas Cirillo's Equatorian opposition force remained a non-signatory to the current peace treaty, outside of the "big tent" into which Salva Kiir was trying to bring all the former combatants.

The crowd continued to grow as more people trickled in. I gave up my seat to an elderly man and stood with the younger locals in the shadow of a nearby tree, taking notes. The equatorial sun was broiling, and the shade made a huge difference. Skinny chickens searched for seeds around our feet, chirping quietly. The handful of soldiers wore faded fatigues. Their weapons looked old, and some were rusty. The weapon of choice here appeared to be AK-47s with folding stocks.

The force commander asked if NAS had the support of the people, but the chief didn't answer directly. Instead, he told a story about a local medical worker who had been shot in the hip, very near this spot, and bled out on the Yei–Lasu Road two weeks ago. The killing of such men had a long history in this area.[2]

The conversation reinforced the importance of one issue that I'd been working on lately. In my notes, I capitalized one word to capture the thought: *There is IMMENSE value in having a language assistant.*

Somewhere in the background, a little girl began to cry. I noticed then that hers was the only female voice that I'd heard since leaving Juba. Not a single woman was in the assembled group of South Sudanese. Clearly, those of UNMISS were not the only ones who struggled with implementing gender integration in this country.

The chief then posed a question of his own to General Tinaikar: "What will you do to protect civilians on the road between Lasu and Yei?"

"What do you want us to do?"

"Send soldiers."

"Doesn't the SSPDF do that?"

"Ask him!" The chief gestured at the SSPDF commander who sat to the right of the force commander. "Anyway, sometimes when the SSPDF goes into the bush to hunt rebels, civilians get killed and tortured."

The local commander clearly wasn't happy with this final observation, and General Tinaikar steered the conversation to safer ground, ignoring the chief's last remark and addressing his military counterpart directly. "When did you last get paid?" he asked.

This question triggered a long reply in Juba Arabic, which our translator reduced to three words: "Not since May." It was now October.

The force commander offered a quid pro quo proposition to encourage the people to move back into their villages: if the displaced civilians returned to the empty houses we saw on our way here, then there would be more UNMISS patrols.

The old men shook their heads, and the SSPDF commander interjected. "They are confused," he said, pausing as the words were translated. "Is there peace, or no peace? The civilians are really suffering."

General Tinaikar gave a vague nonanswer: trust in the peace process, don't abuse the local civilians, obey the laws of armed conflict. His words didn't seem to satisfy anyone, but there was not much they could say in rebuttal.

We posed for the obligatory pictures and were soon headed back to Yei. There, we met briefly with the acting governor, who asked the force commander what he had learned from the visit to Lasu.

"We found the people are living in fear," General Tinaikar replied. He followed up with his own question, repeating what he'd asked the chiefs just an hour before: "What can UNMISS do?"

The acting governor considered. "What can you do? Well, the first thing that is needed is security, because only then can people be productive." No one pointed out that often the governor's own political and military apparatus prevented UNMISS peacekeepers from patrolling the area or that government forces regularly terrorized civilians themselves. Instead, as was common to many such meetings, the local political leaders gathered around the table took the opportunity to present a list of requests for schools, for hospitals, and for water.

We were now only a few weeks from the deadline to form the transitional government, and the acting governor's final request was that General Tinaikar and the Indian ambassador speak with Thomas Cirillo personally and persuade him to end his rebellion. Otherwise, he said, regardless of what would happen on November 12, peace would not come to Yei.

Neither, I thought, *would more peacekeepers.*

33 Strong Medicine for Tanks

To be prepared for war is one of the most
effective means of preserving peace.
—PRESIDENT GEORGE WASHINGTON

25 October 2019. The midmorning sun was oppressive as I stood watching the Rwandan peacekeepers demonstrate how quickly they could put their SPG-9 recoilless rifles into action. I was accompanying the force commander on an inspection of our preparations to defend the mandate—and UN House—if violence returned to Juba with Riek Machar on 12 November.

The gun crew moved swiftly and smoothly. Clearly their actions were well rehearsed, and I saw General Tinaikar nodding his approval. But speed only mattered if the weapons were powerful enough to deal a killing blow. I turned to one of the Rwandan officers beside me. "How well will that work against a T-72 tank?"

He smiled and shook his head, giving me the sort of look that an older brother gives a younger sibling who had asked a sincere but foolish question. "My friend," he said, "this is strong medicine for tanks."

I nodded. I had often seen academics and pundits write disparagingly of the quality of peacekeeping troops from African nations, but in my own opinion, I'd rather have Rwandans and Ethiopians at my back in a fight than troops from many better-equipped armies because those East African soldiers knew what they were doing, having experienced a lot of fighting in this part of the world.[1]

A delegation from the UN Security Council had visited Juba only days before, seeking to pressure Salva Kiir and Riek Machar to hold to the terms and deadlines of the current peace deal, but it hadn't gone well. In the highest level of the mission—and among the diplomats and humanitarians—many suddenly asked a lot of questions about our plans for contingencies, for our own safety and security. The growing feeling was that it was not a case of

12. Rwandan troops demonstrating the use of an SPG-9 anti-tank gun. Author photo.

if fighting would break out but when and where. There was a lot to worry about, but one thing I *wasn't* worried about were caveats. I'd personally engaged with all my fellow senior national representatives and collected a comprehensive list of restrictions on the troops and officers they represented. Of our "combat" forces—infantry, Marines, and aviation crews that included the Rwandan, Nepalese, Mongolian, and Bangladeshi forces—58 percent had no caveats. A few of the big troop contributors—China, India, and Ethiopia—had not responded to my query, but UN Headquarters had noted no caveats on their troops either. There was no reason to think that any members of the force would fail to act in accordance with our plans and preparations.

Today's inspection was a part of those preparations. UN House was vulnerable to attacks from SSPDF positions atop the Jebel, and in 2016 the Tiger Division had blocked the road that led to the city with tanks. The UN's bases had been cut off from each other and had no clear plan to engage in defensive operations outside their own walls. Now, five years later, we still lacked the tactical helicopters, the reconnaissance UAVs, and half the troops that the Security Council had promised to deliver after that previous disaster, but at least we had a plan to do more with what we did have.

Chinese peacekeepers had dug in mortar emplacements that could hit the Jebel, and all our battalions had potent anti-tank capabilities. If the SSPDF launched its attack helicopters, we'd have a harder time of it, but members of the staff and I had planned for that problem as well. I really hoped those plans would never have to be put into action, but there is an old saying in the Marines: "Hope is not a COA."

　　＊ ＊

Of course, preparation for one of our most dangerous threats in Juba wasn't the only thing occupying the force or taking up my own time. Our bases at Akobo and Pibor had flooded, and everyone was saying that this rainy season was the worst on record. I also was busy helping Team America's new guys settle in. Now Emm, Christopher, and I were the old hands; we'd said goodbye to Dave Smith, Drew Ziccardi, Chris Wong, and Ethan Thorpe. They'd been replaced by two more pairs of U.S. Army and Air Force officers: Steve Hansen assumed Drew's position in CIMIC, and Keegan Vaira took over from Chris as our engineer. In the Joint Operations Center, "old Ethan"—Captain Thorpe—was replaced by the "new Ethan," Captain Fairey. Only one American desk sat empty, for now. Dave's replacement was stuck awaiting a letter from the Ministry of Foreign Affairs, just as I had been seven months previously. His weapon and ammunition were approved for arrival, but he was not. Even with the new direct-to-Juba format, it seemed that some things never changed, and one of those was the wild-card nature of South Sudanese politics.

34 Riek Machar versus the World

The Security Council is of the view that nothing is
impossible. Nothing is unsurmountable.

—JERRY MATTHEWS MATJILA, SOUTH AFRICA'S
AMBASSADOR TO THE UN

8 November 2019. Riek Machar had done it again. He had stared down the world, and the world blinked. Machar had been scheduled to meet with Salva Kiir in Kampala the previous morning, but the meeting was postponed by twenty-four hours. Kiir used that time to visit all the other opposition leaders in South Sudan and get their support to form the government on 12 November. When he flew to Kampala to meet with Machar, a day late and now with theoretical support from all the other major political actors, everyone expected the meeting—which was held under the mediation of Uganda's president and longtime Kiir supporter Yoweri Museveni—to result in a declaration that Machar would join Kiir to form the government on 12 November.

Instead, the office of the Ugandan president released a one-page communiqué stating that after meeting in a "cordial and friendly atmosphere," Kiir and Machar had agreed to extend the pre-transitional period for a hundred days due to the "incomplete critical tasks related to the security arrangements and governance" of South Sudan.[1] The communiqué was not only a fait accompli presented to the other countries of the Intergovernmental Authority on Development (IGAD) and to the world but also a slap in the face to the UN Security Council, which had emphatically stated that the unity government had to form on 12 November regardless of whether the conditions for its formation had been met.

How did Dr. Riek pull this off? The answer lay in the flooded bush in Jonglei and Unity States. Large SPLA-IO forces—thousands of men with machine guns and rocket-propelled grenades—had been massing in strategic areas. A heavily armed company of about 150 had passed an UNMISS patrol on the Nile, headed north to Bentiu, and grimly warned the UN "not to get in the way."

    * *

The announcement of the extension was the culmination of a three-week-long political standoff between Machar and the UN Security Council, whose representatives had visited Juba on 21 October for a day-long visit en route to another event in Addis Ababa. But this was no social call. The representatives sought to impress upon both Machar and Kiir the need to form the government as planned this time. The international community had no desire to see a repeat of the extension granted in May.

Talking to reporters at the airport in Juba, the president of the Security Council, South Africa's Jerry Matthews Matjila, made it clear that the issue was money. "No other country has such a huge UN presence unlike South Sudan. No other country has such a very costly peacekeeping than South Sudan. But this comes from taxpayers' money. These resources come from governments and governments have got taxpayers."[2]

The UN's delegation was briefed by the SRSG, who reiterated the political position of UNMISS: while none of the most important preconditions for the formation of the transitional government were complete, the parties to the conflict should reunite in Juba anyway—even without a unified armed force, without a plan for providing security in the capital to former opposition VIPs such as Machar, and without an agreement on the number of states.

Salva Kiir concurred as well. Such a way forward clearly favored him and rewarded his strategy of siphoning off funds, slow rolling the process of cantonment and training of the NUF, and gerrymandering the political establishment by expanding the number of states from ten to thirty-two.

But Riek Machar surprised everyone by pushing back. He had been meeting with Salva Kiir and the heads of their respective security apparatuses when the UN delegation arrived, and the meeting had ended early to allow the rivals to greet their guests. But Dr. Riek already had the key information he required. The South Sudan Joint Defense Board had admitted that the requirement to select and train the NUF could not be completed by the deadline. Training had not even begun, and there were funding shortages for basic supplies.

That being the case, Machar said his opposition party would not form the government on 12 November, noting that while the issue of the number of states and their boundaries also needed to be resolved, his major issue was the military. "The security arrangements must be in place at least," he said.[3] His deputy spokesman, Manawa Peter Gatkuoth, explained why those of Riek were so fixated on this point: "In 2016, Machar was also put under pressure to form a unity government with Kiir before the implementation of the security arrangements, but when fighting erupted again, nobody came from the international community to intervene."[4]

But U.S. ambassador to the UN Kelly Craft was adamant as well. "The Security Council expects that, after we leave here, the parties and stakeholders we have met with will work together to fully implement the peace agreement," she said just before boarding her flight to Ethiopia.[5]

Her fellow delegate Ambassador Matjila shrugged off reporters' questions about funding and implementing the security arrangements. "So, we feel as the Security Council . . . that what Dr. Riek Machar is asking is not impossible to do in the next three weeks, it's possible, it can be done. . . . About the funding, the funding is an issue, but funding is not a deal-breaker. Funds are there, they can be used."[6]

Privately, I believed that these senior UN officials, with their position of "unify without preparation" were setting us up for another round of civil war. It was not my place to raise those concerns publicly, but fortunately others did. Duop Chak Wuol, the editor in chief of the independent South Sudan News Agency, published a scathing editorial that highlighted the unresolved issues that Ambassador Matjila had brushed aside. Duop wrote:

> I would like to remind the United Nations that the agreement states that, a hybrid court to prosecute those who committed war crimes and crimes against humanity should be formed, the current constitution should be amended to reflect reforms, the government should fund the SPLA-iO forces, the number of states needs to be decided, the reunification of the armies should be initiated, and major cities including Juba must be demilitarized. . . .
>
> Do not tell me that all these vital provisions will be implemented after a unity government is formed.[7]

He observed that the only real accomplishment so far was that about a thousand military instructors had been trained but said it was shameful that their uniforms had come from Egypt and their food from China.

"One wonders," he mused rhetorically, "what Salva Kiir is doing with South Sudan's oil money."

Beyond the political posturing and the newspaper editorials, in practical terms what this extension meant for those of us in the mission was that the clock had just been set back. All the problems we expected to face around 12 November still existed, but now the moment of truth had been postponed to 20 February 2020. It also gave us another small window to do more to help South Sudan reform its defense sector, but we would make little use of that opportunity.

35   Until the First Bullet Flies

> UNMISS needs to make meaningful changes to better position itself
> to protect civilians. . . . In the midst of a conflict in which the parties
> have targeted civilians consistently and deliberately, UNMISS has
> often been the only actor civilians can look to for protection. This is a
> heavy burden. But it is a burden the Mission must begin to meet more
> effectively, as the violence in South Sudan is unlikely to end soon.
> —CENTER FOR CIVILIANS IN CONFLICT REPORT, 2016

13 November 2019. The day that we'd all worried about for months had passed without incident, and General Tinaikar had posed an interesting question: "Since we now had more time to prepare for the transition, how could we better deploy the force to implement the mandate?"

I discussed the topic with my team and representatives from the Operations, Intelligence, Logistics, and CIMIC Branches. Predictably, I had to quell a few disgruntled questions. "Hadn't we just given the force commander our best plan for exactly that kind of redeployment in our original operations order? Hadn't our recommendations already been sacrificed on the altar of political expediency?"

Water under the bridge, I told the officers around the table. We were being given a second chance to do what we'd all agreed was important, and we could use what we'd learned about political sensitivities to help guide us. We had this chance to get even more creative, to go further than we'd tried to go before. That point got everyone excited. What came out of our meeting was fairly bold stuff, which I then took into an afternoon discussion with the force commander and my fellow chiefs.

We proposed swapping the locations of Sector South's and Sector Juba's headquarters to provide better command and control in the capital and consolidating one Ethiopian battalion at Yambio to put more peacekeepers in Western Equatoria. We'd redraw the boundaries of Sector East and Sector

North to provide better coordination and increased patrol coverage in Eastern Equatoria and the northern reaches of Jonglei by consolidating the Rwandan battalion in Bor and another battalion of Ethiopian peacekeepers at Tomping. Closing our small outlying bases at Renk and Pariang would let us relocate the peacekeepers from Renk to Maiwut, in response to the continued threat General Ochan posed to civilians, and our troops from Pariang to Koch to support the humanitarian hub that had grown up there. We'd establish a temporary base in Tonj, reevaluate the border between Sector West and Sector Unity in Warrap State, and expand our riverine patrols to include the Nile, Akobo, Pibor, and Bahr el Ghazal Rivers. We would also focus long-duration patrols in sixteen areas that JMAC, the humanitarian community, and our own intelligence had agreed represented "hot spots" where the presence of UN peacekeepers would help deter violence and improve the distribution of aid.

Not everyone was impressed with our proposal to reform our C2 relationships and to realign our forces accordingly. "For me, this is déjà-vu," observed a dour German colonel named Wolfgang Koehler. "I encountered the same situation in Mali. I read several orders, as much as this thick"—he gestured with a thumb and forefinger—"and that is good until the first bullet flies, but then everyone will look to the force commander."

When I looked at General Tinaikar, though, I saw him nodding thoughtfully. He thanked Colonel Koehler for his candor but said that he wanted us to go ahead and draft an order to support the plan we had just briefed. In turn, I handed the task off to the Fantastic Five. The force commander intended to travel extensively to assess the reaction of the country's military forces to the new political reality, and as the plans chief, I was usually on the roster to travel with him. He was particularly interested in talking with was his own counterpart in the opposition, Lt. Gen. Simon Gatwech Dual, who had directed the military movements that had given Riek Machar the political capital to obtain the hundred-day extension.

Gatwech was a hard man to reach. He moved around a lot, inspecting and inspiring his far-flung troops while simultaneously reducing the chances that he might meet with an unfortunate "accident" at the hands of his many enemies, but he had just surfaced at an opposition cantonment site in Unity State. His staff had said he would meet with us if we could get there in the next day or so.

* *

Early in the morning we landed at the airstrip in Bentiu, where I was greeted by my friend Darkwa, a lieutenant colonel who commanded the Ghanaian battalion there. We'd met in Nairobi during September when we attended the security sector reform course together. I rode with Darkwa to the UN base. Along our way, I saw women in bright dresses and a man with no legs riding a hand-cranked tricycle. A wrecked armored vehicle lay on its side, its windscreen spiderwebbed from multiple bullet impacts. I remembered the words of my instructors from O'Gara training—"a rolled vehicle is a bad spot to fight from"—and reflected that somebody's worst day had ended there in the not-too-distant past.

Gatwech was at Ding-Ding, a cantonment site where soldiers were supposed to be gathered for medical screening and other qualifications checks to see if they were fit to serve in the unified force. But before we could meet him, the force commander had a ceremonial duty to discharge. His presence was expected at a medal parade for our colleagues who would soon be departing from the Vietnamese Level II Hospital, which served as our main medical support for Sector Unity.

It was hot even under the visitor's tent. *The officers standing in the sun must be starting to broil*, I thought. The Mongolian battalion had provided a marching band, which played the Vietnamese national anthem. That was followed by the presentation of medals to every peacekeeper, and the force commander gave his personal letters of commendation to a select few. Having served on promotion boards in the past, I knew that such letters could prove important when officers were evaluated for future promotions. As the awards were being presented, it soon became uncomfortably obvious that while 22 percent of the unit were women, only men were being honored with letters from General Tinaikar. It was another example of how far the UN still had to go in implementing the gender mainstreaming that we talked about in our resolutions and orders. The force commander took the podium afterward and gave a short speech to the officers in the sun and the dignitaries in the shade. "You have always won, you have always been victorious," he intoned gravely. "You know what suffering is, so we thank you for coming here to ease the suffering of others."

I applauded his words, as did the delegation from Vietnam, which included the deputy chairmen of several Communist Party central committees. One of the defining aspects of service with the UN was that former adversaries from the bitter wars of an earlier generation now worked side by side to mitigate the effects of war in the present. *I hope that someday soon, someone like me in some other part of the world will watch South Sudanese peacekeepers earn their first UN medals*, I thought to myself as the force commander walked back toward the tent. We spent the next half hour or so with refreshments and small talk; then we were off to meet the opposition forces.

I rode with Darkwa again. Our convoy wound through a market of corrugated tin sheds on a rutted dirt street. Kids flipped us off with a smile. We passed a sad-looking donkey pulling a water cart, then long-tailed sheep, cows, and a man in a bright African print suit. Farther on, a man with one leg hopped along on crutches. Near our destination, I saw a tall youth leading two goats tied to a piece of rope that he held in one hand; in the other, he carried an AK-47. I recalled that the last time the force commander had visited Ding-Ding, Gen. John Turuk had gifted him two goats, and I wondered idly if they might be the same animals.

* *

The cantonment site in Ding-Ding was a massive circle of bare, hardpacked earth on which a large number of tukuls had been constructed. We passed those structures and entered an enclosure created of tightly bound rushes.

Soldiers carrying medium machine guns, their chests crisscrossed with belts of 7.62mm ammunition, flanked the entrance. Within the enclosure sat a large square building made of the same bundles of rushes tied to a wooden framework. It was a sturdy and natural form of construction, perfectly suited to the climate, environmentally friendly, and cheap. This architectural form, I suspected, had not been improved upon for hundreds of years and would probably still be viable a century into the future.

Our host sat at a small, square plastic table topped with a bright red cloth. Lt. Gen. Simon Gatwech Dual, the chief of the general staff of the opposition, was a heavy-set old man with a white goatee and curly yellow-white hair peeking from beneath his beret, but his mustache was still dark. Long, wavy scars ran across his forehead. My first impression was that he could be mistaken for a kindly uncle, but there was a hardness beneath his smile. Dark as his skin was, I could see in him the shadow of the Pale Horse. *Where this man has gone*, I thought, *death has often followed.*

The force commander greeted his fellow general, mentioning that this was his second visit to Ding-Ding and saying that he hadn't forgotten about the goats. Gatwech replied through a translator. "Did you slaughter them?"

"No," said General Tinaikar, "but when the peace comes, we'll have a feast."

Gatwech held forth in Arabic, a quick-moving and melodic flow of words punctuated with pauses to let the translator relay his thoughts. "All around the world, the military is one . . . we follow orders . . . we protect and defend our territory. The rest is up to politicians."

I expected to hear him gloat over the hundred-day extension since his soldiers here in Unity State had provided the leverage Riek Machar used to obtain the additional time, but Gatwech seemed unhappy about the latest political maneuver.

"Only three months to form a government?" He rolled his eyes. "Our people want peace, but this is the peace of Addis Ababa and Khartoum." Gatwech believed the government was stalling and selling oil to buy arms, but he reiterated that as a military man, he would follow orders and continue to support the peace process—for now.

36 Juba Social Club

> Look, it's hardly like living in a monastery. A lot of the time it can be
> fun. There are 125 different nationalities and on Fridays, we have a
> bar night—grass huts, music, the works. Everyone has a beer, listens
> to music, gets up dancing. . . . You can be in a group of a dozen to 20
> people and none of them will be from the same country. They are all
> part of the UN, all part of the team I lead, and that is pretty cool.
>
> —DAVID SHEARER

15 November 2019. The Tulip Inn near the airport was definitely the place to
be on a Friday night. The rooftop bar was packed with a mix of UN staff and
humanitarians, all chatting against a backdrop of 2014 house music. I was
sipping a gin and tonic, and staring across at the airport runway, enjoying
the fading heat of the day and thinking once again about how things stood
halfway through this final deployment. My life wasn't merely Juba good; it
was, objectively, pretty great. I was making more money than I would have
in most other postings, I was eating healthily and working out consistently,
and my job was many things but never boring.

If anything was missing, it was romance and sex, but I had flirtationships
in writing with distant paramours to satisfy the former and the possibility
of a long weekend in Kampala with one of them if I really wanted the latter.
Some of my other single friends had paired off with fellow humanitarians
in Juba. Martin had connected with Claudia, an Italian woman who had
studied at the University of California–Davis and worked for the UN Food
and Agriculture Organization (FAO). Yes, life was good—for me and people
like me—as long as we didn't think too hard about what life was like for the
rest of the people in South Sudan.

Well, for most South Sudanese anyway. A small group of local elites—
politicians, senior officers of the security apparatus mostly, and a few
businessmen—lived very much as we did. These privileged few also enjoyed

the trappings of a modern upper-middle class life: air-conditioning, running water, bank accounts in various countries, cars, electricity, internet service, and international travel.

For the other 10.5 million people in the country, life was pretty Hobbesian. If South Sudan were ten people, six of them would be children. Five of those children would live in poverty, and three would suffer acute malnutrition. Only two would have access to clean drinking water, and only two would be literate.

I was finding this incongruity harder and harder to reconcile, but the trick was to keep my mind occupied on matters in the present. During the week, that meant work and working out, and on the weekends, the go-to method was volunteering, sports, and a social life well lubricated with alcohol.

* *

The next day kicked off the standard weekend routine by meeting Emm and Martin at the Exodus Academy to spend a few hours coaching touch rugby. Martin brought Claudia along, which was par for the course. When people paired off here, one of two things happened: either a new member appeared in your inner circle or someone from your circle disappeared to spend time with the new partner's clique.

In this case, Claudia was definitely making the transition to our little group. Of her own coworkers at FAO, she said, "They're all hippies." She considered herself to be a realist and scoffed when I voiced the hope that one day, some of the kids we were coaching could play for South Sudan's international rugby team—which, of course, did not yet exist.

After a couple of hours, we headed back to UN House, stopping by La Baguette and the flat bread store to restock our respective pantries. We'd been invited to attend a rooftop party hosted by Nonviolent Peaceforce later in the afternoon, and Claudia suggested that we should start a riot at the party to test the concept of "nonviolent peaceforcing," which she cynically suggested was unlikely to hold up against an actual mob.

My mask must have slipped for a moment, and I could tell Claudia had seen the momentary look of dismay that crossed my face. "Come on," she said. "You guys are the violent peaceforce, right?" We all laughed, and the momentary tension was broken because she'd made a fair point. Our peacekeepers went armed and armored wherever they went—a potentially violent peace force, I had to admit.

13. Team photo after coaching touch rugby for kids in Juba. Author photo.

Sonia Hamid was busy, so I volunteered to be our designated driver and navigated to the Tomping neighborhood where Nonviolent Peaceforce had its staff accommodations. The building was a multistory rectangular guesthouse whose rooftop balcony had been transformed into a dance floor for the occasion. As the security guard checked our names on the guest list, I'd noticed that the SRSG's name was on it as well. That came as little surprise since he rarely seemed to miss a good party.

Early on, I chatted with some of our hosts. They had a unique approach to civilian protection, and I found it interesting to hear firsthand about their work. Nonviolent Peaceforce engaged in a practice known as unarmed civilian protection—that is, bringing unarmed and specially trained civilians recruited from around the world to live and work among local civil societies in conflict zones such as this one. Unlike UNMISS peacekeepers, they worked without weapons, which forced them to rely on relationship building and other soft-power approaches. But I was impressed that our approaches to civilian protection had at least one element in common: we both believed that "presence is protection."

Drinking plain tonic water, I hung out on the side of the dance floor, watching the crowd and the clock. We had about an hour left until curfew, at which time those of UNMISS would return Cinderella-like to our bases, leaving our humanitarian colleagues to continue the party. The scene was not that different from the Tulip Inn on any given Friday, with its free-flowing alcohol and the sound of house music.

To be a UN staff officer in UNMISS, I mused cynically, *is to be living a Juba good version of the expat dream. You had well-paid work during the week and a social life on the weekend—all behind razor wire–topped walls manned by bored men with guns that kept you safely separated from the hard world beyond them. You could enjoy that life as long as you could keep your eyes closed to the difference between conditions inside the walls and outside them, and as long as you could keep your mind off hypocrisy and injustice.*

I had been living that dream for most of the year, but now I felt that I was slowly beginning to awaken.

37 Nonworking Group

When you see something that is not right, not fair, not just, you
have a moral obligation to say something, to do something.
—REPRESENTATIVE JOHN LEWIS, CIVIL RIGHTS ACTIVIST

18 November 2019. I started the week in a working group that brought
together all the joint security mechanisms under one roof with a goal of
coming up with a functional security arrangement for the country. What
had not been done in the last six months, we were now trying to accomplish
with two days of planning and ninety days of implementation.

Here I saw Angelina Teny in action for the first time. "We've been given
another opportunity by these hundred days," she said, cautioning the group
convened at the Juba Grand Hotel not to squander this last, best opportunity
to reform the security forces as required by the 2018 peace treaty.

Among only ten women present, out of perhaps two hundred participants,
the most notable was the speaker. Madam Angelina was sixty-six years old,
but her tightly cropped hair was still dark, and she wore a colorful dress that
framed a strong body. "People say that a hundred days is not a lot, and it's
true—so we do not want to waste time going back to the drawing board. . . .
Our challenge is the same. It's money."

As I saw it, money was hardly the only challenge. According to the records,
seventy-four thousand soldiers had been registered in the cantonment sites
already, and while their registration forms had all been shipped to Juba,
many of the soldiers had left the cantonment sites because the promised
food, medicine, and water had never arrived. How many remained exactly?
No one was certain, and no one seemed to care. The 2,292 instructors had
been trained, but most were sitting around in the training sites, waiting for
their trainees to arrive.

So the registration process had really accomplished nothing, but the screening process was the more important part. Suppose a soldier had shown up and registered but was missing a leg or was too old or too young?

As the CDF observed caustically, "The screening is to see if they are fit before money is wasted on training them." Of course, what the screening process actually consisted of was also unclear. Still, money *was* a problem. Only 10 percent of the $100 million pledged to fund the process had been released so far.

After the first plenary session, we broke into smaller groups. I sat with the Joint Military Ceasefire Commission and Joint Transitional Security Committee. Bob Leitch moderated the discussion and tried hard to lead the group toward a solution that was practical given our time frame. Bob worked for the Reconstituted Joint Monitoring and Evaluation Commission (RJMEC), which IGAD had created to monitor and oversee the implementation of the peace agreement. But although the red-faced, white-haired Brit had years of experience in these sorts of negotiations, the South Sudanese officers didn't want to be led. They seemed to have little appetite to arrive at a solution, and having a *khawaja* (the label that the South Sudanese have long applied to Caucasian foreigners) steering the debate was probably suboptimal.[1]

There were six training sites in Upper Nile, three in Western Bahr el Ghazal, and seven in the in the Equatorias. Of these sixteen locations, perhaps four were ready to actually start training troops. Many of the rest lacked even a borehole for water.

A significant faction in the room wanted to spend $29 million over the next thirty days to bring all sixteen sites to a functional condition. This was a pipe dream, as getting the necessary work done in the time we had was unlikely, even if the money did go to the contractors and not into the pockets of the generals and other government kleptocrats. The other major bloc didn't think that the lack of facilities in the training sites was an issue. "It's now the dry season," one general observed pragmatically, "so there is no need for shelter."

I remained quiet, intending to let the South Sudanese work things out for themselves, until I was asked directly for my opinion. "Logistically," I said, "it's a simple problem. You have four functional training sites, and it's going to take eight weeks to train a class of soldiers. If you put one battalion into each training site as quickly as they can be screened and transported, it should theoretically be possible to train four battalions by the fifty-day mark and another four by the hundred-day mark. Priority could be given to training the soldiers for the VIP protection force, and the curriculum and model for their training could be used to train the remaining twenty-five thousand soldiers as the other camps become fully operational."

One of the senior generals shook his head at this notion. "Why do we need a VIP protection force? Juba is already safe. Don't you feel safe here?"

I smiled. "Personally? Of course. But I am afraid not everyone shares our feelings, sir."

After a moment of awkward silence, Bob suggested we break for tea. The discussion when we readjourned focused on how much more money to ask for and whose fault it was that the training had not already been completed.

* *

On the second day, only perhaps a quarter of the original participants showed up. Notably absent was the entire South Sudan Joint Defense Board. We started half an hour late and later discovered that the missing group had been next door the whole time, holding its own meeting outside of the plenary. In the group's absence, it had been decided that an additional $10 million would be needed to accomplish the training of the unified force, and most of the rest of the day was spent lining out how that money—if it could be found—would be spent.

Heading back to the base at the end of the day, I noticed something interesting: crews were erecting power lines along several of the main roads and affixing streetlamps to the poles. It was a small thing, but it represented improvement. On a day such as this one, any sign of progress was cause for hope.

* *

Elsewhere in the country, hope was thin on the ground. The one notable success was in the Equatorias, where a Rwandan patrol on the road to Kajo-Keiji succeeded in chasing off a group of armed bandits and rescuing two civilians from their clutches. Our peacekeepers exchanged fire with the robbers without anyone getting hit.

In Sector West, the government had set up a series of checkpoints near Wau for the supposed purpose of disarming civilians and combating criminality; instead, of course, as with most checkpoints in the country, they were used for criminal activities. Local community leaders and female civilians reported that the armed men at those roadblocks harassed civilians, conducted aggressive body searches, and extorted cash.

The year appeared to be headed toward an inauspicious end, but I thought there was still plenty of time to change the course of local history, if anyone could be troubled to do so.

38 Friendsgiving

Inconsistent and at times competing international engagements
have failed to put pressure on the parties to respect the [peace]
agreement. . . . This approach has favoured the absence of
war over building the conditions for durable, inclusive and
genuine peace for the millions of exhausted civilians.

—UN PANEL OF EXPERTS ON SOUTH SUDAN

25 November 2019. In July the UN secretary-general had appointed a panel of
five experts in the fields of humanitarian affairs, natural resources, weapons,
finance, and regional issues to gather, examine, and analyze information on
illegal arms sales, trafficking in illicit goods, and violations of human rights
in the context of the ongoing sanctions regime. The panel's interim report
had recently been released, and it made for upsetting reading.

The panel informed UN leaders that the South Sudanese government
was continuing to obstruct the peace process by failing to release the funds
that had been earmarked for its implementation and by encouraging the
defection of General Ochan by providing him with weapons, ammunition, and intelligence. This had allowed Ochan to attack Maiwut and the
surrounding areas, burning one village to the ground and conducting a
localized campaign of killing, looting, and sexual violence.

The report also noted that government forces in the Equatorias used sexual
violence against women and girls as a standard tactic in the campaign to
suppress support for the insurgency led by Thomas Cirrillo. Additionally, the
panel found that natural resources such as teak and mahogany were being
illegally exported and that generals in both the SSPDF and the SPLA-IO used
the funds to purchase weapons and supplies and, of course, to line their
own pockets. The looted lumber flowed through Uganda and on to India,
where much of it was turned into furniture that was bought by European

stores. As illegally logged timber flowed out, illegally imported weapons and ammunition flowed in and were used to kill civilians.

These experts made five recommendations, but none of them were for UNMISS. They did not suggest that we should take action to protect the people of Maiwut from General Ochan or the inhabitants of the Equatorias from the SSPDF and NAS. It was very disappointing. The mission was taking no action of its own to protect these at-risk populations, and none of the UN's oversight bodies made any recommendations to the secretary-general to suggest that we should. More problematically, no one who presumably read these reports—António Guterres and his staff, the members of the Security Council, the UN General Assembly, or even the media—seemed to notice this glaring discrepancy. That fact weighed on my mind as another week passed with the usual mélange of events both surreal and ordinary.

In the DRC, our sister mission was under siege. Its base at Beni was attacked by a mob of residents who were angry because there, too, UN peacekeepers appeared to be doing nothing to protect them.

"We are protesting because no one is doing anything to protect us. Everyone—the government soldiers and the UN soldiers—have failed to protect us," one of the demonstrators had told reporters. Another said, "They should either protect us or leave our country. We have been killed while they just watch. What are they here to do?"[1]

The sentiments expressed were apropos to our mission as well. In the last month alone, more than a hundred people had been killed, raped, or abducted. The only difference was that no one was demonstrating against the UN in Sudan, so there was little international news coverage.

＊ ＊

On Thursday, I briefed the new commander of Sector Unity, Brig. Gen. Taef Ul Haq, on the current state of security in the mission and in Unity State. One of the new items of interest was that a notorious South Sudanese general named Gordon Koang had just been reinstated as a county commissioner in Unity State despite that a recent human rights investigation had found him responsible for the commission of atrocities that likely amounted to war crimes in southern Unity in 2018.

The Bangladeshi general shook his head and wrote in his notebook. Looking up, he asked, "Is any political action being taken by the mission?"

I told him that I wasn't aware of anything but that before he departed

Juba to take command of his new sector, it might be worth discussing that question with General Tinaikar.

* *

That night, we celebrated Thanksgiving with a "Friendsgiving" dinner at the Tukul, inviting all the Americans from the various elements of the mission. Hugh and Martin joined us to add a little international flavor. I chatted with Maureen Nealon, a slim woman with pale blonde hair who worked in the mission headquarters. I knew her from CrossFit, and as we ate pizza, she told me that white rhinos had supposedly been seen somewhere the middle of the country and that an old European man traveled here to search for them from time to time. She also talked about safaris down the Juba–Nimule Road in the "good old days" of 2015. Those times were long past—this last month had seen several attacks on travelers along that route—but perhaps once the transitional government was formed, security would be sufficiently improved that UN staff would again be able to explore South Sudan's national parks on the weekends. Those parks appeared in green on various maps but existed, for now, mainly on paper and in the minds of people who had been in the country for many years. It was sad, because the parks represented the only part of the East African ecosphere to have remained largely untouched by humanity and its machines for over a half century.

* *

On Sunday I had an invitation to join Canadian ambassador Douglas Proudfoot at his residence. He was a large, genial man with graying, curly hair and a thick beard, and his residence was on the fourth floor of a fairly nice apartment complex that was notable for its lack of the heavy security that I associated with the housing set aside for senior U.S. diplomats.

His excellency was hosting an afternoon cocktail party to introduce the senior national representatives of Norway, the United States, Denmark, and New Zealand to a party of visiting policy wonks from the Canadian government. Colin Townson and Bradley Pye worked for the peace support operations program of Global Affairs Canada, Tania Roth was with the Department of National Defense, and Lt. Col. Andrew Nicholson was the Ethiopia-based defense attaché who was also responsible for South Sudan, Djibouti, and the AU. They were in town to assess UNMISS before making their recommendations for updates to the mandate and for consideration of Canadian support for the mission, and this informal session was a way for them to gather information and evaluate the human terrain prior to beginning their formal work on Monday. Colin and Bradley were a Laurel and Hardy pair: the former, stick thin in a tailored suit; the latter, stressing the seams of a rather large jacket. Tania was small and serious, while Andrew was tall and just as loquacious as I expected an attaché to be.

I was frank about my concerns regarding the protection of civilians, the checkpoint corruption, the lack of a focus on DDR, and the issues we had with freedom of movement. On this last topic, I highlighted the problems with the mission's failures to make any improvements to the roads and bridges that lasted more than a single rainy season. Colin said that the local roads didn't look too bad, but I laughed and said that no one should judge South Sudan's infrastructure based on what they saw in Juba. "The force commander is leading a patrol up the road to Bor next week," I told him. "I can try to send you some photos from there that might paint a different picture."

My phone buzzed. In a break between conversations, I glanced at my email and felt an unexpected thrill when I saw a short note from Jayde, who had finally replied to the letter that I'd sent in August. Somewhat to my surprise, she still wanted to come visit—preferably in the early part of the next year.

The week was ending on a high note, I thought.

Then my phone buzzed again. A note from the force commander's aide said there had been fighting north of Rumbek, and we were deploying peace-keepers to intervene. Was I free to travel with General Tinaikar tomorrow? My answer, of course, was yes.

39 Clash of Clans

The form of military force that is inspiring perhaps the greatest hope
is the United Nations peacekeeping force. It inspires optimism because
it seems to perform military duties without being militaristic.
—CYNTHIA ENLOE

2 December 2019. We'd flown from Juba to Rumbek in a turboprop plane
early in the morning. Such planes could not land without a proper runway,
so now we were waiting for an Mi-8 helicopter to carry us the final sixty-four
miles north to a village called Maper. It was the epicenter of a deadly week in
Sector West with seventy-nine people killed and over one hundred injured
in fighting between two local clans, the Gak and the Manuer. Yesterday, we'd
flown in seventy Nepalese peacekeepers to stabilize the situation, and now
the force commander was going to meet with the Gak community in an
attempt to break the pattern of violence that was expected to continue. This
vicious cycle was driven by revenge and amplified by assault rifles, according to Leopold Kouassi, who was accompanying us to Maper because it fell
within his political purview as the acting head of our Rumbek field office.

According to Leopold, both the Gak and Manuer were ethnic Dinka, but
their clan allegiances were apparently stronger than their shared tribal identity. Often the victims weren't even the people whose actions had triggered
the call for vengeance; anyone from the offender's clan or social group was
considered fair game. Leopold told us about a Kenyan truck driver whose
vehicle had struck a local chief and killed him earlier in the year. That incident resulted in the killing of two Ugandan teachers in May. I remembered
hearing about that attack when I'd first arrived in-country and thinking
at the time it had seemed a senseless act of violence. Now I understood.
A foreigner had killed a member of the clan, and the next foreigners who
appeared in the area had been killed in retribution.

The latest fighting had been triggered when a Manuer trader was murdered by gun-wielding Gak youths. Around 15 percent of civilians in the area were armed, according to a study by the UN Development Programme.[1] The figure sounded low until you factored in age and gender. Primarily, teenage boys and adult men were the ones who carried guns. Since they made up only about a quarter of the population, that meant two out of three civilian men had weapons—usually AK-47s. The murder had triggered an attack by the victim's clansmen on the Gak, starting a series of raids by both groups that had lasted for three days. The fighting had continued despite the arrival of a small SSPDF contingent that had killed five Manuer attackers near Maper, but the raids had ended—at least temporarily—when our peacekeepers deployed to the area.

The Sector West commander, General Wang, also joined our delegation. He told General Tinaikar that in this part of the country, most of the ammunition was sold by the soldiers of the SSPDF. They made only 7,000 South Sudanese pounds a month—about $54—when they got paid, which was infrequent. But the government kept them well supplied with ammunition, which they could sell for around $10 for a fully loaded magazine of thirty rounds. The rest of the ammunition, Leopold interjected, came across the border from the DRC.

* *

I considered everything the local experts had shared as we lined up to board the helicopter. It was a lot to think about, but once we were airborne, I found myself contemplating less depressing subjects. I was strapped into the best seat in the chopper, the one farthest back, where I could open one of the bubble windows and enjoy a fresh breeze. A dirt road connected Rumbek to Maper, but we had been told that it was impassable due to the recent rains. From the air, the road looked fine, and the country on either side was wide, flat, green, and empty. I remembered my conversation with Maureen about the old Englishman who was convinced that a handful of white rhinos still lived in South Sudan. I'd asked where, expecting her to say the Equatorias. Those states bordered Uganda, where I knew that rhinos lived, and the heavier vegetation seemed a good place for a three-ton beast to hide. But Maureen had surprised me by saying that the eccentric zoologist thought the rhinos were in Lakes State, the same area I was currently flying over. I kept my eyes open, scanning the dry, scrubby ground below, but I saw no sign of them or animals of any sort, for that matter.

* *

When our helicopter landed at Maper, we found the ground dry and cracked, the cornstalks brown and broken. Chickens, goats, sheep, and cows wandered around, as did children. A few melons stood out—bright spots of glossy green against the dark earth—but it didn't look as though there were nearly enough to sustain the number of people in the village. Using a large wooden pestle nearly as tall as she was, a young woman pounded grain into flour in a mortar consisting of a hollowed-out log. We made our way past her and the sun-bleached walls of an old UN base that had been abandoned in 2014. The Nepalese troops who arrived to secure the area were not staying there, and it was unclear to me just where they *were* staying. I had no time to investigate this as we were already late for our rendezvous with the governor and village elders, who were gathered around a bare circle of earth beneath several towering acacias that created a cool area of shade under the hot afternoon sun.

We reached the meeting spot to find the governor addressing a circle of perhaps six hundred to eight hundred people. The inner circle consisted of the elderly and the chiefs. The latter were very old men, distinctive in their ancient colonial uniforms—worn khaki trousers and jackets adorned with sashes of red and gold—and aged military-style caps perched on their bald, weathered heads. They were seated on the ubiquitous plastic chairs; in front of the semicircle, an office desk and five or six beaten-up office chairs had been set up for the dignitaries. The force commander, Leopold, and General Wang were ushered into a trio of the seats, while the rest of us found places in the crowd.

Behind the chiefs and elders were arrayed men and women, most of them very young. Seventy percent of South Sudanese were younger than twenty-five years old. All were standing, listening intently to the governor, who continued to speak as we arrived. "I've heard what you have said, and documented it," he said. "I've heard all your problems and what you need from us."

The governor's bodyguard—a sharply dressed member of the National Security Special Forces, according to his shoulder patch—stood closely behind him. He carried what appeared to be a clean, new U.S. M-4 carbine;

had a pistol in a leg holster; and wore a good tactical vest over a U.S. Army woodland-patterned camouflage uniform complete with neat new boots. This young man presented a far different picture of military discipline than the numerous other members of the police, the military, and the local militia in and among the crowd.

His boss continued to speak, apparently responding in detail to the chiefs' litany of requests, which they had delivered just before our arrival. The governor said that he understood the need for network coverage and would speak to MTN South Sudan, the national telecom provider. The crowd responded with muted applause. Some of them—but by no means everyone—clapped slowly.

As for the community's request for soldiers and judges, he agreed that the army needed to be present for the mobile court to function but said that bringing soldiers would present a logistical challenge. The governor also wanted a certain quid pro quo from the village. "Some soldiers were killed here in the past," he said and told the elders that they should talk among themselves and hand over the killers as a show of good faith.

The chiefs had requested food aid. Flooding and looting had left the community stricken, and the young people were all with the cattle in the bush. As if on cue, a baby started to cry somewhere in the back of the crowd—a loud, inconsolable wail. The governor said he would see what could be done.

The elders also wanted a real hospital. All they had was a primary healthcare center, a basic clinic run by an Italian aid organization. But the governor told them, "You must have peace if you want a hospital. Who will run it? Foreigners. So they must hear that Maper is peaceful and know that it is safe to walk at night."

The baby stopped crying.

The governor closed his remarks by saying that this was a good opportunity for the UN to be present and to hear the community's demands directly from them. He gestured Leopold forward, and the acting head of the field office surprised me with the way he chided the assembly. "Last year the UN negotiated a peace between the Gak and Manuer," he began, "but if one little incident can trigger this sort of violence, I don't think there was any sincere desire for peace." He went on to remind everyone that the UN was impartial. "We're here today, talking to you, but we'll go to the Manuer and pass the message of peace to them too."

There was no applause this time. Leopold then yielded the floor to the force commander.

"We are concerned with the number of people who've lost their lives," General Tinaikar began. "Disputes happen, but they should not be settled by killing each other. Is there any mother here who has lost a son?" he asked. "Let them come forward. Let them tell me if they are happy."

This caused a stir in the crowd, a muttering, and a shaking of heads. No one came forward.

"There are Manuer mothers who have lost their children and feel the same way you do," he said. "We have noted your concerns, and we'll see how we can help, but the fighting must stop." He paused. "Now," he asked through the interpreter, "does anyone have a request for me?"

The paramount chief slowly rose and spoke in Dinka, pausing between sentences to make sure the translator had time to tell the general what he said. "Tell the Manuer that although we still have some grievances, we've stopped the fighting now. Tell them we must all stop fighting. Those who lost sons, just seeing you helps. It shows that their lives were important, that you have come all the way from Juba to talk to us. Tell the Manuer there should be no more fighting."

Behind me, one of the young armed men laughed quietly and derisively, and he said something low to his comrade, who laughed as well. I thought of what Leopold said earlier over breakfast in Rumbek: "If you are not able to cleanse the heart, the fighting will continue."

* *

Before we flew out, we walked about half a mile to the local clinic. We hoped to visit the wounded, but most had already left. We met one of them, though—a skinny young man, perhaps fourteen years old, wearing a camouflage ball cap and a bright yellow sheet wrapped around his shoulder. He pulled the sheet back to reveal his left arm in a cast, the bones broken by a gunshot wound. When asked if he had participated in the fighting, he wouldn't say, but the injury seemed to speak for itself.

On our way back to the helicopter, we encountered an SSPDF patrol dressed in the usual motley assortment of uniforms, some with boots, some with sandals, some barefoot. They carried AK-47s and rocket-propelled grenade launchers. I noticed that the barrel of one weapon was completely plugged with dirt. Although we had resorted to helicopters to get here, they had

14. South Sudan People's Defense Force (SSPDF) "technical." Author photo.

come by road in a pair of "technicals"—old, battered Toyota Land Cruiser pickups with heavy machine guns mounted in the back. The cabs had been cut off, and the vehicles were painted in green camouflage with a red stripe on the hood, marking them as military police. On the door panels in bright yellow was stenciled "Division 6" with a stylized crocodile above it.

These soldiers were far from the Division 6 headquarters in Maridi, which lay 276 miles to the south. We exchanged greetings with our South Sudanese counterparts, took a few photos, and headed to the chopper. The presence of the SSPDF patrol begged the questions of why they could get here in trucks, but we couldn't, and why neither government nor UN forces had arrived in time to prevent the worst of the attacks. But there was no time to gather details through our translator. It was getting late, and we had to get back to Juba before the airport closed at 6:00 p.m.

Flying back, I mulled over the problem of getting beyond "early warning" and achieving a "proactive response." We knew about the murder that sparked this fight and had enough historical data to know that it would almost certainly be followed by a major clash. Our presence did seem to forestall violence, but we still failed to arrive until after it was too late. What could we do differently in the future to prevent the killings in the first place? I believed that answering that question was the most important work that we on the force staff could do.

40 The Road Less Traveled

> When other people's lives depend on you, you cannot be bold
> without having firsthand knowledge of the on-ground situation.
> I am responsible, ultimately, for the lives of both our Blue
> Helmets as well as the communities we are here to serve. I can't
> be comfortable sitting in an air-conditioned office in Juba giving
> orders. . . . Unless you meet and talk to people who are suffering,
> appreciate their challenges, it's impossible to take sound decisions.
> —LT. GEN. SHAILESH TINAIKAR

3 December 2019. The word "petrichor" describes the unique smell that rises from the earth when the first big droplets of rain begin to thump against dry soil. I'd first heard the term from a woman in Uganda with whom I'd had a brief but passionate affair, which had consisted mainly of torrid messages exchanged on WhatsApp. Its consummation on a weekend visit to Kampala in August, I thought, had been a little less than either of us had hoped.

Now I smelled it again through the open window as the clouds overhead finally made good on what they had threatened for the last few hours. I shook my head. Rain meant mud, and mud meant we might find ourselves stranded. But we were on the cusp of the seasons, headed into the overdue dry months, and the shower soon passed.

Our convoy slowed shortly afterward to let a large herd of cattle pass. Three young men drove the thin, heavy-horned animals. One man carried an AK-47; the other two carried long spears. *This was a dangerous business*, I thought. I estimated the animals represented a value of around $25,000—a great prize for anyone who could capture them, although I suspect that would be easier said than done.

* *

We'd gotten back late from our trip to Maper, so I had only managed to get a few hours' sleep before waking to make the drive to Bor. General Tinaikar

15. Herd of cattle on the road to Bor. Author photo

led the convoy, driving as fast as conditions allowed, but the roads were so bad that our speed never got above twenty miles per hour. I was reflecting on how much I'd enjoy a break from driving when the lead vehicle pulled to the side of the rutted red-clay road. The rest of us followed suit. It was time for tea. In a dry circle under a towering baobab tree, the force commander's aide set out a handful of chairs. General Tinaikar walked over, accompanied by Bob Leitch, who had been riding with him. I'd hadn't seen the ruddy-faced Englishman since the working group back in November.

"Come, Carp, sit," said General Tinaikar, waving me to an empty chair. "Let us eat."

Food was brought out—samosas and small sandwiches—and water and tea. The force commander rarely ate much, preferring meals to delay him no more than courtesy allowed, but today, with the scent of rain heavy in the air, he seemed a little more relaxed.

Bob, a former colonel in Britain's Royal Army Medical Corps who had spent much of his life in South Sudan, began to spin stories of his days with the rebel armies. He described men too tall to fit completely inside their Russian-made tanks and told of summary executions and grotesque injuries. The stories were unbelievable, but in this country, the truth was often so much stranger than any fiction one could imagine. The force commander rose suddenly, causing Bob to pause mid-sentence.

"Let's try the road again," General Tinaikar said, as he headed for his vehicle.

I stood, stretched, and walked back toward the column of once-white SUVs now filmed with red dust. It had already been a long drive, and we still had much of it left.

* *

We continued north, roughly parallel with the east bank of the Nile River. We passed checkpoints manned by lethargic soldiers. At one, the officer on duty leaned back in a plastic chair, a baby in his lap. They didn't shake us down for money, as they would have any passing civilian or humanitarian vehicles, and they rarely asked if we had clearance papers. Freedom of movement was only a problem in areas where the government didn't want us to be, and it didn't care about transit along this road because it wasn't the current focus of any particular conflict. Our pace only slowed because freedom of movement was influenced as much by the weather and road conditions as by the security forces. North of Gemieza, the ground changed from hard, red laterite soil known locally as *murram* to a cracking, dark clay that proved treacherously soft and deeply rutted. I had to put my vehicle in four-wheel drive just to keep moving.

We made it to Bor around nightfall, and I had a chance to catch up with Marius Undlein, the Norwegian major whom I'd first met months ago during our in-processing in Entebbe. His hospitality was top rate. We drank aquavit and ate reindeer sausage in his accommodations while he told me about life in Bor. It wasn't all that different from mine in Juba, but here, the rooftop parties were mainly held by baboons. A troop of them lived on the base and apparently enjoyed lounging on the roof of his containerized housing unit from time to time although I never saw them. As I returned to my own quarters after dark, I did see an incongruous selection of smaller creatures: a cavorting mob of mongooses, which I knew were endemic in East Africa, and a solitary hedgehog, which I had wrongly believed were native only to Europe.

* *

The drive from Juba was just the first leg of a trip that would take us farther north and east into the country; from Bor, we traveled on to Lankien, which was new to me, and Akobo, which was not. Unfortunately, it appeared there was nothing new to Akobo, either. None of the decrepitude I'd seen three months earlier had been repaired; if anything, the base was in worse shape than before. Granted, the conditions there were still much better than what most of the civilians in Jonglei lived in, but they were also worse than what the UN's own regulations required it to provide its peacekeepers.

The experience reinforced my belief that the keys to solving South Sudan's problems lay in education, infrastructure, and disarmament. The Equatorias were dangerous, but at least there I had seen schools and children in school uniforms. Not so on the road to Bor. Nor anywhere in Jonglei, where the World Bank had reported that adult literacy was 15 percent, only 50 percent of the children had access to education, and 68 percent of the teachers were volunteers. Roads, where they existed, were bad at the best of times, and more men carried guns in Jonglei than anywhere else in the country.

When we talked with civilian leaders, their messages were consistent: they asked for support in education, health, and security, and had little illusion as to where they currently stood. "I think India is a first world country, maybe second," one of them told the force commander, "but I don't think we are even in the third world. . . . We're in the fourth world."

General Tinaikar replied that peace through unity was the first step in the path to development. "The process is slow," he said, "but have faith and do not take any steps back."

＊ ＊

Back in Juba, some new faces were in our headquarters building, and some familiar ones had disappeared. Among the latter group was Hugh McKeown, who had returned to Australia. Maj. Andrew "Andy" Stewart introduced himself as the "new Hugh," which seemed appropriate, given that our new Australian's sideburns were just as impressive as his predecessor's. Stig Rogne and Bin Cao had also returned to their home countries of Norway and China. Bin had been loud and funny. His replacement, Maj. Donglin Bai, was quiet and serious. My first impression was that while Bin had been the life of the party, Bai's life *was* the Party. I was sorry to see Stig go but glad to discover that his successor, Maj. Hilding Runar, was a veteran of a previous tour in UNMISS. I was sure his experience would serve our team well in the months ahead.

41 Up the Creek

Peace is like water, you cannot stop anyone from drinking of it.
—LT. GEN. GABRIEL DUOP LAM

13 December 2019. En route to a meeting with more opposition military leaders at their remote headquarters in Diel, we visited the UNMISS base at Malakal, where Sector North was headquartered, so that the force commander could inspect one of the battalions from his home country and award its personnel their UN peacekeeping medals. The viewing stand was filled with civilian and military leaders. Governor Peter Chol was there, as was Indian ambassador S. D. Moorthy and Maj. Gen. Akul Majok, the SSPDF Division 2 commander.

I watched as the force commander, standing erect in an open-topped jeep, rode to inspect the formation. In earlier times, he would have ridden his horse down the line of soldiers, casting an appraising gaze across their ranks, but there were few horses in South Sudan. I knew this because the Mongolian battalion in Bentiu had tried to find enough horses for their patrols and failed; instead, they went patrolling on mountain bikes. Truth here really was much stranger than any fiction.

When General Tinaikar completed his cursory inspection and returned to his seat in the audience, the battalion marched past in review. Their mustaches were outstanding, and the pomp and circumstance was top notch. After the ceremony, the audience adjourned for a light lunch. Then our party from Juba headed over to the Bangladeshi Marine outpost on the edge of the Nile, where we loaded on Zodiac boats for the trip to Diel.

Each boat mounted a heavy machine gun in the stern and, along with its pilot and gunner, carried a complement of six to eight peacekeepers. Our force protection was sourced from the Rwandan battalion.

Traveling by boat proved much smoother than driving on local roads, and I made a mental note that we should have more riverine assets to take

16. Patrol boat on the Nile. Author photo.

advantage of this. The river's surface was flat; the water, a dark greenish brown. The sun was hot, and the artificial breeze created as the patrol boat's powerful engines sent us skimming over the water felt refreshing. Palms dotted the right bank, and as we passed the shell of Malakal on the left, I found myself wondering if the town was intentionally destroyed to keep it from supplanting Juba.

Malakal had been the second-largest city in South Sudan before the civil war in 2013, and it had soon become a heavily contested battleground. In the years that followed, it would change hands twelve times and, in the process, be completely destroyed. Gone along with the buildings was any real faith in humanity for its surviving inhabitants as government and opposition forces alike had used such tactics as castration, mass rape, and the burning of people inside their homes. In February 2016, with much of Malakal razed to the ground and largely abandoned by the 150,000 residents who had once lived there, the final attacks were against the last place where significant concentrations of people could still be found in the area—the UNMISS POC camp.

Those attacks, in which government forces breached the perimeter of the POC camp and of the UN base itself—killing thirty civilians and damaging key infrastructure—had represented a serious failure of the UN's role as protectors of civilians. It had been the first incident that General Cammaert investigated in South Sudan, and his report's very abbreviated summary, which the UN finally released, concluded that "once the security situation began to deteriorate, the Mission, at all levels, failed to manage the crisis effectively."[1] Other reports by outside agencies went further. A Médicins Sans Frontières (MSF) report stated that as many as sixty-five civilians had been killed, that 2,326 shelters had been burned, and that "UNMISS seems to have been simply *missing in action*."[2] It was a harsh indictment of the failure of a previous cohort of UN leaders to enforce our mandate, and I hoped our current leaders would do better if faced with similar challenges.

* *

The shell of the city disappeared behind our Zodiac boats as we buzzed southward down the Nile. Periodically we passed long, slender canoes paddled by two or three people. One carried a large load of charcoal, a dozen white plastic bags stacked precariously on its narrow hull. Later we passed a stranger sight—the tail end of a transport plane sticking up out of the river at a sharp angle. It was the remains of a WFP flight that had crashed here in 2015. No one was killed, but as with the hulks that lined the runways in Wau and Juba, it was a reminder that every time we boarded a plane out here, we were "rolling the dice" again. On the surface in South Sudan, things seemed peaceful, but all around us were signs fraught with danger. Just this morning, I'd heard about another round of intra-clan fighting—but with a twist. By now, I was used to hearing about cattle as a vector for violence, but fish? Reports were that eighty-six people had gone missing after an attack on Cuet-Akuet, a fishing island in the Nile whose ownership was disputed by two Dinka clans and whose location seemed to be a mystery to everyone else. As with so many places here, it appeared in different places on different maps and, sometimes, nowhere at all.

* *

My train of thought regarding Cuet-Akuet was broken as Diel—a cluster of tukuls near the water's edge—appeared on the left, and a group of uniformed men waved us to a landing site. It was one of those places that didn't appear on Google Maps, but here it was. We drew up in the boats, then climbed down, shaking hands, saluting, and exchanging greetings with our hosts. Diel seemed to be much the same sort of village I'd seen elsewhere: hardpacked dry ground, neat little tukuls, and natural shade provided by large trees. General Tinaikar observed that it seemed a charming location and that it probably would be most pleasant to sit here in the evening and drink a beer. It was hard to disagree.

Calves wandered the shoreline, nibbling at tufts of grass. I reached out to pat one on the head, but it shied away. This elicited smiles from several of the members of our welcoming committee. Their expressions of amusement seemed a bit at odds with the machine guns the young men carried and the ammunition belts draped across their tall, lean bodies. The weapons and the ammunition looked old, even older than the men who carried them.

As we walked toward the center of the village, I noticed the South Sudanese escorts and our force protection detail were casually sizing each other up. There was no hint of aggression; it was just the sort of appraisal that comes naturally to armed men, to fighters. *If I had to, could I take them?* I'd had similar thoughts in other circumstances. The locals' glances at our Rwandan peacekeepers made me notice things that I hadn't before. One of the Rwandans stood out—to me—because he was casually carrying a rocket-propelled grenade launcher, which suddenly seemed a bit . . . excessive. I shook my head and had to remind myself that it was a standard infantry weapon in many armies throughout the world, and to our hosts, it wouldn't appear out of place at all.

This was the SPLA-IO's general headquarters, and in the usual fashion, we quickly found ourselves seated around a picnic table set in the shade of a large tree. Goats bleated, and solid dance beats were coming from a radio somewhere in the camp—near enough to be audible but far enough not to distract from the discussion at hand.

Lt. Gen. Gabriel Duop Lam was the deputy chief of staff for the opposition and the youngest-looking general I'd met so far. He welcomed us warmly, saying that he appreciated the UNMISS mandate and our neutrality.

The force commander asked Duop whether he thought the peace would continue to hold.

Duop smiled, but his words belied the friendly expression. "You cannot just sign the paper and then fail to implement the agreement," he said. "You know, the primary responsibility of any government is to maintain public order. But if it doesn't do that, and becomes a threat to the people . . ."

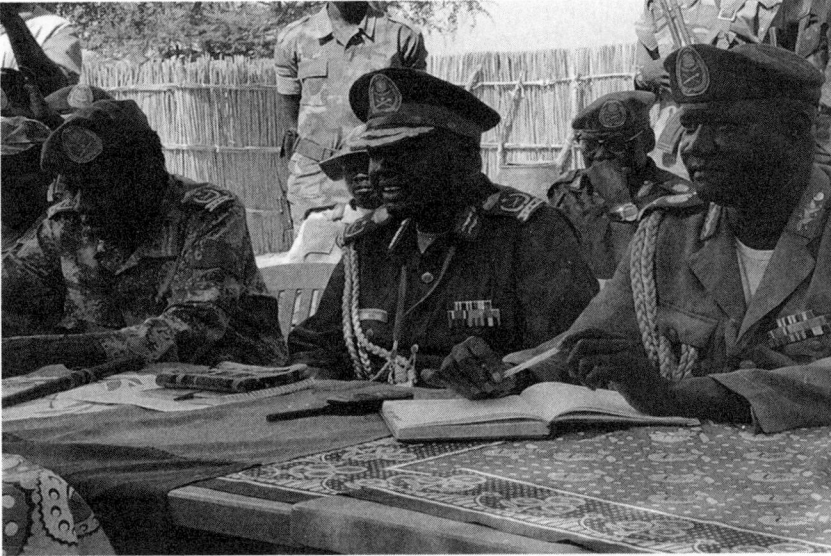

17. Meeting with the opposition general staff at Diel. Author photo.

Lt. Gen. John Both Teny cut in then, speaking through our translator. He looked old—old and tired—and his words recalled the earliest campaigns against Khartoum and the latest uncivil conflicts. "Some of us were born during the war, and now we're growing old during the war. . . . In South Sudan, all the women are widows. We here don't have children. They've all been killed. We've been six years fighting. They didn't defeat us, we didn't defeat them. We need to find a middle ground."

I thought, *It was a good sign that the opposition general staff understood that there was no military solution to the country's problems.* But when General Mawich began to speak, I realized that not all of these generals saw things quite the same.

"We love peace," he said, "but our brothers in Juba? They are not for peace." He referenced General Ochan, who he believed was being supplied with ammunition by the government in violation of the current ceasefire.

I raised my hand and identified myself as Lieutenant Colonel Carpenter, the chief of plans for the force commander. General Tinaikar and I had spoken earlier, and he knew what I would be asking, but before I could pose my question, our hosts had questions of their own.

"Like Jesus?" Laughter.

"You build houses?" More laughter.

My name seemed to be a source of amusement for the South Sudanese—as it had been in a few places around the world—and I had my answers ready. "Yes, I can build with wood, but not very well. That's why I had to become a soldier."

The generals nodded, smiling, and I took it as an invitation to ask my question: "How are the hundred days going, from your perspective?"

Duop replied that there was a lack of political will, because the oil was still flowing.

Mawich seemed to be the hard-liner in the group. "Let me tell you, if there are no security arrangements, there will be no peace in South Sudan. Our forces have gone to cantonment, but there's no food, water, shelter, medicine. . . . If these are not provided . . ." He trailed off. There was an unspoken threat there, as in Duop's less heated reply, which suggested that the oil could be cut off, if necessary. It had been done before—in 2013 and 2016.

General Tinaikar did not address the veiled threats directly but said that as professional soldiers, no one at this meeting should focus on arbitrary deadlines set by politicians. "One hundred days may become two hundred, two hundred days may become three hundred. . . . The important thing is that we don't return to fighting."

Duop didn't set much store by politicians. "Nuer and Dinka are brothers. We made peace with the Arabs last time and we had a different language and religion. So why is it so difficult for the people of South Sudan to make peace? It's the manipulation by the elites."

As the meeting drew to a close, our hosts asked if anyone else wanted to ask UNMISS for anything. The senior civilian from the local IDP site stood up and requested that we send humanitarians with food, medicine, and schoolbooks. General Tinaikar promised to pass the request to the HOFO at Malakal, and it was a reminder that while UNMISS talked about its POC sites as if they represented the only refuge for their inhabitants, the reality was that only 15 percent of all IDPs lived in those sites, protected day and night by UN forces, and the rest were scattered in far-flung locations such as this one.

The last speaker was Maj. Gen. William Deng, the director of police, who told us that he had spent five years living in the POC camp in Juba. "I was a former IDP, but now I am a general," he told us, with no trace of irony. His question was the same one I'd heard before in Akobo: "Why are there no UNPOL officers with you today?" The force commander said it was an oversight and that he would ask the police commissioner in Juba to remedy it. "It would be good if they would conduct some workshops," said Deng, and all of us nodded in agreement. Any opportunity for engagement and professional development of the police forces seemed a good idea in this country, where justice was hard to come by.

* *

The boat ride back was uneventful until just upriver from the port of Malakal I saw a dead woman floating in the river, face down, naked, bloated, and discolored. To my surprise, we didn't stop. The Bangladeshi commander said their standard practice was to notify their UNPOL colleagues, who would relay the message to the local police. Our translator, Buay Deng Chuol, told me the fisherfolk often murdered each other in territorial disputes, drawing his thumb across his throat to drive the point home. But based on the speed of the current and the state of the body, the corpse was probably not local, and I suspected that it would never be pulled from the river. As bad as communications were, by the time the local police were notified, the body would have floated many miles north from where I saw it. There were no forensics experts here, and she wouldn't have identification. It was strange that something that would be headline news in America was so completely unremarkable here.

Who was she? How did she die? Was she a victim of the violence on Cuet-Akuet Island? Was she drowned or murdered? No one would ever know. No one would ever care.[3]

42 A Long December

> No better example exists of how the U.S. military can perform
> a quiet, low-cost, yet influential role in multinational,
> comprehensive engagement. . . . [G]reater DOD [Department
> of Defense] commitment to this multinational opportunity
> would go far to enhance U.S. foreign and security policies.
> —CHRISTOPHER HOLSHEK ON THE VALUE OF U.S.
> CONTRIBUTIONS TO UN PEACEKEEPING

29 December 2019. Looking back, how much I'd somehow managed to pack into the last month of the year seemed strange. Flying back from my latest trip with the force commander, our usual mode of travel prompted me to note it in a journal entry: "It occurs to me that I'm finishing my career very much like I started it—in the back of a helicopter. Thirty years ago, I was as a crew-chief on a UH-1 'Huey'—one of America's most iconic helicopters. Now I'm a passenger in an Mi-8, the Cold War workhorse of the Soviet Union." I could never have imagined it when I began my military journey, but I found it somehow uplifting. People and countries—even federated superpowers—could change, and change for the better.[1]

　　　＊ ＊

I returned to Juba just in time to meet with a visiting delegation from the U.S. State Department. Like the Canadians I'd met at the end of November, the Americans were in town to assess matters before weighing in on the mission's new mandate. The State Department representatives wanted assurances that we were focused on eliminating sexual exploitation and abuse committed by peacekeepers against vulnerable populations. We took the issue very seriously, I assured them, and committed significant time to both prevention training and thorough investigations of all complaints. For my part, I wanted the State Department to encourage the Department of Defense to implement a strategic plan for developing U.S. military officers as effective peacekeepers and to earmark $10,000 annually for the American contingent in UNMISS to use for QIPS.

When they asked what I meant by a "strategic plan for officer development," I explained that unlike other countries, the U.S. military was haphazard in staffing its limited number of UN positions. Most of the officers who ended up in South Sudan were on their final tour before retirement, so their experience was lost almost as soon as they returned to the United States. The UN system valued and rewarded officers who did several tours with the organization. Its best practice was for an officer to serve as a captain or a major in a junior staff position and then return as a lieutenant colonel to serve as a branch chief, as I was. The third deployment with the UN would be as a colonel, filling a deputy chief of staff's billet, and if the officer was very good, that person might return to serve as a brigadier general in the position of force chief of staff.

The State Department team agreed that with this context, it made sense to do a better job of developing and placing U.S. military officers in positions within UN missions. I left the meeting hopeful that the conversation had advanced the interests of both the United States and the United Nations.

＊ ＊

It seemed as if everyone was interested in visiting the mission as the year wound down. I also met with Lauren Spink from the Center for Civilians in Conflict, a DC-based NGO that was focused on civilian protection. She had recently returned from doing research in Yei. What she had learned, she said, was that while the local people liked UNMISS in general, they viewed the force itself as weak. They wanted to see our patrols in action, protecting them from the depredations of both the SSPDF and NAS.

"I'm not surprised," I said. "That aligns with what I heard when I visited in October."

What did surprise me was her response to my concern about the checkpoint corruption that I'd now managed to validate from several sources. Her take on the bribes that the WFP and other humanitarian aid drivers paid was that "it's equivalent to the way the government is charging foreigners $4,000 for a work permit."

I didn't think it was the same thing at all. While the increased work permit fees were a problematic approach to government fundraising, they were still a formal policy, whereas checkpoint extortion had been specifically prohibited by presidential decree.² But I was in a minority in thinking that spending WFP funds on bribery was a serious problem, so I let it go. I had more pressing matters to focus on.

* *

The force commander and the SRSG had "approved in concept" the proposal we'd drafted for realigning the force, but not everyone was as happy about it as I was. The Mission Support Center wasn't keen on moving troops. From its perspective, it meant more work in terms of transportation and building—I got it—but this work had to be done if we expected to do better at enforcing the mandate in 2020 than we had in 2019. Indeed, even as we prepared to execute our realignment, General Ochan was again attacking SPLA-IO positions near the Sobat River and carrying out a campaign of atrocities against civilian communities in the area. No matter how quickly we could get this plan approved and implemented, it would be too late for many people.

* *

I finally took leave again, this time to visit my family for Christmas. My niece Haley lived in Bielefeld, Germany, with her fiancé, Fabi; her mother and brother were also flying in for the holiday. Transiting through the airport in Egypt's capital, I found myself looking forward to returning sometime to visit the pyramids and was struck by a thought: *Is not Cairo International Airport just as marvelous a work of architecture as the pyramids and more functional?* We moderns didn't always credit ourselves that much for our great works; we took so many things very much for granted.

As I scanned the news between flights, I saw that the Trump administration had launched a "Prosper Africa" initiative, which sought to open markets for U.S. businesses, to promote youth employment opportunities, and to enable the United States to compete with China in Africa. I was pleasantly surprised by the announcement. I thought it represented a real opportunity for U.S. firms to help South Sudan build its infrastructure, expand its agricultural and environmental tourism sectors, and extract its extensive natural resources in a legal and less exploitative manner than currently was the norm.

On the second leg of my flight to Germany, I found myself in a contemplative mindset. *The world was, quite simply put, an incredibly complex place. What influence could a single person have? What should I do with my life after retirement, when I would have so much time and freedom to decide how to best to use it?*

I put the deep thoughts aside for the next week and pushed through the momentary culture shock to immerse myself in the comforts of reconnecting with family and enjoying the European standard of living. Drinking glüh-wein in the brightly lit Christkindlesmarkt, eating roast goose with Fabi's family, and indulging in saunas and trips to the local parks and castles—all were a welcome change of pace. But a part of me couldn't wait to get back to the mission, where I knew that violence never took a vacation, and the hundred-day extension Riek Machar had secured in November was already halfway gone.

43 The Far Edge of the Empire

The Zande language predominates from 23° to 30° Long. E. and from 3° to 6° Lat. N. . . . It is remarkable that, without any technological superiority, those who built this empire were able to conquer such vast territories and to weld their inhabitants into a nation.

—SIR E. E. EVANS-PRITCHARD, BRITISH ANTHROPOLOGIST

7 January 2020. There are a few things you never want to hear from your flight crew as the small plane you're in banks hard at low altitude, and the words "Problem with left engine, we go back to Juba" in a rough Ukrainian accent were pretty close to the top of my list.

I was again traveling with the force commander. We were supposed to be headed to Yambio, but General Tinaikar opted to delay the mission for a day once we were back safely on the ground. The next morning, I woke early and caught a ride to the airport with my friend Andreas. An officer in the Swiss reserves, Andreas was a doctor in civilian life, but in the military, his specialty was intelligence.

This time there were no problems with the plane, and we arrived in Yambio after a pleasantly uneventful flight. I linked up with the local military observer, Major Everitt, and rode with him to the base. Yambio had dusty town roads, but everything was well marked and signposted. We drove past two local celebrities: one, a naked madman; the other, "Michael Jackson"—a local traffic cop who danced out his hand directions to traffic at one of the three roundabouts in town.

Major Everitt laughed at the expression on my face. I thought I'd seen it all, but no. "You get used to it," he said.

I was here in part to assess the potential of the existing base infrastructure to support more troops as part of our force realignment, and the Ethiopian coffee ceremony honoring the force commander gave me an opportunity to do so. Most peacekeeping contingents had some unique cultural or culinary tradition, and this was a perfect example. A woman in a white dress—she was a soldier but dressed in traditional attire for this occasion—roasted the coffee beans in a little pan over open coals. Then she brought the pan full of the still-smoking beans to each guest, starting with General Tinaikar, who wafted a handful of the fragrant smoke into his face, inhaled, then nodded and smiled his approval. His face said one thing, while his body language said another. The force commander was impatient to get on the road, but we couldn't rush an Ethiopian coffee ceremony, and he knew it. This wasn't his first time at such an event. Nor was it mine.

Once I'd enjoyed the fragrant smoke, I knew from my place in the serving order that I'd have some time while our hostess returned to her fire, ground the beans in a mortar, added a copious quantity of sugar, and then poured boiling water over them. While she was preparing the drinks and everyone else was talking, I slipped out the back and walked through the Ethiopian company's area on the base. I found it was not in particularly good condition, and there was no room for more troops here. They'd have to be housed at the auxiliary base out by the airport. My inspection didn't take long, and I was back in time to graciously accept my coffee. Served in tiny china cups, the brew was strong and sweet and accompanied with popcorn. We downed our cups, thanked our hosts, and hit the road.

We were headed to Lirangu, about thirty minutes to the north, and the opposition's main base of operations in Western Equatoria State. I rode with Major Everitt again, asked questions, and listened while he shared his thoughts about the area and described the challenges that he faced as an observer, especially in integrated patrols. The terrain was flat and heavily forested. Everitt said that neither checkpoints nor food insecurity were issues here. The roads tended to be bad, so their convoys would only average fifteen miles per hour. More problematic were the differences in equipment and interests. The Ethiopian troops slept on the ground, under the open air, unless it was raining; then they would put up tents. They brought their own food and water, and they were self-sufficient. Observers like himself had been issued special tents and cooking gear, so they, too, were able to camp outdoors. Civilians from other divisions in the mission didn't have that kind of equipment, and the force protection platoons from Ethiopia were neither funded nor required to cater for anyone else's food and shelter. Instead, for every day spent in the field, the civilians got extra money that they were supposed to use to shelter in hotels and buy food in the local markets. So while the civilians wanted to ensure every patrol ended in a town at the end of the day, the observers wanted to make connections with people in the countryside, and the Ethiopians just wanted everyone else to make up their minds. It sounded problematic from many perspectives.

When we arrived at Lirangu, Lt. Gen. Alfred Futayo, the opposition commander for the region, and the local police commissioner met us in a grass hut. I wondered if we would be chided again for not bringing any UNPOL representatives with us.

General Tinaikar asked how the peace was going, what General Futayo needed from UNMISS, and if food had been arriving.

Futayo replied that his soldiers were ready to follow orders and to be trained as part of the unified force. He said he had heard that food had finally been delivered to the training site in Maridi, where his troops were meant to go, so he had sent them there. That explained why this camp seemed largely deserted. He also said he hoped that UNMISS would ensure that his soldiers would be safe in the training sites and that they did not stay there long. They should go, be trained, and redeployed.

General Tinaikar asked how long the training would last.

Futayo didn't know but said it should not take long. "They are already soldiers, so they won't train in military skills. They will just learn how to be a part of the new organization."

Now the force commander raised a sensitive subject: the opposition forces here had recently been spotlighted by the UNMISS HRD for allegedly recruiting child soldiers and holding women against their will. What did General Futayo know of these matters?

Futayo picked his nose while the question was being translated, perhaps to indicate impatience or unhappiness with the question. He said something to one of his aides, who walked away, and when the general finally answered, his reply was delivered at a noticeably increased volume and with extensive hand gestures. The civilians in and around Lirangu were the families of the soldiers, he said. Anyone who was here, was here because they wanted to be. His soldiers hadn't "captured" anyone. Futayo snorted and rolled his eyes. "It was the government who was killing and capturing people during the conflict years!"

Two women appeared—one in a bright blue dress, another in a pink skirt and a white tank top. They said that they were the general's daughters. Both looked to be in their twenties.

"Here are the women in my camp," he proclaimed. "If you tell me to release them, how can I do that? Release them? They're my daughters. I'm stuck with them until I die."

Futayo said that all his officers had sisters, wives, and children living with them. He added that if the UN created a housing center for such families, the women could go there. Otherwise, they would stay with their soldiers.

He ended the meeting by requesting that the force commander pass a message to David Shearer. "Tell the SRSG to talk to Salva and Riek, and tell them to put the peace into action. The people deserve to live free of mines, free of gunshots, free of torture . . . and those UN reports that there are abductions in Lirangu—those reports are false and should be investigated."

We headed back to Juba by way of Yambio. On our way to the airport, I noted with interest the tomb of Gbudue, the last of the Azande kings, who had been buried here in 1905 after his death at the hands of British colonial troops.[1] *Would this corner of the Equatorias be any better off*, I wondered, *if it was still governed by a local monarch rather than an ex-general in distant Juba?*

44 History Will Judge Us

For the record I fully support the observations and conclusions
drawn by Chief U5. This is in line with both what I have
stated internally and in my reports back to Norway.
—BRIG. GEN. BJØRN GAUTE HERLYNG

14 January 2020. Jayde and I had been emailing back and forth occasionally, discussing our plans for her visit, which was tentatively slated for March. When she'd asked what I'd been up to recently, I'd written a bit about my visit to Maper and about the ethnic violence and the disconnect between our words and our actions. She'd replied with a list of challenging questions: Why did Dinka clans fight? Could the elders really make peace, or would the young men go off to kill regardless? Were all health facilities run by foreigners? Her final question really got to the heart of the matter. "Biggest question," she wrote. "If you were in charge, how would you stop the violence?"

My answer was simple: deploy our forces, preferably in advance of any fighting, where and when early warning from JMAC or the force's own historical experience suggested there was likely to be trouble. And where violence was already occurring, deploy to prevent it from continuing, as we had done in Maper.

The final call was not mine to make, but her question encouraged me to try harder to get the decision-makers to take action. I drafted a letter calling for UNMISS to deploy peacekeepers to Maiwut to protect civilians, but I did so in a manner that definitely pushed the envelope of military protocol. Normally, I would have sent such a letter to my immediate superior, Colonel Bahizi, and perhaps copied the force chief of staff. If I persuaded them, then they would route the issue to the force commander, who would decide whether to take it to the SRSG. Then perhaps a decision would be made.

But Colonel Bahizi and the force commander had already heard my thoughts on this issue several times since General Ochan had first launched his campaign of terror in Maiwut County in August 2019, and nothing substantive had been done. It was time to try something new, something a bit riskier.

I drafted a detailed assessment of the issue and sent it to the three people who I believed would support my argument and whose own unique positions in the mission might actually allow us to get peacekeepers into the area. The three addressees were General Herlyng, my friend Brent, and the force's new legal adviser.

Gentlemen—I would like to draw your attention to the following notes from the HRD and our own Intel branch—the fighting in Maiwut has continued, shows no sign of abating, and is known to have caused the murder, rape, and displacement of civilians. If our primary pillar is POC, it is hard for me to see how our current approach of doing nothing as a Force is fulfilling that mandate....

In the past few days, I have heard many people within our ranks say that "history will judge us harshly" for our failure to act here. It is not too late to do something—better late than never.

Landing a significant force at Mutthiang—Company-sized, preferably with APCs and 1–2 Sri Lankan or Rwandan helicopters with door guns mounted in a direct support role to provide air cover, life [*sic*] and CASEVAC [casualty evacuation]—and making a deliberate approach by road to the Maiwut would have the effect of focusing the attention of the South Sudanese government, IGAD and the international community on the fact that we have a month-long shooting war that is a major violation of the cease-fire and has resulted in the rape, murder, and displacement of civilians.

Sector North has submitted a recommendation to use Jikou as our entry point—my assessment is that this would "preference" the Opposition, while Mutthiang represents a better "hub" and is also connected directly by road to Maiwut.

However, any action would be better than none, and it is good to see that Sector North is putting forward military options—now it is time to take action.

> In light of the reports below, we cannot pretend that we do not know
> what is happening—although I suspect that we do not know the full extent.

I pasted in some extracts from the latest reports of the mission's Human Rights Division and our Intelligence Branch that noted General Ochan's attacks on SPLA-iO positions near Jikou had resulted in gang rapes, extrajudicial executions, destruction of civilian property, and forced displacement of civilians. Then I signed the note with "best regards" and waited to see if it resulted in orders to plan a patrol or in a firm reminder about the limits of my leaders' patience. The answer, unfortunately, was neither.

＊ ＊

Lt. Col. Børge Hatlebrekke, the Norwegian military lawyer who had replaced Ronald Gilissen as the force's legal officer, had proven to be less outspoken but just as attentive to the issues as his predecessor was. His response came quickly. As the force's legal adviser, he supported my recommendation and believed that such a proactive deployment aimed at protecting civilians was in line with our mandate and our rules of engagement.

Brent was the next to reply, noting that he was meeting with the SRSG over lunch and that he'd personally raise the topic with his boss and fellow Kiwi over their meal. He also noted that the SRSG might then want to talk to the force chief of staff about the issue in the early afternoon.

So far, so good.

General Herlyng wrote back to Brent, saying that he was ready to discuss the issue with the SRSG and indicating that he also supported my assessment and recommendations.

But then, nothing.

I was disappointed but no longer surprised. Moreover, I was determined to keep trying. What I could see so easily in others, I was still blind to in myself—that is, manifesting the definition of insanity by doing the same things but expecting different results.

＊ ＊

I could definitely see that definition was true of our approach to seasonal road repairs. Only 28 percent of the work had been done so far, and the unprecedented flooding was setting us back, especially in Jonglei. In stark contrast, where we had made significant changes, we were seeing improvements. Sector Unity had proven highly effective under its new leadership structure and was leading the way in long-duration patrols on both the land and the waterways. Its Mongolian battalion had conducted a riverine patrol using small Zodiac boats on the Bahr el Ghazal River, and the Ghanaians were in the midst of a two-week-long expedition to one of the most problematic areas in Unity State.

This report made me hopeful that the two-phase realignment of forces that we'd been planning would have similar effects throughout the country. We'd already released the orders for the first phase, which would solve the c2 problem in Juba and the Equatorias before the hundred days was up, and we were now working on the order for the second phase, which would rebase three battalions and realign sector boundaries to improve our ability to conduct robust and proactive patrols—if we were allowed to do so.

45 Hub and Spoke

Transparency is a casualty, and sincerity is notable by its absence.
—LT. GEN. SHAILESH TINAIKAR REMARKING ON
THE SECURITY TRANSITION ARRANGEMENTS

16 January 2020. Outside my window, the propeller of our transport plane's left engine whirled at two thousand revolutions per minute, and the green expanse of the South Sudanese bush passed below me. I was on my way to Koch, by way of Bentiu and Leer, traveling again with the force commander to inspect one of our hub-and-spoke patrol bases. Finally, this initiative was getting off the ground; our deployments to Maper and Tonj had been a start, but those were reactions to local violence. This patrol was the first truly proactive one that we'd sent out utilizing the hub-and-spoke approach that Brent and I had been working to implement since we'd arrived in-country, and reports indicated that the Ghanaian infantry had been doing an excellent job. Hopefully, the other sectors and battalions would take note and follow suit.

＊ ＊

As the little plane carried us north toward Sector Unity, cruising through blue skies en route to our destination, my mind was elsewhere. I was thinking about how we needed to start the strategic dialogue with the SSPDF and SPLA-IO about what the future role of the South Sudanese military should be and about what needed to be done after the unity government was formed to make that a reality. South Sudan had no external enemies, and its neighbors had put a great deal of time, money, and effort into making sure it succeeded in remaining a functioning nation.

Certainly, some forces were required to garrison the borders, which were not yet formally demarcated, with Sudan and those borders with the CAR and the DRC to prevent cross-border criminal activity. Beyond that, I thought the country's focus should be on development vice defense. If South

Sudan had a large corps of engineers based on the American model, those troops could build the roads, bridges, dams, and levees that were vital for the country's development.[1] With expanded riverine forces—using the U.S. Coast Guard for its model—the Nile and its tributaries could be cleared of floating debris, marked, patrolled, and made safer for commercial traffic and fishing. That was one vision for the future—a new army for a new country. And one of the first things that such an army would need was uniforms, but it needed a way to acquire them without violating the current embargo on military equipment.

To my mind, the importance of a uniform for a military organization could not be overstated. In a unit where the soldiers were wearing six different patterns of camouflage and some with boots, some with flip-flops, some with bare feet—well, those weren't really uniforms. They were just clothes. The main point of a military uniform was to be, well, uniform. Among other things, it distinguished a professional military from a militia. New, standardized military clothing would provide a visual cue that the NUF was different from—and better than—the various armed groups from which it was meant to be created.

Egypt had already furnished four thousand uniforms for the NUF instructors, and I had recently met the Egyptian defense attaché, Staff Col. Mohamed Abdelkarim Baiomy, at a going-away party for Kyle Walton. We had been standing in the late afternoon sun on the patio at AFEX, watching the brown water of the Nile swirl past the stationary wreck in front of us, when I'd asked him if Egypt would consider donating enough uniforms to outfit all of the NUF. He had said it was possible but that the South Sudanese government would need to make a formal request.

Later that evening, during a party at the tukul, I had a chance to chat with the SRSG. I first offered my condolences on the recent rugby World Cup results, where New Zealand had finished third after a disappointing loss to England in the semifinals, and then I mentioned the topic of the uniforms. Thanks to Brent, I knew the SRSG had an upcoming meeting with the Egyptian ambassador, and I thought that if I could get enough people talking about the idea, maybe it would actually happen. I'd also raised the issue with my bosses in both the force and USMOG, but it remained to be seen what would come of it.

My ruminations were cut short as we began our descent into Bentiu.

* *

Stepping off the plane into the dazzling sunlight, I was greeted by my friend Darkwa, whom I hadn't seen since we'd met with Lt. Gen. Simon Gatwech in November. Here, as a lieutenant colonel commanding his battalion in the field, Darkwa was in his natural element, and I had to admit that I was a little jealous. Not long ago, I, too, was a commander, and within my sphere of influence, I had a great deal of freedom to act, to give orders. Now, as a staff officer, I could only give advice.

We transferred to a helicopter for the short flight to Koch. Only seventy-three miles by air, it would have been twice that on the ground and slow going over bad roads. The skeleton of an old UNMISS camp—HESCO barriers and wire—was at the airfield, but Darkwa told us his troops had set up their patrol base some distance away, next to a humanitarian hub and borehole. This pattern was becoming repetitive; the force had neglected these premade bases in conflict zones such as Koch and Maper for so long that it had forgotten they existed. We only rediscovered them on trips such as these. I shook my head.

The new sector commander, Brig. Gen. Taef Ul Haq, was here as well, so the force commander rode with him, leaving me free to ride with Darkwa to the Ghanaian patrol base. As we drove, I was struck, not for the first time, by the numbers of women walking along the side of the dusty road, headed to and from the borehole with large, yellow plastic jerricans of water balanced on their heads. That so many hours of so many lives were spent just getting water was a massive waste of human potential.

* *

The temporary camp was well laid out in a semicircular arrangement within a razor wire enclosure. Two officers and fifty-three enlisted soldiers, including ten women, in addition to security—all were focused on civil affairs support and health initiatives.

When they went on their patrols, the officers carried, among other items, slingshots. "For the hyenas," they told me, and I believed them. Pythons, dik-diks, and large monitor lizards were at UN House, and baboons, mongooses, and hedgehogs were at our base in Bor. It came as little surprise that Africa's most abundant predator could be found here in Koch.

Darkwa explained that while locals told them that they felt safer with the peacekeepers around, what excited them most was that one of the Ghanaians was a veterinarian. His free clinic had made the local herders very happy.

The people here were Nuer. Koch was close to where Riek Machar was born and had historically been a stronghold of his supporters, but the area was now controlled by the government, which had forced the opposition out in a brutal months-long campaign before the signing of the 2018 peace treaty. The push to secure the area had much to do with the oil field in Thar Jath, twenty-five miles to the southeast. Run by a consortium of Malaysian, Indian, and South Sudanese companies, it had three operational wells and others under construction, but the haphazard extraction of the oil had proven an environmental nightmare.

Drilling fluids festered in open mud pits, and local boreholes contained high levels of heavy metals. People and their animals near the sites suffered terribly from disease and birth defects. All this pollution had been documented for years by the UN Environment Programme, the UN Human Rights Council's Commission on Human Rights in South Sudan, and by media organizations, but nothing had been done about it. And it seemed unlikely that much ever would be.

* *

We took a walk to meet the infamous Gordon Koang in an old plaster building with no electricity. Darkwa told me that both the opposition and the government were violating the ceasefire terms by recruiting young men in the area. "Join us or turn in your weapon" was apparently the standard pitch used by both sides.

But when we met with Koang, he claimed that he was not forcing anyone to join up these days. He'd changed, he said. He was no longer the notorious militia leader from 2018 who had led his troops on a brutal, months-long offensive on behalf of the government. "Then I was a commander, now I'm the county commissioner," he offered by way of explanation.

But he had been a county commissioner when he led those attacks too.

Regarding the presence of the UNMISS troops, Koang said that the returning IDPs liked having them around, considering them—incorrectly—to be a part of the peace deal. "Overall, our people are ready for the UN to be here, and for peace to form. We are all ready for it." Koang's face and voice conveyed sincerity.

We're definitely getting the full political charm offensive here, I thought, and reminded myself that this man had led very different offensives in the past: hanging men from trees, raping women, running children down with tanks, burning families alive in their tukuls.

The commissioner, oblivious to my thoughts, continued to speak. "We have a lot of challenges. Lack of access is a great problem. The UN is now repairing the road from Bentiu to Leer." He wanted the road to a nearby locale known as Bwau cleared as well. Following a deadly ambush in 2018, vehicles had avoided the track for almost two years, and now trees were blocking it. If the path was cleared, it was the best grazing land in the region. The force commander nodded to General Ul Haq, who told Koang that the Ghanian officers would survey the route and that he would discuss the matter with his engineering company at Bentiu.

We bade the problematic commissioner farewell and headed toward the training site at Muom. I'd read and talked lot about these places, but this would be my first time seeing one in action. En route, we stopped by our austere operating base at Leer to let the generals thank its small detachment of peacekeepers for their willingness to brave the challenging conditions. Leer was similar to our bases at Akobo and Kodok, in that it was remote and under-resourced, but it was being expanded to provide a more stable UNMISS presence in a known hot spot for violence. An IDP site with 1,720 displaced people had grown up outside its walls, where local NGO camps had also located. They all seemed to find comfort in having a hundred well-armed men and women watching over them, and considering the history of the area, it was not hard to understand why.

The company commander at Leer told us much the same story that we'd heard in Koch. There was no cell signal here, but there were no illegal checkpoints either. However, he said, you had to watch out for the hyenas and pythons at night. I told Darkwa it was a good thing that we were not sleeping there because I'd forgotten to pack my slingshot.

      * *

We drove about nine miles over the dry, parched earth. The road was rough, so the journey took about half an hour. The training camp at Muom sat on a flat stretch of land overgrown with weeds and shrubs. A few gnarled trees offered the possibility of shade. On paper, over 1,400 soldiers were supposed to be here, but we saw only a handful, who were working to thatch the skeletal frames of huts.

Darkwa pulled over to the side of the dirt track, indicating that we have arrived, although not much seemed to set this spot apart from any other. There were no buildings and no vehicles in sight besides our own. We walked a little way into the bush, toward the spot where a lone acacia tree loomed higher than its stunted neighbors, and there we met our hosts, Maj. Gen. Samuel Dok Wanjang and the deputy governor, Abraham Koey, who welcomed us to sit with them at a picnic table covered in a green-checkered tablecloth.

The ground was hard and cracked, and the breeze was hot, even in the shade. The men around the table were old, their faces deeply lined. Thuraya satellite phones were in evidence, but there were few other signs of modernity except for the guns.

The deputy governor spoke first and invoked the need for the international community to support the establishment of the training site. "You can't talk to a hungry, angry man," he said. He seemed very unhappy—I couldn't blame him—although his demeanor made a strange counterpoint to his military colleague's apparently boundless optimism.

"Since you've come here," said General Dok, "I believe all our problems are going to be solved because you are the ones responsible for the peace in South Sudan. Tonight we will sleep very happy."

But it didn't seem as if there was much to be happy about in Muom. The site had one borehole for water and food for two to three days. There were a few men here, with some women and children. They had no shelters beyond a handful of torn tents and the huts that were slowly taking shape in the distance.

The general had four requests: water, medicine, food, and a grinding machine. "It's hard to make flour," he said, "if you can't grind the grain." I wondered how they had managed so far, recalling the young woman I'd seen in Maper in November, pounding grain in the hollowed-out log. General Tinaikar said he would see what could be done and that he would carry word of their problems back to Juba.

On the ride back, Darkwa and I talked about the situation. He said he would have his soldiers bring a water truck from their camp at Leer. We knew grain was sitting at the port in Adok only a few miles away, so I'd try to get the mission to transport it to the camp. Neither of us could do anything about medicine, but I gave Darkwa a hundred-dollar bill and asked him to buy a grinding machine in Bentiu and take it to the troops at Muom. It seemed the least I could do.

46 Not All Lives

> I co-founded Black Lives Matter because I actually believe
> all lives matter—and so when we hear stories and read
> reports that make it clear that Black lives aren't valued
> in the US, it's our moral duty to change that.
>
> —AYỌ TOMETI

22 January 2020. Thirty-three people died in the raid by Arab Misseriya tribesmen against a Dinka village called Kolom. People were shot, houses burned. And suddenly, the world cared. Over the next few days, stories appeared in outlets from *Al Jazeera* to the *Vatican News* and even on the Voice of America. The United States and the UN Security Council publicly condemned the attack, as did the South Sudanese president, Salva Kiir.

But all of those statements left something out. Dinka villagers weren't being killed only in Kolom, a small town in the Abyei Administrative Area on the border between the two Sudans, but also in even greater numbers less than a hundred miles away in South Sudan itself. In the last two weeks of January, while voices were raised and action was taken in Abyei, more than twice as many Dinka would be killed in Warrap and Lakes States. Nothing would be said or done about it, even though the principals who spoke so vociferously about the violence in Abyei all knew it was happening.

Why didn't all Dinka lives matter?

In short, there was one reason, and her name was Caroline Anne Cox. A middle-aged white woman who had been visiting Abyei as part of her own personal mission of charity and advocacy work, Cox also happened to be a member of the British nobility.

* *

Abyei was a small quasi-state on the border between Sudan and South Sudan that remained in a special administrative status pending an ultimate decision on which country would control it. The Abyei Administrative Area was of interest to both nations not for its people but for the oil beneath its sands. A separate mission in the disputed region—UNISFA—had a mandate to "protect civilians under imminent threat of physical violence," something it had failed to do in Kolom.[1]

Baroness Cox was a peer of the House of Lords and had frequently spoken there about the conflict zones that she visited in her self-appointed role as an "eyewitness to a broken world."[2] As a result of the unfortunate coincidence of the timing of her visit to UNISFA and the attack on Kolom, she was able to tour the ruined village the day after it was burned and see the charred and mutilated bodies, the still-smoldering tukuls, and the survivors digging a mass grave for their relatives. Through her online platform, she was able to give the survivors a chance to ask the question that could have been asked of so many similar events in South Sudan: "Why didn't the UN protect us?"

She called upon the UN to "launch a full investigation into the massacre" and raised the issue personally with the British ambassador to South Sudan, who maintained purview over the Abyei vis-à-vis the UK government. But none of January's other Dinka dead had a baroness to bear witness to their devastated villages, to mourn over them, or to call for accountability.

In one of our morning meetings a few days later, Col. Theodomir Bahizi noted the different outcomes for the similar events. General Herlyng replied, "The difference is that this incident had an international presence with the right contacts to blow it up into the media." He went on to observe that the problem was not that the Kolom killings had received media coverage when so many similar events didn't—but that they happened at all.

Of course, he was right.

UN leaders in Abyei were sweating in the spotlight because their peacekeepers had failed the civilians they were charged to protect. *But, I wondered, were we really doing any better here in South Sudan?*

47 A Sad State of Affairs

It is clear to me, and I'm sorry to say so, but I've never seen a political
elite with so little interest in the well-being of its own people.
—UN SECRETARY-GENERAL ANTÓNIO GUTERRES
SPEAKING ABOUT SOUTH SUDAN

24 January 2020. I was in a helicopter again and headed to Mapel in Sector
West, another training area for the unified forces. Muom had been a disappointment, but it might have been an anomaly. It was an opposition site
in a government area, so it wasn't completely unexpected that it would be
in bad shape. But Mapel was in a government-controlled area where the
United States had previously built a proper training facility, so I was cau-
tiously optimistic that the training could be done well here.

We landed as close to the site as possible and packed ourselves tightly
into a few vehicles for the final leg of our journey. Peacekeepers from Wau
had driven the UN SUVs and their accompanying force protection vehicles
overland on a long and dusty trip; their efforts had ensured that we VIPs
would not have to endure it ourselves. We dropped in comfortably by air
and would depart just as easily. Local people and their dogs had come to
see the spectacle of the helicopter, but they were kept at a distance by our
watchful Bangladeshi force protection troops. I wondered what the people
made of us—so very similar to them in our DNA, so very different in our
lives and livelihoods.

Our short drive took us past some buildings with a distinctly military
appearance. The United States had previously built this training facility as
a noncommissioned officer training school, but that was before the civil
war. It had been designed to comfortably accommodate three thousand
personnel and would have been perfect for a training base, but alas, no. It
had been set aside for training the NSS, and although only thirty members

of South Sudan's militarized intelligence agency currently occupied it, the NUF had to be trained elsewhere.

Elsewhere, in this case, was a few miles onward to a rough camp set up in the bush that was home to 2,519 soldiers. Most were men, but 207 women—some of whom were pregnant or still breastfeeding—were here as well. Last November, Simon Gatwech had been adamant that the opposition would not send fighters to the cantonment here, referring to the grim history of the area. Nuer soldiers had been massacred here in 2014 when they had shown up for a similar sort of reunification exercise before the previous ceasefire had dissolved in gunfire on the streets of Juba. Yet the chief instructor, a brigadier general, was from the opposition, and so were 1,300 of the troops. Along with their counterparts from the government, they were overseen by 170 instructors, and we were told that the training had started three weeks ago.

That training, it turned out, consisted only of a single military drill—marching and saluting. The force commander said he'd like to support them with classes on human rights, the Geneva Conventions, and similar nonlethal subjects, but the chief instructor who ran the camp said his needs were more material in nature. "To unify them, we need one uniform for them," he said, waving an arm toward the patchwork troops moving in the camp around us. Many had no uniforms at all.

He also asked for cooking utensils, medicine, and sleeping mats. "They are now lying on the dirt," he said of the sleeping arrangements in the camp. They only had seven cooking pots for all the soldiers, so groups took turns to cook their food, eat it, and pass the pots on to others who were waiting. Hygiene was a major problem. There were no toilets; the people just went "to the bush."

The troops here had zero mobility, as their general had no tactical vehicles and, even more problematically, no ambulance. He did have sixty cartons of mixed drugs but no doctor to diagnose conditions or administer the right medicines. He seemed hopeful that we would be able to help, confident that he and his troops were doing their part. "We have become a non-party army for South Sudan," he said proudly. "And with your help, we will achieve victory over our problems."

After our meeting with the leadership had concluded, it was time for a parade. The troops formed into a three-battalion square. They wore no caps and few boots; the men and women wore a motley assortment of mismatched uniforms and civilian clothes. Here a tank top, there a suit jacket. But there was no question that they had good discipline, for they formed their ranks quickly and in good order.

"You are the pioneers," the force commander told them, "the first soldiers of the new South Sudan." The translation of his words was met with loud cheering. There was a single woman in our party, an observer from RJMEC, and on command, the women in the formation broke ranks and ran over for a separate meeting with her, trilling and ululating as they went. But that meeting did not last long. The women soon returned to the ranks of their male counterparts, who had been waiting patiently in the heat, and then these pioneers, these first soldiers of the new South Sudan, were dismissed to wander back to the shade of the camp's scrubby trees. We were off to see another camp at a place called Mas Na Bira, the site of an old beer factory on the outskirts of Wau.

We went down a single-track road, rutted and red. I found myself riding in the back of a vehicle with Bob Leitch. "We keep running into each other in odd spots!" he exclaimed. Then he launched forth into more stories about his many decades working in the region; they were a continuation, it seemed, of the tales he'd regaled the force commander and me with at the side of the road to Bor, two months ago and half a country away.

We veered around sad donkeys sluggishly pulling carts. An old beggar gestured mutely for food. Small children smiled and waved. *These smiles are one of the things that will stick with me*, I thought, *always*. Children who had absolutely nothing yet were still happy, who ran out to see our white SUVs passing down the dusty roads fronting their tukuls, who waved and smiled, and who, unlike me, had no idea of the degree of privilege that separated my life from theirs.

In Mas Na Bira, little remained of the colonial-era beer facility. Now it was the place where the officers of the organized forces—park rangers, police, and prison guards—were supposed to train. All of these elements of the state security apparatus often went forgotten, but they were still, at least in theory, uniformed and armed officers of the state whom—as with those in the army—the war had split into opposing groups. Likewise, too, now a sufficient number of these organized forces were supposed to undergo the cantonment and training process to reunify them. That was what had brought these women and men—5,678 of them in total—to this dusty parade deck. The sun was hot, and the dry breeze was redolent of cow dung. As in Mapel, the personnel had no uniforms, no bedding, and no transportation, and the opposition trainees did not get paid. But here they at least had shelter in the dilapidated beer factory.

The instructors told us that of the 732 women trainees, 110 were either pregnant or mothers with young children. They complained that there seemed to be no coordination between the various government agencies responsible for the camp. Morale here seemed decidedly lower than in any of the purely military training sites that we had visited.

"It's a sad state of affairs," the force commander observed to the staff as we walked toward our waiting vehicles to begin the journey back to Juba. Later that night, I made a note in my journal that described what it was like:

> To see, for the first time, thousands of men and women mustered for training, marching on dusty parade decks, and to see that they need so little to make them successful. Cooking utensils to make their food, uniforms to give them identity and a sense of belonging, a paycheck, however small. A mat to sleep on, some sort of shelter. Boots for their feet.
>
> To see that they have Brigadier Generals who know all these things, but who don't feel they have the power to obtain them. Who don't even have a vehicle. And to know that in Juba, there are tons of donated stores sitting in warehouses, undistributed. To know that 50 million dollars has been pledged to this process and that these troops have gotten none of it.
>
> To know that the Generals in Juba, the ones in the JDB [Joint Defense Board] and the JTSC [Joint Transitional Security Committee] and JMCC [Joint Military Ceasefire Commission] and NPTC [National Pre-Transitional Committee] all know how bad it is, and they do nothing. To admit that we see have seen firsthand how bad it is and that we too do nothing. At least the trainees we saw today have water and some food, which is more than those in Muom had . . .

And at least in Mapel the trainees weren't dying—not there, not yet—but the same could not be said for all the training sites. The media had just reported that two soldiers in a training area in Torit State had died of pneumonia. The SPLA-io spokesman, Col. Lam Paul Gabriel, had spoken to Eye Radio. "It's kind of very cold," he said. "The forces here at the training center lack shelters. They also lack beddings. No blankets. So these soldiers just sleep on the ground."[1] It was one thing to hear this on the radio, but it had been something else to see it firsthand.

But the miserable situation could also be viewed as an opportunity for the mission—for the force—to do something positive and set an example for what could and should be done. We had doctors at the Chinese Level II Hospital in Wau, and we had planes and trucks capable of moving matériel from the warehouses in Juba to where it was needed. We could put a patrol base adjacent to the training site in Mapel and assign just enough troops to provide security for a small medical team and a few vehicles for transportation. We could send an engineer detachment to dig latrines. We could demonstrate how a field camp could and should be set up, and we could engage with the right countries to provide uniforms for the NUF. Someone needed to do these things, and if no one else was going to do them, why not us?

I believed this sort of assistance would be in keeping with our mandate task to "support the peace process, including advice or technical assistance, within existing resources," but I seemed to be one of the few people who saw it this way. When I suggested these sorts of measures, the answer came back that it wasn't our responsibility and that the South Sudanese had to do this themselves. But it was clear to me that they simply would not do so of their own accord, any more than they would feed the starving civilians throughout the country. Humanitarians focused on those poverty-stricken noncombatants, but no one seemed to be interested in the rag-clad soldiers who were seemingly just as disadvantaged.

This point was driven home to me a few days later, as I sat in the latest meeting of the Security Supervisory Mechanism, the group responsible for the implementation of security arrangements in this pre-transitional period. The topic of the conditions in the training camps was raised, but it was brushed aside as trivial. When asked about the lack of a training curriculum, the JTSC chairman, Lt. Gen. Wesley Welebe Samson, replied with a rhetorical question: "As a lieutenant general, with twenty-six years of service, what are you going to teach me about running a camp?"

I wanted to raise my hand and say, "General Samson, I'd teach you to care about your troops, teach you the importance of a national force having a standard uniform, and teach you to embrace the leadership principle of 'leaders eat last' instead of 'leaders live in hotels while their troops sleep under trees in the training sites.'" But of course, I held my tongue. I also held my applause when the CDF arrived and, in his role as head of the Joint Defense Board, pronounced that he was pleased with the progress being made in training the NUF.

It was a sad state of affairs indeed.

48 The Chance to Make a Difference

> The world is a dangerous place, not because of those who do
> evil, but because of those who look on and do nothing.
> —ALBERT EINSTEIN

1 February 2020. On Saturday, I started the weekend by visiting the POC camp next to our base with Elisabeth Nilsen, an UNPOL officer who was trying to establish a library there. As she drove us through the camp, I stared out the window and was struck again by the disparity in circumstances between my life of privilege and what I saw of the camp.

A small child was shitting by the side of the road; a man missing a leg hobbled by on crutches. Farther on, another man held a young boy by one arm and whipped him with a stick as the child howled and danced. *That was me, once,* I thought, *a child being beaten because it was the cultural norm. . . . And now I have grown up to be one of the adults that said nothing, did nothing when it happened.*

None of the minor human tragedies along the camp's interior roads appeared to register with Elisabeth, and I realized that she had probably seen it all, regularly, and probably much worse. Peacekeepers from the force stared outward from the walls, but UNPOL did much of its police work, at least in UNMISS, inside the POC camps. It was the only UN mission where they had the responsibility of policing such camps. Military staff officers like me were discouraged from visiting the POC sites, perhaps because no one wanted us to see what the conditions were a few hundred yards from where we slept in air-conditioned comfort. But many of our UNPOL colleagues saw them every day.

At the optimistically named Hope School, which served three thousand children, I met with some of the teachers and saw the room that had been set aside for the library. It was a rough place. The bare dirt floor was not even smooth, and rocks were poking up in places. The room didn't look like much, but it was a chance to make a difference. I decided to ask Capt. Keegan Vaira, our American engineering officer, to take a look and see if we could make some improvements.

I'd looked forward to a lazy afternoon of reading, but when I got back home, I heard email notifications coming from my laptop and discovered that my senior leaders were finally beginning to pay attention to the violence in Lakes State. After five incidents of violence were reported in the last seventy-two hours, General Tinaikar had tasked the Sector West commander and General Herlyng with taking action. "We can't be bystanders," he wrote. "Please formulate a robust response." The attacks had already taken the lives of thirty-four civilians and wounded at least twice as many. Although as with the UN's mission in Abyei, we were too late to prevent the violence, now we were being given the green light to rein it in. It felt as if it was another chance to make a difference.

General Herlyng sent out a directive to Sector West with orders to devote all available peacekeepers to patrolling, and General Wang responded quickly. He noted that his staff had already conducted an elaborate study on seasonal violence due to the cattle migration, had marked the hot spots where violence was likely to occur, and had a basic deployment plan ready to implement. The Nepalese battalion from Rumbek would establish a temporary operating base in Pacong within twenty-four to forty-eight hours, and the Bangladeshis in Kuajok would shift their operations to Turalei while maintaining their temporary operating base at Kuajena. They would be prepared to shift that latter force to Mapel if violence threatened. Meanwhile, the Ghanaian company would keep a platoon on standby as a quick reaction force to go wherever they were needed in the sector.

My job was to prepare an order to get more peacekeepers moving toward Sector West, guiding the actions required to surge an additional two hundred troops to the area. I double-checked the load capacity for Mi-8 and Mi-17 helicopters, and figured out how many flights we'd need to move the required peacekeepers and their equipment. I brought our colleagues from JMAC in to validate Sector West's assessment of which villages to focus our patrols on and to map them for our planners.

It took an extra day to establish our first new temporary operating base at Pacong because, as usual, the SSPDF and NSS delayed signing the SOI. But sign they did, and the troops moved out on 3 February—a mere twenty-four hours behind schedule.

But then the politicians pushed back.

As soon as the first additional patrols began to move out, the field office in Rumbek got a call from the local governor's office saying that UNMISS should not deploy in the area. It gave no justification. The force commander recommended that the peacekeepers should hold their position at Pacong while UNMISS negotiated with the government for permission to conduct security patrols in the area. He himself requested a meeting with the CDF to engage in those talks personally, but he said that if those negotiations were unsuccessful, then we would have no option but to withdraw. I fumed inwardly.

Of course, we had options. There was nothing in the mandate or in the status of forces agreement that suggested we had to negotiate with anyone if we were deploying peacekeepers to protect civilians. And that General Tinaikar had been obliged to frame his guidance as a recommendation and not an order? It was a sign of how political expediency was allowed to trump military necessity—with civilians paying the price.

But the decisions of local South Sudanese and UN political figures were again allowed to override the mandate. The acting HOFO in Rumbek spoke with the acting governor, who claimed that the violence was taking place in swamps where civilians weren't being affected. They agreed to withdraw our peacekeepers, and General Wang was ordered to shut down the base at Pacong. Our mission to keep the peace in Lakes State was over before it began. Another chance to make a difference had been wasted.

* *

General Herlyng, who could almost always put a positive spin on a bad situation, spoke for us all at the next staff meeting. "This decision has consequences," he stated gravely. "It cements this belief that South Sudanese politicians in Juba can tell the UN to go and we'll withdraw. . . . Yesterday we were on the ground, and all it took was a phone call to get us out."

I'd first noted this problem while working on the operations order in July. The HOFOS expected that the military forces in their areas would ultimately follow directions from them and not the force commander. When those directions were driven by local politics instead of mandate tasks, protecting civilians became exponentially more difficult for our peacekeepers.

18. The Hope School "Library Construction Team." Author photo.

Fortunately, I was already on the schedule to brief the issue of freedom of movement to the SRSG and his core team in a few weeks. So I channeled my frustration resulting from this latest failure into creating a set of carefully worded slides that I believed would convince the SRSG to take action on the linked issues of political will and the civil-military C2 relationship at the field office level—problems that only he had the power to solve.

* *

The one bright spot in the week was the library project at the Hope School. Keegan had acquired a dump truck's worth of gravel to improve the floor of the building, and I'd returned to the POC site with a joint team of force and UNPOL members to carry out the refurbishment. I'd also sent out a tweet asking for donations of books, and dozens of generous people were sending boxes our way, making me wonder how much trouble I'd get in with the embassy mailroom. But compared to everything else that was going on, I figured it would be trouble of the best kind.

49 Maybe Just Once

> We appeal to the UNMISS field office in Rumbek to
> offer humanitarian assistance and stable security to
> the displaced community of Malek County.
>
> —WILLIAM MACHAR CHOL

8 February 2020. Leadership and self-improvement experts recommended not writing emails when one was angry, but this rule of thumb was becoming harder and harder not to break. On Saturday, I'd finally had enough. After scanning the news headlines, I fired off a note to Brent and Lauren Hutton, with the subject "Early Warning without Action Is Useless."

Dear Colleagues;

I'm attaching a news article from yesterday and would like to point out that Malek County was identified by both JMAC and Force as a location for Long-Duration Hub and Spoke patrols to prevent the type of violence that is currently sweeping Lakes.

Now, the press is reporting 9 people dead and 150 tukuls burned and the local leaders asking for our help and still nothing is being done for the people of Malek County.

This mission likes to TALK about being "robust, proactive and nimble"—but I do not see that our actions indicate that we are ANY of those things at present.

Please advise your thoughts if there is any way to actually mobilize and get troops on the ground where our best intelligence says they should be to actually BE proactive for once.

I, for one, would like to be able to say that maybe just once in my year here, we showed up BEFORE the killing started, and thereby prevented it.

I signed off with my usual "best regards." Then I went for a run to burn off my still-simmering rage while I awaited a response from two of the people who had a direct line to the SRSG.

Lauren's reply came quickly. "I totally understand and concur with your sentiments below," she wrote, but the rest of her letter gave no indication that anything would be done to address the matter, at least not from her end. Brent's reply focused on taking a bureaucratic approach, with "the issue needing to be raised within the UNMISS governance framework." That was hardly useful in dealing with fast-moving crises involving men with guns.

Nothing changed as a result of my letter, except perhaps the level of cortisol in my bloodstream. It seemed that I could do very little to get us to actually intervene to protect civilians, but I would still keep working the issue into my own briefs to senior leaders, such as the one that I would give Lt. Gen. Carlos Humberto Loitey later that day and the one that I was scheduled to give the SRSG at the end of the month.

　　　* *

General Loitey was the military adviser to the secretary-general—in essence, the highest-ranking military officer in all of UN peacekeeping. He was here to make his own assessment of the UNMISS Force, and I had the lead on briefing him. My slide deck contained a basic overview of our personnel, operations, equipment, and challenges. I showed that we were deficient by 2,088 troops, that only 4 percent of our peacekeepers were women, and that we needed more translators. I highlighted the importance both of supplying UNMISS with all-terrain quad bikes, additional boats, and light, tracked amphibious vehicles to increase our mobility and of delivering the reconnaissance drones and tactical helicopters we had been promised in 2016—a promise that remained unkept.

I ended my presentation with a one-two punch, a little "bad news, good news." Government interference in the form of SOI was preventing us from enforcing the mandate in many areas, I told him, but where we were free to operate, the hub-and-spoke approach was working well. I left unspoken my belief that our own lack of willpower had prevented us from operating when SOI was not granted or when we were ordered to withdraw even though we had it. General Loitey was a smart man, and I was sure that he would read between the lines. I'd save my mandate-specific metrics and polemics on political will for the SRSG, who was the one person I believed could really do something meaningful about it in the short term.

* *

In the meantime, I had another important communication task to attend to. The safari lodge on the Masai Mara National Reserve in Kenya had asked me to provide some information for my planned adventure with Jayde. "Would you prefer single beds or a double bed? Do you have any special interests while on safari? Is this trip in celebration of a special event?"

I sent an email to collect Jayde's input and laughed when I read her reply. "I hadn't even thought of what my 'special interests' are on safari!" She had checked the block for single beds, so I did the same, but where she'd left the final question blank, I wrote, "Anytime I spend with Jayde is a special event!" Just how special remained to be seen.

50 Reconciliation and Rumors of War

There is a persistent pattern of peacekeeping operations not
intervening with force when civilians are under attack. . . .
UNMISS has been noted as having a "pattern of non-intervention"
and was less than effective during the November-December
2012 crisis that resulted in more than 600 civilian deaths.

—UN OFFICE OF INTERNAL OVERSIGHT SERVICES REPORT, 2014

19 February 2020. On Wednesday, I saw reports from Sector East of an
impending large-scale attack by the Nuer White Army against the Murle
in the Greater Pibor Administrative Area of Jonglei State. Humanitarian
agencies had confirmed the mobilization, and some people had already
been displaced by attacks in Bich-Bich and Lokurmach at the borders of
the territories where the Murle homelands abutted those of the Lou Nuer
and Dinka Bor. I recalled that similar attacks in 2011–12 had marked the
beginning of a massive wave of ethnic violence, which was one of the "most
dangerous" COAs that appeared in our operations order. So I wrote to the
force commander, the head of the field office at Bor, and the Sector East
commander, attaching copies of reports and pictures from 2012 to highlight
the seriousness of the issue. I concluded that "I would recommend, if it has
not already been done, to immediately order an aerial reconnaissance of
the area to establish the size of the Nuer forces, and that Force should be
prepared to rapidly deploy additional troops to the area for the Protection
of Civilians and Deterrence of Violence."

Fortunately, the key leaders to whom I wrote seemed to take the reports
seriously this time. The Sector East commander planned to send patrols to
the major population center of Likaungole and the grazing lands around
Bich-Bich.[1] The force commander endorsed General Alam's plan and offered
his support, asking his subordinate general both to get troops on the ground
as soon as possible and to let the FHQ know if there was any difficulty. Bor's

head of field office, Deborah Schein, had been in contact with the area's former governor, David Yau-Yau, who had been supportive of the planned three-day airmobile patrols.[2]

Within the next forty-eight hours, a patrol was dispatched to check the conditions of the Lilibok River crossing en route to Likaungole and found it was passable with four-wheel drive vehicles. Women, children, and animals were wading through it on their way south toward Pibor, while armed Murle youths were moving north, spurred by the rumors that the Nuer militias were within thirteen miles of Likaungole. General Herlyng ordered the Operations Branch to prepare a plan to reinforce Sector East with additional troops. It looked as though we might actually be able to do something meaningful for a change.

* *

The local newspapers seemed unaware of the potential trouble brewing on the savannas east of the Nile. Instead, their focus was on Juba, where Salva Kiir had just given a surprise announcement at a weekend press conference that by presidential decree, he was unilaterally reverting the country to its previous ten-state arrangement, which meant that many of his supporters who had held positions as governors or county commissioners were now suddenly out of a job. That was a big deal, especially since it was completely unexpected.

Kiir was supposed to have been in Addis Ababa in further IGAD-hosted negotiations on the issue with Machar. Instead, he announced on Friday that he was going to "tactically withdraw" from the negotiations and called his own meeting in Juba with his deputies, national ministers, parliamentarians, presidential advisers, and state governors. The opposition was not present. Most of the voices in the room would have had personal incentives to stick with the new thirty-two-state arrangement. But Kiir did the opposite and passed the hot potato to his opponent, saying, "The compromise we have made today is one of the most painful decisions I have ever made but it is necessary if that is what will bring back peace and preserve the unity of our people."

His public statements made it clear that the concession came with a cost. "The compromise we have just made is in the interests of peace and the quest for peace should not be one-sided," he said. "I expect the opposition to reciprocate the same and allow the country to move forward."[3]

But the so-called compromise wasn't quite what it seemed. While Kiir publicly said ten states, his decree actually established "ten states and three administrative areas." One of those areas—Abyei, the disputed territory with Sudan that remained in an indeterminate status pending final negotiations with Khartoum—already existed and wasn't especially controversial. But the other two represented significant attempts at gerrymandering. The Ruweng Administrative Area effectively split off the top end of Unity State to create a Dinka stronghold that sat atop massive oil reserves in a state that was otherwise majority Nuer. And the Greater Pibor Administrative Area essentially carved out the territory that was already largely controlled by the Murle in Jonglei—a move that looked like a juicy bone to be tossed to David Yau-Yau in exchange for his support.

Dr. Riek and his supporters were not happy, but they did not have much time to argue the point or offer an alternative. If they resisted the ten-state solution, they would merely frustrate an increasingly impatient international community and play into Kiir's narrative that the opposition was delaying the formation of the government.

* *

Four days later, the cabinet had approved Kiir's "Ten Plus Three" resolution, and Riek Machar had returned to Juba, temporarily living and working out of the Pyramid Hotel. The VIP security forces were said to be ready, even if the troops of the unified forces were still without uniforms and sleeping in the dirt. The government's formation now seemed assured; it was simply a matter of time. The countdown to the new deadline passed quickly and was, for me, consumed with administrative minutiae. I continued the work to get four vehicles from the U.S. Embassy, to refine the force's input for the secretary-general's ninety-day report, and to coordinate the delivery of books for the library at the Hope School.

Then, on Saturday, it was done.

The transitional government formed quietly and on schedule with the dissolution of the existing government and the swearing-in of three new vice presidents: Riek Machar, Rebecca Nyandeng, and Hussein Abdelbagi Akol. Taban Deng Gai and Dr. James Wani Igga retained their status as vice presidents from the previous administration, and it was understood that ministerial positions and state-level appointments would come next.

The country was, at least officially, now at peace.

51 | Peace on Paper, Army on the Move

Who or what will respond to tomorrow's Rwanda? There
is a nagging suspicion that perhaps no one will. . . . How
moral is it not to act? . . . [P]articularly where a failure to
respond results in the death and abuse of civilians?

—DAVID SHEARER

24 February 2020. The unity government had finally been formed. It should
have meant peace throughout South Sudan, but the conference room in
the mission headquarters building was anything but tranquil—and that
appeared to be my fault.

The SRSG was livid. "You've come here to tell me nothing that I don't
already know," he thundered at me, "but please, go ahead!"

Seated to his right, his chief of staff, Paul Engunsola, was in a similar
mood. He held up a paper copy of the brief I was about to give. "This brief,
if it got out—it would make us all look very bad."

"Sir," I told him, "this brief only contains information that is already well-
known and documented. It's already out." I plunged ahead. I only got as far
as halfway into the first slide, where I had highlighted that more civilians
had been killed in 2019 than in 2018, before the SRSG blew up again.

"Quite frankly," he said, "this is bullshit. Most of those people were killed
in intercommunal violence, which isn't our job to prevent."

"Sir," I replied, "the mandate is quite clear that we are to protect civilians
and deter violence—without respect to the source of the threat."

"Well, I disagree," he said.

I forged ahead with the brief.

When I finished speaking, Victoria Browning, the director of mission
support, cleared her throat. "I think that there really is a problem with the
understanding of the chain of command, because the HOFOS are, as Carp

said, 'mini-SRSGS.' They are the area security coordinators, so they have the power to direct the use of all forces in their area."

Had they ever used that power to deploy peacekeepers to enforce the mandate, the number of deaths would be going down, not up, I thought to myself. Aloud, I clarified that I had no misunderstanding of the current chain of command. I simply believed that we needed to put decisions related to the protection of civilians and UN personnel in the hands of the military professionals during times of crises involving armed actors—particularly the crisis that was currently unfolding in Sector East and whose scale I had just now seen.

* *

I understood the scope of impending disaster in Sector East because while I'd been waiting to give my brief to the SRSG and his inner circle, I had heard Lauren Hutton, the chief of JMAC, give her assessment of the current security situation. I was shocked. JMAC had known for weeks about the problems in Jonglei, starting with raids two weeks before by young men from the Murle tribe, who had stolen children and cows. JMAC had known that weapons were being sold in Akobo and that the White Army leaders were planning an imminent attack on the Murle. JMAC had known but had told the force nothing.

On Tuesday, 18 February, JMAC knew that the White Army forces had moved out from Akobo but still said or did nothing. On Thursday, the first attacks began, and only then did it come to the attention of the force, as women and children began to show up in Pibor, having run about twenty-one miles to seek safety at the UN base. The weekend had come and gone, and still the mission had no idea exactly how big the Nuer raiding party was, where it was, or where it was headed. Nor did anyone appear to be making a serious attempt to find out.

"We've lost track of the organized forces," Lauren stated. She believed that while the White Army had the opportunity to hit several large towns, they had chosen not to do so. This led the SRSG to wonder aloud if the Nuer were just making a political statement rather than carrying out a true revenge attack or a serious attempt at cattle raiding.

One straightforward way to find the missing army was with aerial patrols. The discussion turned to the fact that the mission had not been able to get a plane launched since Friday, not because the government was preventing us, but because our own Risk Assessment Committee would not approve the flights. Now I watched in dismay as the mission's most senior leadership twisted themselves into knots over risks and rewards, arguing over the difference between flying at two thousand feet or five thousand feet and, in the end, deciding not to fly at all.

＊ ＊

This was the context in which I had been asked to go ahead and present my slides on freedom of movement, which, of course, dealt with just this sort of scenario. The brief highlighted four factors that restricted our ability to move freely: weather, interference by the government, inadequate equipment, and our own lack of political will.

The first two were beyond our ability to control, and the third was a work in progress. Our logistics chief, Lt. Col. Charmaine Benfield, was on hand to explain our plan for acquiring new types of vehicles that would allow us to operate more easily regardless of the weather and across a wide variety of terrain. Some vehicles we could test in-country by trading a few of our suvs to unpol for all-terrain vehicles (atvs) and by borrowing the big-wheeled sherp transports from the wfp, but most of the technical solutions would take time, money, and cooperation from un Headquarters and nations such as the United States and Norway.

The final factor restricting our movement was ours alone to fix. At the mission level, I said, "these violations happen because we let them happen. The only way one man with an ak-47 and a piece of rope stops an armored vehicle from driving down a road is if the organization with the armored vehicle lacks the will to keep going." At the regional level, I noted that hofos should not tell sector commanders to withdraw a patrol from its hub or to retreat from a roadblock; only the force commander should do that and only if the srsg directed it.

I closed by highlighting that in 2019, 2,536 civilians—that we knew of—had been killed on our watch, and that was 261 more deaths than the previous year. We knew that the presence of peacekeepers had been proven to reduce violence, but we had to be present to protect civilians.[1] "What will we do today," I asked rhetorically, "to make sure that next year, the number has not risen again?"

The answer, as it turned out, would be nothing.

＊ ＊

After our short and heated discussion, the SRSG thanked me coldly for my contribution and indicated that my presence was no longer required. I left the principals to their meeting and returned to my office to continue working on the various issues on my day's agenda.

Later that morning, I got a short email from the SRSG, who apologized for his tone in the meeting but not for the substance of what he said. I didn't give a damn for Shearer's apology. It was hardly the first time in my career that a senior official had shouted at me for highlighting a serious organizational problem that had a simple, legal, and commonsense solution.

What I did care about—and what troubled me deeply—was that even after having time to cool off and consider the issue, the SRSG stuck by his statement that intercommunal violence was not our job to prevent, that the mandate did not require us to protect civilians from ethnic militias.

I had done my part—spoken truth to power—and received an answer that explained why we weren't deploying peacekeepers to Maiwut and why we had pulled back from Pacong. It revealed the real reason we weren't present in Lobonok or Lasu, and why our patrols accompanying the HRD were always eventually able to arrive at the site of violence but only *after* the killing, burning, and looting had been accomplished and never before. The SRSG's words echoed in my mind: "This is bullshit . . . those people were killed in intercommunal violence, which isn't our job to prevent."

It was bullshit, all right, and it only seemed to lend credence to what Bishop Santu Laku Pio had told the Human Rights Commission in 2015: "No one will be talking about accountability or human rights or those things. The international community will be coming here just to count the dead."[2]

＊ ＊

That afternoon the FHQ held a short ceremony to award those of us who had been in the mission six months or longer a UN medal. It was one of those military rituals that had meant a lot to me when I was younger but had lost a bit of its luster over the years. I was more excited for Sergeant Prasad than myself and would have happily traded the shiny bit of metal and ribbon for the opportunity to have one of my calls for proactive deployment acted upon. In the picture from that event, my smile was bright. It occurred to me that when you wore a mask long enough, it came to fit as naturally as a beret shaped in the proper Australian fashion.

19. The author with Sergeant Prasad after a UN medal ceremony. Author photo.

Later in the day, I received an email saying that my leave was approved and my trip to Kenya authorized. That was definitely the highlight of my week. Now more than ever, I was looking forward to spending some time alone with Jayde. Among other things, I wanted her advice about how I might best make a difference in the world, because it surely didn't seem as if I was accomplishing much as a senior staff officer here.

52 Troubled Waters

The British brought together the chiefs to discuss the
future of South Sudan. They asked what should be done,
but they did not listen to what the chiefs said.
—DENG KOOCH

25 February 2020. The Jur River meandered lazily below us as our little plane
bounced in the strong winds on its approach to Wau. A month had passed
since our last visit, and as I looked toward Mas Na Bira, I saw orderly rows
of blue tents in a once-barren field. At least some of the training areas were
getting the matériel support that they should have had from the start. As
in Jonglei, the land here was still brown and dry; only a little green was
visible along the riverbanks. Below us I spotted herds of cattle, which I had
expected to see, and brick kilns, which I had not. People were firing red
mud to build new houses, which seemed a good sign.

We were on our way to Tonj and stopped in Wau only long enough to
trade our prop plane for a helicopter and to take on a delegation of staff
officers from Sector West. Much smaller than Wau, Tonj was a frequent hot
spot for intercommunal violence, so it had been chosen as the site of our
newest temporary operating base.

Along the banks of the river from which the town got its name were more
artisan kilns, more bricks being made, more signs of hope. I even saw a
small farm with row crops sprouting in neat lines. This was the first time
I'd seen that level of organized agriculture in South Sudan.

Our temporary operating base was located in an octagonal compound
that had once housed a local school. While the school had long since been
abandoned, its brick buildings were still in good shape, and the compound
itself was fenced and gated.

It was not all blue helmets here either; the integrated patrol was diverse
and a good model of what we had been trying to achieve. The patrol included

a community liaison assistant, who helped translate and provided cultural insight, and a member of the Civil Affairs Division. Also present was a South Sudanese officer who was a representative from the Joint Verification Monitoring Mechanism, an organ of the security forces that the government used to control the movement of UNMISS forces by issuing or denying SOI. Here, their representative Lieutenant Marac was quite helpful because our purposes aligned, which was not always the case.

The local commander briefed us and showed a map of exactly the sort of engagement that we wanted to see from such a unit—short-range patrols to various smaller villages branching off from the hub in Tonj. We'd be going on one of those patrols today to a small village called Wanh Alel on the banks of the Tonj River farther north of here.

* *

After the briefing and a quick lunch, we headed out on patrol. Past the airstrip with its wrecked planes, past sheep and goats, and the "Tonj Comfort Hotel," we set out along a dusty red dirt road. Periodically we passed scenes that struck discordant notes in my perception of the ordinary. Here a sleeping dog, there a small group of women chatting in the shade of a mango tree. An old man walking along the side of the road and carrying a spear. Farther on, a cluster of soldiers wearing camouflage clothing in the U.S. Army's combat uniform pattern stood barefoot, AK-47s with folding stocks hanging loosely at their sides.

Our convoy passed a young man on a motorcycle who was wearing a bright pink puffy down jacket despite the heat. Outside of Tonj proper, we passed the Himango International School, where the few pupils in its courtyard waved as we drove by. The road got rougher, and our SUV jumped and bounced across the ruts. Two men in brightly colored shirts herded three emaciated cows down the middle of the road, causing our vehicles to divert to either side. A few minutes later, we passed a teenager wearing a green-striped shirt with an AK-47 slung casually over his shoulder. And then for long minutes we saw nothing much. The land was flat with scrub brush as far as the eye could see, and our convoy hurtled along, bearing us ever closer to our destination—Wanh Alel, which was about nineteen miles northeast of Tonj.

Tukuls dotted the landscape, usually in ones and twos, sometimes in small clusters. *Who chose to live out here*, I wondered, *so far from the nearest village, and why?* I was surprised to see a young child of about ten years old walking alone down the side of the road, miles from any visible sign of human habitation. But our convoy didn't slow down, and the small figure was soon lost in the dust and distance in the rearview mirror.

As we passed Malual, the bush gave way to savanna, stretching horizon to horizon, and presently we turned right off the main road and headed almost due east along a mere track in the vast plain. We saw movement up ahead—a large herd of cattle attended by one small boy armed with only a stick.

* *

"Welcome to Wanh Alel," said a tall man who turned out to be James, the executive director of the village. As usual, our meeting took place while sitting in plastic chairs under a large tree. James told us of trouble with the nearby village of Manyang Gok, whose inhabitants would fire at any man they saw approaching the riverbank. He asked if our patrol had come to protect the local civilians, but the force commander replied that we were only there to say that the people should not kill each other.

"The bad feeling in the hearts of the people is still high," said one elder, speaking through our translator. "Thus, we need the deployment of UNMISS."

It occurred to me that we weren't much different from the British colonials. We came to these places and asked the local leaders what they needed, but we didn't really listen to what they told us. They asked us to provide security and to protect civilians, but we simply told them "not [to] kill each other." It hadn't exactly been working out very well so far; we were again doing the exact same thing and expecting to achieve different results—insane. I felt anger building and pushed it back down where it belonged. I didn't want any bad feelings in my heart.

A tall man in a purple jacket, Abor Deng Matioc, explained the history of the conflict. Goats were stolen routinely, people were murdered occasionally, and so it had gone for the past ten years. But it was getting worse. Now only women could travel village to village or go down to the river to wash clothes, draw water, and fish because men would be shot on sight.

James said we should see for ourselves, but the force commander said he didn't want to be shot. "Don't worry," said James. He observed that some government troops had swept the area today in anticipation of our visit, and, anyway, those of Manyang Gok had no interest in shooting at peacekeepers.

We made our way to the riverbank, where our guide pointed to fresh gouges in some of the trees, the results of errant rifle fire. Looking across the slow-moving brown water, I could not see the village of Manyang Gok itself—only bush—but I am sure it was there. I could feel the void staring back into me.

Having seen the lay of the land, we returned to our chairs under the tree. Now it was the force commander's turn to speak. "You've lost a few sheep and goats," he said, "but human lives are more valuable." General Tinaikar recommended negotiation, but James said he needed security. He wanted military assistance to create a safe zone on both sides of the river and to bring an end to the raids.

Lieutenant Marac, the South Sudanese officer traveling with us, said that the government forces could not maintain such a presence here because they lacked the logistical support to do so. He said that UNMISS was better prepared to do this, and I agreed.

The force commander said he would raise the issue in Juba but couldn't make any promises. Then he was up and moving, shaking hands with our hosts and preparing to play his role as one of the public faces of the mission. A film crew from the Public Affairs Office had come along to record the day's events, and they wanted the force commander to give an interview, leaving the rest of us to our own devices for a few minutes.

A group of smiling men beckoned me over. None of them spoke English. I didn't speak any Dinka, and my Arabic was too rusty to be of use. But smiles were universal, as were many simple gestures. Other cues were more confusing. The men raised their arms, pointing at bone-white bracelets encircling their wrists. "Akol!" they shouted in unison, gesturing at my wrist, which was shrouded by the sleeve of my camouflage uniform. I raised my hand to the sky, too, revealing my bare wrist, which became the source of much amusement. "Akol!" they repeated. I assumed it referred to a cow's horns, which were what I imagined the bracelets must be made of.

I asked our South Sudanese escort what *akol* meant, and to my surprise, he said "elephant." The bracelets these men wore had been cut from ivory tusks, not mere horn. "They get it from the bush," Lieutenant Marac said, anticipating my next question, and waved in a vaguely southerly direction. The men smiled and said, "Akol!" in unison again while pantomiming the act of spearing some great and invisible beast.

20. The author with members of the village of Wanh Alel. Author photo.

The laughter and cheers earned us all a stern look and another universal gesture from one of the public affairs reps—"Shhhh!!" Didn't we see that the force commander was trying to give an interview? In a picture snapped a few moments later, I was still surrounded by the smiling faces of seven men, two women, three children, and one baby. That photo would haunt me in the months to come, but in the moment, I too was smiling.

When the force commander finished his interview, we left the people of Wanh Alel in much the same condition as we found them and made our way back to our air-conditioned bungalows in Juba, our shelves laden with plentiful food and clean water. Back to a place where the question of whether we would be attacked in the night didn't ever seriously cross our minds.

* *

On that long return trip, I had plenty of time to consider the elements at play in this area. As in Maper, the violence around Tonj was not between ethnic groups but within them. The inhabitants of Wanh Alel were Dinka, as were those across the river. It was strange to think that people who seemed so similar could maintain such enmity over such a long period, but then I remembered the Hatfields and McCoys, two American clans very similar to those of Wanh Alel and Manyang Gok. They, too, had been separated by a river and carried on a decades-long feud based on thefts of livestock, killings of clan members, and attempts to leverage local political forces against each other. It was just one of many historical examples I could have chosen. An officer from another culture might have thought of another example, but it would likely have shared many similarities with Tonj today and the Appalachian Mountains of America in the 1800s.

Limited resources, strong kinship bonds, a recent civil war, poor policing, and relatively weak governance—all were features common to deadly feuds past and present. Here we had the power to deter the violence with our presence, but at the end of the day, we had only admired the problem. A platoon of peacekeepers could have solved it temporarily, and with some development aid, it might have been fixed permanently. But who was going to make the effort?

53 This Is It, Your Excellency

There is no medicine and we sleep in the open where it's
cold and the needs for female soldiers are not met.

—CECILIA BUTUL, FEMALE NUF TRAINEE

26 February 2020. From the air, the Equatorias still appeared green despite
it being the dry season. I was in the back of an Mi-8 helicopter on my way
to Maridi for a military training review with the force commander, an *Al
Jazeera* film crew, and ambassadors from South Africa, Norway, and the EU.

The unity government had formed in quite an anticlimactic fashion. The
White Army was still on the march, locusts had invaded the country, and
how the hundreds of excess generals were to be pensioned off remained to
be seen, but for the next few hours, I'd be focused on other matters.

We'd come to assess the progress of the military training being conducted
at the Maridi site. This visit was a first for the ambassadors and the news
crew, but not for those of us in the force. As usual, we met our hosts beneath
several trees and sat on plastic chairs in the rough rectangle that served as
the open-air "conference room" for both the Maridi Training Center and
the SSPDF's Sixth Division Headquarters.

The division commander, Maj. Gen. Johnson Juma Okot, greeted us with
a warm smile. "Today, this morning, we are very happy to have you." Small
chickens scurried underfoot beneath our chairs, chirping quietly. Water
was handed out in half-liter bottles.

The officers who ran this camp told us that so far, only food and water
had been provided. They had received no blankets, no shelters, no uniforms,
no medicine, no vehicles for transportation. There was no generator, so
they had no electricity. There was no firewood nearby, and it took hours to
gather it from the bush.

The former administrator of Maridi State represented the local civilians.
He was worried about the progress of the training or lack thereof. "With-

out help, this training will come out half-cooked," he warned, "and no one wants to eat a half-cooked meal." He pointed to the strain that the troops were putting on the area. The camp was surrounded by villages, and the wood that the soldiers collected caused problems for the local women, who needed it for their cooking fires.

The Sixth Division commander acknowledged the issues. "There are a lot of things, basic struggles, but we are continuing in our own way," said General Okot. "We have lost a few people. My own car has become an ambulance for us."

He recited a list of agencies that had visited him so far, an alphabet soup of acronyms—RJMEC, JTSC, AU, CTSAMVM (Ceasefire and Transitional Security Arrangements Monitoring and Verification Mechanism)—and concluded ruefully that "all those visits in vain." He said he was hoping that the ambassadors visiting today would bring some change. "We have a lot of people suffering in this training center."

Sinéad Walsh, the EU's ambassador to South Sudan, asked about the curriculum and the background of the troops. In answering, chief instructor Ayok Lier held up books on the peace agreement, the laws of war, and leadership. "Togetherness, forgiveness, discipline, and march," he stated, but I was fairly certain those topics did not appear in any of the old, faded books he displayed. Lier said troops from both sides had taken off their rank for the training. Only the instructors stood out from the crowd, wearing green Adidas track suits given to them at their train-the-trainers course. The trainers had all received a hundred dollars—a "motivation payment"—at the beginning of the training as well. Otherwise, money had not appeared. "Nothing at all," said the chief instructor. "We hear there are tents in Juba, even uniforms. But they haven't come."

"How long will the training last?" asked the South African ambassador.

No period of training had been specified, according to General Okot, but water was only being provided for sixty days. "When the water stops coming, the training will end."

The crowd was silent as people did the math in their heads. A rooster started to crow.

The general pivoted the focus from the training to the trainees, telling us that the camp was home to 1,505 soldiers, 71 of whom were women. Sixty-one of those women already had children, and twelve were currently pregnant.

General Okot noted that he had no "dignity kits"—no basic feminine hygiene supplies. As a result, "we have lots of difficulties with the ladies."

Dignity kits were not the only things missing when it came to health and hygiene. They had no soap, and seven or eight soldiers shared each set of utensils for cooking and eating. The senior doctor—a tall man wearing an emergency-yellow vest marked "Medical Team"—said that he saw about sixty-four patients per day. Upper respiratory tract infections were the biggest problem, the result of sleeping on the ground without shelter. The troops also suffered from dysentery, peptic ulcers, hernias, malaria, typhoid, burns, and snakebites. There had been two deaths—so far.

While screening the trainees, the doctor had discovered eleven pregnancies, seventy-one cases of hepatitis, and eighty-five cases of HIV, of which only thirty-five were being treated. He couldn't offer the soldiers condoms to prevent pregnancy or disease. He had seven doctors and fifteen nurses working for him—the most I'd ever seen at a training camp—but clearly medical staff without medicine and matériel wouldn't get them very far.

"When you visit the clinic, you will see we have a problem with infrastructure," the doctor explained.

"Where is the clinic?" asked one of the ambassadors.

The doctor waved in the direction of a ruined building. "Oh, it's just over there." His team did their routine consultations outdoors under the trees. The limited space in the building was saved for more serious cases. That "ward"—one of the few buildings in the camp with a roof—housed three cases of dysentery. The men lay on blankets spread on the concrete floor; there were no hospital beds, because there were no mattresses.

Most of the men slept in grass huts that they had constructed themselves, but General Okot said there were quarters set aside for female soldiers.

"Where?" someone in our group asked.

"Over there." Okot gestured to another shell of a building across from the clinic and on the other side of the dusty path leading toward the parade ground. The women's quarters consisted of a single-story building with brick walls and a concrete floor but no roof. It was partitioned into three rooms that had no furniture. A clutch of small children sat together; their mothers were on the parade ground, awaiting our inspection along with their male peers. A pot of half-eaten beans and *ugali* sat next to a pair of pink plastic shoes.[1] There were few visible possessions. Clearly the women and their children slept on the bare concrete.

The ambassadors appeared somewhat taken aback at these sights, but they had little time to dwell on the sad tableau because we were the guests of honor at the next event. We made our way down the dusty lane to the parade deck and watched as the assembled troops displayed what they had learned. "Togetherness, forgiveness, discipline, and march" was what the senior instructor had said. These soldiers seem to have learned those lessons well. They had no rifles; wooden sticks took the place of real weapons. The officer leading the parade used a machete as long as a man's leg in place of a ceremonial sword.

After the troops halted in a box formation in front of the assembled visitors, the dignitaries took turns to speak. As they did, I scanned the ranks. Some very young faces were among the soldiers and some very old ones as well. As usual, they had no uniforms to indicate that they were soldiers, and footwear was the exception rather than the rule.

The South African ambassador referenced the latest AU initiative. "This is the year of 'Silencing the Guns,'" he said.[2] "Well, you have already silenced the guns . . ." That proclamation was met with silence, but later the soldiers rewarded the end of the EU ambassador's speech with a song. Deep male voices offset the trilling ululations of the women.

General Okot spoke of "loyalty and professionalism," reminding the troops that "victory is certain." The Norwegian ambassador told them to "stay strong and work hard." Then she turned to me and asked me when I thought training would start.

"This is it, Your Excellency," I replied. "This is the training."

　　* *

When I arrived at UN House later that afternoon, I found that the Fantastic Five had finished the final draft of the new order for the second phase of realigning our forces, so I took it to the force commander to sign. I met him in the hallway, and as we walked to his office, he asked, "Have you heard what's going on in Manyabol?"

"No," I replied, "but I'm guessing it's not good."

He shook his head. "There's been some shooting, and now the HOFO wants us to withdraw . . ."

Not good, I thought to myself. *Not good at all.*

PART 3

The Ordeal

54 Crimes against Humanity

I saw—in the distance—a bird eating a body on
the road. One of those giant cranes.
—SHELDON WARDWELL

27 February 2020. The rising sun was burning the mist off the Nile as our small turboprop rose smoothly from the runway at Juba and banked east over the river. I was headed with the force commander to Bor, the first stop on a daylong trip that would take us to Pibor and, I hoped, to Manyabol, where I thought that seeing the effects of our withdrawal might finally spur us to action.

When our plane landed in Bor, the news was grim. Back on the ground and with cell coverage again, the messages began to come in. WhatsApp notes from the U5 with situation updates confirmed that Manyabol had been attacked the previous night just after our patrol withdrew and that refugees were arriving in a small village called Anyidi, only twelve miles from where I stood. Nineteen miles north of our base in Pibor, Nuer militias had also overrun the village of Likaungole. All reports suggested that the attackers were now approaching Pibor from both the north and west.

We loaded in a column of SUVs and headed to the base, passing an outbound patrol on its way to reinforce Anyidi. Their four armored personnel carriers and an assortment of other vehicles were pulled up in front of the ubiquitous "rope across the road"; local government forces didn't want them to proceed. When we stopped to assess the situation, the patrol leader gave us more bad news: two thousand Dinka fighters from Duk Padiet were supposedly headed to reinforce the Nuer against their mutual enemy, the Murle tribe. Displaced people were pouring into Pibor and forming a makeshift camp outside the walls of the UN base.

We left the patrol leader negotiating with his SSPDF counterpart at the rope and were soon passing through the gates of the UN base. I assumed that this stop would be for a quick situation brief before continuing to either Anyidi or Pibor as it appeared we were too late to do anything for Manyabol.

But no. We were headed to a medal parade, fiddling while Rome burned. I looked at the giant marabou storks, East Africa's preeminent scavengers, perched in the trees around the parade deck. Others like them had already been feasting on human flesh in Jonglei this week. Many more would be doing so if this massacre in the making wasn't stopped.

We spent the next hour and a half watching a parade, making speeches, eating Sri Lankan delicacies, and watching a live calypso music show—all while somewhere less than a hundred miles away, armed men were marching with murder on their minds. Besides me, only one person seemed concerned by this—the sector commander, Brigadier General Alam, who beckoned me over during the force commander's speech. He gripped my wrist tightly and spoke quickly and quietly. He wanted to ensure that the time lines in our latest order that pertained to reinforcing sectors in crisis were sufficient to address the operational realities here in Jonglei. I assured him they were.

Finally, with all the social niceties observed, we joined the head of the Bor field office, Deborah Schein, for a crisis management team meeting. She was visibly agitated, and the county commissioner was worried about an attack on Anyidi. No one seemed to know much.

"There's a lot of rumors," Deborah said defeatedly.

But we'd made no real effort to collect intelligence, I thought. *This is all our own fault.*

We did know that three thousand refugees were in Pibor already, with more arriving in steady streams from the north and west. Deborah took a phone call and told someone on the ground in Pibor to let the leaders of the refugees know that UNMISS "will protect lives, not property." The attackers were now allegedly eleven miles from Pibor at a river crossing called Lilibok.

Refugees were still arriving in Anyidi as well, though in smaller numbers. Forty-four families and twenty unaccompanied children had arrived so far, seeking help. Where were those children's parents? The stereotypical Nuer approach was to kill men and to kill or kidnap women, so these kids were probably already orphans.

I sent a WhatsApp message to the acting defense attaché at the U.S. Embassy in Juba asking for current satellite imagery but got no reply. The expression "flying blind" came to mind, because we were about to do just

21. Marabou storks will scavenge from any dead bodies, animal or human. Photo by Jennifer Watson, iStockPhoto.com.

that. Our group from Juba and the sector commander would fly onward to Pibor to assess the situation and organize a defense, while the Indian battalion commander here in Bor would travel to Anyidi by ground to do the same.

* *

At 11:40 a.m. we were back at the airfield and walking toward the chopper, having wasted two and a half hours. The plan was to fly at twenty-five thousand feet, so we wouldn't be able to see much detail of activity on the ground. Walking across the tarmac with the force commander, I asked him if he had spoken to the force chief of staff in Juba.

"Why," he asked, "is something wrong?"

"To tell him the situation here, have him convene the force crisis management team, sir," I explained.

"Maybe after we see how things are in Pibor," he replied.

I sent a WhatsApp to my team asking them to forewarn General Herlyng. Then we were airborne, and the cell signal faded. The air was hazy, and the brown, parched land stretched beneath us. Eventually as we started descending, the landscape came into focus.

Connected by footpaths, small homesteads reminiscent of the Skywalker farm on Tatooine dotted the landscape. I could make out cattle but no people. How would such isolated places get the word of an impending attack? How many, farther north, had been overrun already?

Counting the little clusters of huts, I realized that given the vastness of the area, even this relatively sparse distribution of habitations represented a very large number of vulnerable people. As our Mi-17 approached the airfield at Pibor, I saw a growing refugee camp pitched against the wall of our base and under the watchful cannons of the APCs guarding its walls.

We crowded into vehicles for the short drive from the runway to the base; then we made our way to the small conference room where Adewuyi "Ade" Adewumi, a civil affairs representative and the senior civilian in Pibor, led the brief. Starting at around nine o'clock the night before, he said, refugees began arriving from Likaungole. Many people had been killed and injured there, he told us, but no one was sure of the exact number. MSF had pulled its staff out before the town was overrun and was focusing its efforts on treating the wounded in Pibor. This had all happened yesterday. Deborah had known about all of this, but it was news to us—another example of the mission's poor internal communications.

The former state information minister weighed in. "They are coming from this way, and they are coming from that way," he said, pointing at the map pinned to the wall, indicating Likaungole to the north and Manyabol to the east. "They are converging on Pibor to seize us."

The commander of the Indian infantry company that garrisoned the base said his plan was to hold his ground and defend the refugees outside his walls. The force commander said that we would reinforce Pibor with another company—about 130 soldiers—and gestured across the table for me to contact force headquarters. I nodded and started working my comms. There was no cell signal here, but with my satellite phone and tactical radio, I relayed the orders to my team in the U5, which would inform General Herlyng and get the process in motion.

The government's SSPDF brigade commander arrived and briefed us on what he knew about the progress of the ethnic militias. He had been up the road toward Likaungole as far as the river crossing at Lilibok, where he said he had turned back because he was low on fuel. He planned to try again in the afternoon and offered to take us along. Also, he claimed that he didn't have enough troops to defend Pibor because they had already been sent to training.

The information minister spoke up again, demanding that UNMISS obey its mandate to protect civilians. "In 2012 there was a whole brigade here, well-armed, and the town was still sacked," he said. Clearly he didn't believe another company would be enough, and he was not the only one. I thought we needed a full battalion and that we were about a week late in getting them deployed, but for now, I was here to listen, not to talk.

"If they attack, will the peacekeepers open fire?" asked the local WFP representative.

"Of course," said the force commander.

The humanitarian shook his head. "They didn't last time."

The force commander wanted to know about casualties, and the South Sudanese brigade commander laughed grimly. "We will count the dead when they have left," he said.

A tall, skinny young man spoke up. "In Murle culture, when someone dies in this kind of thing, you don't tell people for about two weeks," he said. "If someone asks you where they are, you say, 'Oh, they are still coming.'"

Ade nodded and told General Tinaikar that the speaker was Minny-Minny, the local language assistant. The force commander asked Minny-Minny to accompany us, because instead of waiting to travel with the SSPDF, we were heading north immediately on our own.

* *

Traveling in a small convoy of four SUVs, we passed through Pibor proper, a town that seemed barely more than a refugee camp itself in terms of infrastructure. Carrying spears and assault rifles, groups of armed men sat or stood in the shade of trees.

The road to Likaungole was dry and dusty, with dark gray soil instead of the red clay that I was used to seeing around Juba. Not far north of Pibor, we saw a group of armed men walking from the north and stopped to talk with them. Their leader carried a customized M-16 assault rifle and a whistle, and wore a leather hat.[1] He told us that he'd come from Manyabol and that the attackers there had four vehicles with mounted machine guns. "They will reach Pibor," he observed laconically. "I don't think they're just here to raid cattle."

We continued north along the narrow single-track trail through the bush, stopping each time we encountered a group of refugees or fighters.

22. Murle fighters retreating from Manyabol. Author photo.

One group consisted of three women, six children, and one dog. They had been walking from Likaungole, a distance of some twenty miles. The oldest woman appeared to be blind; her middle-aged daughter was leading her, with each one clutching one end of a bamboo pole. They said they had been part of a larger group, according to the youngest woman, "but five were killed on the other side of the river."

We encountered two more small groups of fighters before the force commander decided we should turn back. On the road back to Pibor, we met several more groups. Clearly, people were coming from the west as well as the north. We stopped to talk with another group of six well-armed men carrying spears, M-16s, AK-47s, and charred meat—goat or antelope, perhaps—that dangled from woven strings of grass.

"They burned the dwellings at Lilibok," said their spokesman. "We got scattered. We don't know how many died or got injured. They are so many." The speaker stretched his arms wide to indicate the large size of the attacking force.

The force commander thanked them for this intelligence, and we all continued south—we in our air-conditioned vehicles, they on foot in the dusty heat.

Back in Pibor, the market was being stripped of everything of value. All the little stalls were bare, and shopkeepers carried their goods on their

23. Murle women displaced from Likaungole and headed to Pibor. Author photo.

heads or in wheelbarrows toward the presumed safety of the UN camp's outer wall. We sped past them, through the still-growing refugee camp, and on to the base.

There, we ate a quick snack and reconvened with Deborah, who had more bad news: Kongor had been burned to the ground, and the raiders held its river crossing. But we couldn't stay. The SRSG was having a cocktail party for VIPs in Juba to celebrate the peace deal, and the force commander was supposed to be there.

I entreated first General Tinaikar and then our Sri Lankan pilots to take off in a big loop to the north so we could try to observe the situation and see what kind of force we were dealing with. They adamantly refused. Instead, we flew directly west toward Bor and Juba.

We would be blind for another day, I thought, *with no one to blame but ourselves.*

* *

We arrived in Juba late in the day, and I immediately went to work on a message to my commanders. Just before 8:00 p.m., I pasted the final draft into an email and sent it, copying the force legal adviser and the senior national representatives of Canada and Australia. Now there could be no pretending that the United States, China, India, Australia, Norway, and Canada were unaware of the severity of the situation.

> Respected Generals—I am writing to convey my extreme concern that we are unprepared as an FHQ for the worst-case scenario, which is that around 2300 tonight, Pibor will be hit by a pincer attack from the North and West, wherein a force ranging between two Regiments and a full Division will strike a town guarded by approximately one company of SSPDF, several hundred Murle militia fighters, and one UN company sitting behind the HESCO, with 3000 IDPs as a literal human shield outside the walls of the base.
>
> Our best intelligence is that both Likaungole to the North and Manyabol to the West were taken last night—2300 was the time quoted for Likaungole being overrun. We know the Nuer forces are within striking distance of Pibor, and again, everything we learned today suggests that they are not raiding cattle, but destroying towns.
>
> Several point [sic] MUST be made.
>
> 1. This White Army must be called what it is—a threat to civilians—the greatest organized and mobilized threat that we have seen since 2018.
> 2. There is a Unity government, so there is no "iO" [opposition] anymore—this threat, which appears to encompass both Dinka from Duk Padiet and Nuer mobilized from throughout Jonglei and across the border in Gambella is a threat to BOTH the government and the UN mandate. As such, we should be cooperating and engaging closely with the government forces to put an end to this rampage.
> 3. There is a political / religious element—these types of assaults are usually led by a prophet and with the blessing of chiefs. However, it must also be stated that the last time an assault of this magnitude was launched, in 2012, no less a figure than Riek Machar himself met with the White Army "leaders" to try to dissuade them from marching on Pibor, and failed. Thus, the solution is unlikely to be political, though all levers should be engaged.
> 4. We have often discussed when in a "Juba" situation the control in the IOC [integrated operations center] should switch from Police

to Military—in the Sector, I strongly question why the military is not in the lead in solving what is clearly a military problem.

5. Our greatest weakness right now is lack of real intelligence. We do not know how big our enemy is, where they are located, in what direction(s) and how fast they are moving.

6. We need to get aerial reconnaissance completed to remedy this.

7. We know they possess "technical[s]" (gun-mounted trucks) and have used them to threaten and probably kill civilians. Those trucks need to be located and destroyed; once their 12.7mm weapons have been neutralized, our air assets will be able to fly more freely.

8. Based on the size of the enemy force, locating them, blocking their advance on Pibor, and creating the space for a political solution is not the work of a few companies; it is a task for a full battalion, augmented with all the enablers and reserves we can offer them.

9. We need to push up the Bor-Pibor axis, clear Manyabol and re-establish our ground "Lines of Communication" to reinforce Pibor.

10. We need to push up the Pibor-Likaungole axis and secure the Kongor River crossings to block an enemy advance to Pibor from the North.

Time is of the essence—I have therefore laid out 10 key points. I personally believe that we do not have the luxury of sleeping comfortably in our air-conditioned cottages tonight—rather, we should engage a Force Crisis Management Team and convince the Mission that it is far better to mobilize for a threat that fades away, than deal with the aftermath of not having acted when we still could (though clearly, a full 10 days past when we SHOULD have started these same measures.)

Otherwise, in the words of the SSPDF Brigade Commander whom we met today in Pibor, when asked about the casualties in Likaungole—"We will count the dead when they have left."

Instead of my traditional "best regards," I signed this letter "sent with my most urgent concerns."

Within forty-five minutes, the first response came from the force chief of staff. General Herlyng noted my concerns, but he had spoken with the force commander, the SRSG was aware of the situation, and the decision was to let Sector East proceed with its plans and reassess in the morning.

Then I received another reply, this time from General Tinaikar himself. He was cordial, saying he appreciated my views and agreed the situation was grave with a high probability of an attack within twenty-four hours. While acknowledging that our job was to protect civilians, he said our options were limited against the White Army. Protecting our own bases and any civilians who sought refuge there was the best we could do. But, he observed, the Murle militias were armed, and David Yau-Yau had returned to organize them. The general didn't believe we could stop the violence between the White Army and the Murle fighters. In his view, it was the consequence of long-standing grievances, and they would have to be allowed to battle it out. The UN was not currently a target and did not wish to become one. We would support Sector East's attempts to hold the base at Pibor and protect the huddled masses in front of its walls, but more than that we would not do.

I was not prepared to accept that answer without protest. I knew I'd be pushing the limits, but this was the moment of truth. To remain silent now would be to betray my own principles and, I believed, the principles of the UN itself. I replied with another long letter describing what I believed was at stake.

Sir, I am glad we both share the concern that the next 24 hours are critical in the vicinity of Pibor.

However, I will note that no outside observer would expect as much, given the darkened halls of our headquarters and fact that the Mission leadership is literally enjoying the best social events that our little base can offer.

You ask "how do we stop two groups bent on inflicting untold harm on each other?"

I would reply that we have seen only one of those groups—the Murle—and they were all in retreat. I saw not one Murle fighter moving TOWARD the direction of their opponents. Only retreating toward Pibor for a defensive "last stand."

I would also point out that none of us have seen the other group—we have made no significant attempt to observe them by any military means that I am aware of—and that remains a problem—but that every person we talked to today indicated that they were moving south, in large numbers, killing and burning.

The way you stop a group like that is to put better armed and armored forces in their path. We have had the opportunity to do this for 10 days. We failed to garrison Likaungole. We failed to hold our position in Many-abol. We have been told by multiple sources that both those towns were seized by the White Army last night, their civilians sent fleeing, men killed, women and children abducted.

We are the only organized armed force in this country. We have the majority of the air assets, and the majority of functional armored vehicles; the majority of personal protective gear (i.e. helmets and flak jackets)—none of this makes us supermen or invulnerable—but it does give us a significant tactical advantage over militia fighters—especially when our Rwandan and Sri Lankan helicopters have machineguns, and every battalion has anti-tank weapons. It would be nice to think we can rely on the SSPDF—but in 2012, more than 500 of their soldiers stood by and let the White Army pass. They, too, found that their "neutrality" protected them—but it did not protect civilians.

When you say that "We just can't stop the violence outside as both parties, as a consequence of long nurtured mutual grievances, battle it out" it sounds as if we are saying that we will be bystanders to a potential mass battle between the White Army and David Yau-Yau's militia forces. That does not sound like deterring violence, to me.

The report on the 2012 attacks states that "UNMISS itself preventively deployed its troops and equipment to areas in Jonglei where attacks appeared likely. It was nevertheless constrained by the availability of troops devoted to undertake active protective field operations and its own asset shortages, as the military strength authorised by Security Council Resolution 1996 and the concomitant air assets needed for the mission had yet to be realised."

The strength mentioned was only 7,000 troops—we have more than double that, and significantly more air power—yet we have not even matched the efforts made by our predecessors.

The report further notes that "the objective of the December/January attacks appears to go beyond retaliatory reprisals and more towards the depopulation, displacement and possibly even destruction of the opposing community and their livelihood, as well as undermining the credibility of the State."

This is entirely consistent with what we heard today—and it is highly reminiscent of the UN's own definition of genocide:

> In the present Convention, genocide means any of the following acts committed with intent to destroy, in whole or in part, a national, ethnical, racial or religious group, as such:
>
> (a) Killing members of the group;
>
> (b) Causing serious bodily or mental harm to members of the group;
>
> (c) Deliberately inflicting on the group conditions of life calculated to bring about its physical destruction in whole or in part;
>
> (d) Imposing measures intended to prevent births within the group;
>
> (e) Forcibly transferring children of the group to another group.

If the scale of 2012 is repeated, we can expect approximately 1,000 Murle to be killed—including at least 88 women and 88 children, with about 400 more abducted. Adults will mainly be shot, and children will be primarily killed through machete blows—this assessment again based [on] the 2012 report.

You say we can only "[aid] the civilians that seek protection at our base." But that is not at all what the Mandate or the ROE [rules of engagement] indicate.

Today, I saw what "Protection of Civilians" means in practice, to the people of South Sudan. It appears to mean that IF you can cross a swollen river, leaving five of your less fortunate friends dead on the other side and can walk 40 kilometers with your children and your dog, leading your blind mother who holds onto the bamboo pole you clutch—IF you can make it to the nearest UN base, then we will protect you. Otherwise, you can expect to die in the bush, because despite dry road terrain and armor [sic] vehicles and helicopters and thousands of soldiers, the UN will not protect you otherwise.

Of course, perhaps tomorrow all will be well. The Nuer and Dinka will return north, and our inspection of the villages they have seized will discover that they harmed no one, burnt nothing.

But it appears much more likely that there will be a "June_2020_Jonglei_Report"—what will that report say about us? Will it reflect that we made every effort?

They say the pen is mightier than the sword—which is why I write this in hopes that we as a Force will take more decisive action in this case. More than this I cannot do—but neither can I remain silent in the face of what I perceive to be the greatest threat that the Mission and Force will face during my tour with UNMISS.

I knew that this level of candor was risky and signed off "with the greatest respect" to convey clearly that I still understood where the power to make the decisions lay.

This time, there was no response.

55 Come to Count the Dead

> The concept of human rights assumes that all human life is of equal value. Risk-free warfare presumes that our lives matter more than the lives of those we are intervening to save.
> —MICHAEL IGNATIEFF

28 February 2020. To his great credit the force commander asked for my opinion along with those of the other gathered officers at his morning staff meeting. He patiently listened as I recited the major points from my unanswered email. Then he sighed and said, "I have heard all your recommendations. We will continue with our plan to hold Pibor."

The meeting was short to facilitate the day's planned visit to the training site at Rejaf, but I managed at least to convince General Tinaikar that we didn't have enough troops in Pibor to discourage an attack; it had helped that General Herlyng agreed with my assessment. The Operations Branch would therefore prepare an order for the Nepalese reserve battalion to deploy a company of troops by helicopter, and the U5 was directed to assist as needed. I tasked Andy and Emm with the support role and sought to attack the Jonglei issue from another angle.

I had opted out of the visit to the Rejaf training camp, certain I would see nothing different there from what I had already seen on my recent visits to other training sites: Muom, Mapel, Mas Na Bira, and Maridi. Instead, I stopped by our Intelligence Branch and asked Andreas to go to JMAC with me and talk to Lauren. I hoped we could convince her to give us a written assessment that we could use to influence the force commander and the SRSG to authorize the deployment of a full battalion into Pibor to avert the coming crisis and surge peacekeepers in the area to restore security. I was not surprised that she refused—I was still fuming that she'd cut our intelligence team out of the loop for almost two weeks—but the reason for her rejection caught me off guard.

"Carp," she said, "I've been telling the SRSG that we needed to do something for two weeks. Even if you could get your reinforcement plan together, he's not going to authorize your action. The mission doesn't want to get involved." She said she was on her way to Tomping to catch a flight out of the country but that she could talk for a few minutes if it would help.

"It's a good day to be going on leave, I suppose," I said. We shared the sort of bitter laugh that dark humor often inspires. Then I took her up on the offer to pick her brain. Our conversation focused on the immediate crisis in Pibor and what she saw as the larger one to come—that is, what would happen when the Nuer wave broke against the banks of the Lotilla River and retreated north to the home territories between Yuai and Akobo, where small Murle war parties were already at work. Starvation had created a humanitarian crisis there, she noted, that would only worsen if the fighting rose to a level where aid workers could not operate. Former government and opposition fighters in that part of the country still held a great deal of arms and ammunition. Now ostensibly they were on the same side, but . . .

The "but" lingered. We both knew what she hadn't said: there were no UN bases in that area, nowhere for those at risk from a counterattack to take refuge. Everyone in that region was at risk, at least everyone who wasn't carrying a weapon: the women, the children, the elderly. "You'd think this is when the mission might convene its crisis management team . . . ," she said, her words trailing off again.

"But instead," I said, "they'll be drinking cocktails and enjoying their air-conditioning like they did last night." We shared another bitter laugh. Then she was out the door to catch her flight, and Andreas and I were off to do what we could to avert the coming disaster.

"Andreas," I said, "you'll have to come up with a force intel assessment that sums up what we talked about in there." I motioned back toward Lauren's office as we walked away. "A one-pager on the crisis in Pibor basically stating that if we can land a battalion in the next twenty-four to forty-eight hours, we might hold the town."

He nodded.

"And then a follow-on assessment of the next phase of the conflict in the north."

"Roger," he said, breaking off toward his cubicle as I headed back to my desk to see how the order for the Nepalese battalion was coming.

* *

Andreas finished his assessment just after lunch, so I was able to review it before heading to the U.S. Embassy to finalize plans for obtaining our vehicles. It was well written and hit all the key points, so I forwarded it to the force commander, the deputy force commander, and General Herlyng. When I got back from the embassy, Andy cheerfully reported that the first reinforcements were on their way to Pibor. The 130 troops—not the full battalion for which I'd advocated—had been ordered only to reinforce our base and not to intervene in the slaughter. It was another performative action—too little too late to stop the killing—but I had to console myself that it was better than nothing.

* *

Throughout the weekend, we continued to monitor the situation in Sector East from afar. The force commander agreed to prepare additional reinforcements but not to deploy them unless requested by the Sector East commander, who believed that he could hold Pibor without them. The irony was not lost on me that what was happening now had also happened in 2012, as narrated by the chief of JMAC's own seminal paper, "Prolonging the Agony of UNMISS":

> During the violence in Pibor in 2011/2012, UNMISS deployed over 550 personnel and armoured personnel carriers to protect Pibor Town and UN assets. . . . [A] military force of this size should have been capable of deploying sub-units to areas within 3-5km [2-3 miles] of Pibor Town. However, there is little evidence to suggest there were any attempts to protect outlying communities.[1]

The only difference now was that although we had more than twice as many troops in the country, we'd deployed only half as many to Pibor. Even with the benefit of historical knowledge and that of people who had literally written reports on the topic, the mission was failing to do anything better or indeed different than it had eight years previously.

* *

Sector West had also asked for reinforcements to cover their scheduled rotation of troops but was told that no additional reserves were available at that time. This was exactly why we had wanted to reconstitute the full Nepalese battalion as a reserve force in our original operations order last year, but it hadn't happened.

Meanwhile, we were slowly gaining a better picture of what was going on. The Nuer had apparently taken heavy casualties in their attack on Likaungole and were now negotiating to have the ICRC fly their wounded to Akobo for treatment. The fighters, the Akobo County commissioner, and the HOFO— all were in discussions about it. That was proof that these leaders had the ability to communicate all along; they had just chosen not to as long as their offensive was going well.

* *

Scanning the latest news reports before Monday's brief with the force commander, I noted that the issue of dividing government ministries between the various political parties remained fraught and that non-signatory groups, including NAS, were indicating they might be willing to join the political process. Then, midway through my review, I saw a story that took another tragic event and exposed, with ironic humor, some ridiculous aspect of hope.

Victor Lugala was a South Sudanese journalist, poet, and author who'd published *The White House*, a poignant story of life in Juba during the worst times before South Sudan won its independence. Now he had written an editorial claiming that the current plague of locusts, "bad as it is, has turned out to be a blessing in disguise." While the insects were consuming every bit of vegetation they could find, the famished South Sudanese were also eating them.

> Locals may call it manna from the sky. They are harvesting the insects en masse, and with the dry season heat, the natural oven is conducive for drying the bumper harvest. Bags of these have hit the Magwi Corner of Soukh Custom in Juba, where on a fine day, a housewife on a shoestring kitchen budget could sample some of the delicacy, plus some raw cassava, and a meal for the day is assured.[2]

Only in South Sudan could a journalist write such a feature, a story meant for the consumption of the elites in power and for the foreigners with their mandates to do good. Given that literacy was only 35 percent and that there was little access to print media outside of Juba, how could it be intended otherwise? I sighed and headed upstairs for the morning meeting, where the force chief of staff held forth on what he'd seen at Rejaf on Friday's visit.

"What is happening is a big fraud in front of our eyes," he announced. "I told this to the Norwegian ambassador. There's no money for training. The training will last for sixty days. Why? Because then the water will be shut off. They have no uniforms, no shoes. . . . A lot of donations have come in, but there's no accountability for the supplies. The government soldiers are getting paid, the opposition are not. Rejaf has 7,641 people. It looks more like an IDP camp than a training camp . . ."

That was pretty much what I had expected to hear after repeatedly seeing the same thing at other training sites, but Rejaf was only a few miles from Juba. It was supposed to be the "showcase" site for the Joint Defense Board and the other elements of the security mechanisms, where they could usher visiting dignitaries to show them how well the training of the NUF was going and how scrupulously their funds were being spent. If Rejaf was as bad as everywhere else, then it meant no one—not Salva Kiir, not Riek Machar, not the international community—cared about even maintaining a pretense that the security arrangements required by the peace treaty were going to be met now that the government had formed.

A representative from the mission's Political Affairs Division had come over from the mission building to give us its interpretation of the situation in Pibor, but it was soon clear that the group had no idea what was actually going on there. "This sort of cattle raiding is pretty common, and you'd expect to see it at this time regardless of the political instability . . ."

I shook my head at yet another example of how the mission was failing to see the crisis for what it actually was and how information about the reality on the ground was not being circulated to all the people who needed it. As the meeting progressed, the intelligence chief noted that Manyabol had been burned, that the number of displaced people in Pibor was up to five thousand and rising, and that the Murle were counterattacking near Kongor. I noticed our guest speaker's expression became worried as the gravity of the situation on the ground was revealed. Maybe what was happening wasn't "pretty common" after all.

I pressed again for sending out long-duration patrols, particularly a reconnaissance-in-force patrol to Likaungole, but the force commander was adamantly opposed. "Without full armored protection, I will not go there," he said. But he knew we *had* armored vehicles in Pibor—namely, BMP-II amphibious infantry fighting vehicles that were specifically designed to cross rivers and were quite capable of crossing the Lilibok, the same small stream that hundreds of women and children had forded in their flight to

Pibor. Short of main battle tanks, which the Nuer militias did not have, the BMP-IIs were the most powerful armored vehicles found anywhere in South Sudan and were capable of driving over vertical obstacles two feet high and trenches eight feet wide. Their armor could withstand not only small arms and medium machine-gun fire on all sides but also attacks from heavier weapons on their frontal armor. But clearly the mission leadership had made up their minds to take no action.

* *

The next day, Andreas asked me to provide some information for a strange request. With Lauren Hutton on leave, David Shearer had apparently asked the next-most-senior civilian in JMAC, Rory Morrison, for a short summary of the situation in Jonglei, including what UNMISS had done, where we had deployed peacekeepers, and what towns had been destroyed.

JMAC didn't have the answers, so it asked the force for them. This meant that the mission's senior leaders had gone not only the entire weekend but also the next two days without having any idea what was going on in the deadliest conflict in the country since the peace treaty was signed in 2018. Was the SRSG—the one person with the power to do something—really that uninformed? Or was this request simply a way to create plausible deniability later? I believed that it could only be the latter. If David Shearer *hadn't* known what was going on, that would have meant that no information from the force, from the Bor field office, from the humanitarian agencies—not even from high-level political figures such as David Yau-Yau—was reaching the mission. Any one of those avenues of communication might have failed, but to think that all of them had and simultaneously? It just wasn't believable.

56 Potemkin Would Be Proud

> The women and girls that I have met this week fill me
> with confidence that South Sudan has the right women to
> work alongside their male counterparts to bring about a
> lasting peace for everyone and a more equal country.
> —PRINCESS SOPHIE, COUNTESS OF WESSEX

5 March 2020. Unfortunately for the Murle, the Baroness Cox was not in South Sudan, but a member of the British royal family was. The Countess of Wessex, on hand to celebrate International Women's Day, had flown to Malakal to speak to survivors of gender-based violence and to present medals to the British engineering company based there. Her flight path would have taken her directly over some of the very areas where stolen women were still struggling to escape their captors, still mourning their dead male relatives and their abducted children.

I, too, was in the air—on a similar flight path but at a lower altitude and, unlike Princess Sophie, headed to Yuai, a village in the far north of Jonglei. I was again traveling with the force commander, and our group was on its way to meet with senior leaders of the Nuer communities whose young men had been killing, burning, and looting their way through the Murle territories to the south. We also planned to visit the only long-duration patrol that we had out in the sector—a platoon of Ethiopian peacekeepers that had deployed to the area from Bor a few days earlier.

In my breast pocket was an envelope with $200 and an ATM card that I'd promised to deliver to a guy named Pierre in Bor. Just before our flight boarded, a security officer had walked into the waiting area and asked if anyone could pass the envelope to his colleague, and I'd volunteered to help. I'd often been the beneficiary of the kindness of strangers, and I tried never to miss an opportunity to pay it forward. At Bor, our chopper touched down briefly to take on the rest of our party—the sector commander and a few of his staff officers. I jumped out, found Pierre, handed off the card and the cash, and hurried back to strap in again for the second half of the trip.

When we landed in Yuai, I discovered another existing HESCO-walled temporary operating base beside the airstrip that was similar to the abandoned bases in Koch and Maper, but again, our troops weren't occupying it. They had come north from Bor in armored vehicles and were stuck on the other side of a shallow river about six miles from the village itself.

I sighed and checked my phone for any notes from the team in Juba, but there was no cell signal here. In this remote part of the country, communication was possible only with Thuraya satellite phones. *Who*, I wondered, *paid those bills?* There wasn't time for much reflection on that subject as we approached the large, low, tin-roofed shed where we were meeting the Nuer leadership in Jonglei. As we made our way to our seats, I was conscious of the somber expressions from the older men in the room and of the near-total absence of the young men carrying weapons who normally guarded such assemblies. The youngest man in the room stood in the back by the door and was armed only with a dazzling smile and surprisingly good English. "Good morning," he said, waving us toward a row of seats near the front of the room. "You are most welcome."

There were no women among our assembled hosts, but that was not unusual; the only woman in the room was Col. Vanessa Hanrahan, the force provost marshal. While UNPOL handled civilian policing, Colonel Hanrahan oversaw the 116 military police that enforced discipline among the peacekeepers assigned to the mission. I was glad that she was with us, in part because it was important that the FHQ set the example for diversity in our patrols, but also because, in my mind, we were here to address issues of criminal violence: murder, sexual assault, kidnapping, theft, and arson.

As usual, the force commander started the conversation by asking about the security situation and how we could help. Our hosts told us that "the people are not in good condition. This week, there were a lot of ambushes. Even today."

I wonder why, I thought to myself. Out loud, I asked instead if the young men from Yuai had gone south to attack Pibor.

A chief, distinctive in his time-worn khaki uniform and red sash, answered. "Yes, the young men went from here because their cows and women and children were taken, so they followed them. And then they met their brothers the Murle in the plains. Even now, you can find them two hours away. They went to fight for several days. They went, but they didn't return, so they are still there."

The force commander asked if this was in response to the political instability in the area.

His answer came from the paramount chief of the area—the tallest man I had ever seen—who dismissed as ridiculous the idea the attacks had anything to do with the recent reversion to the ten-state solution. "We cannot say it is political, because it's in their blood," he declared, noting that the Murle had been raiding in the area since before his father was born, and he was now an old man. He shook his head. "When a Murle is born, he is taught to hide and steal. . . . Murle can't produce children, so they take the children of other men." He also advocated for a final solution to the problem of intercommunal conflict in the region. "If we all get together, we can go to Pibor and stay permanently."

Unspoken was the corollary that if the Nuer went to Pibor en masse, it would be over the Murle's dead bodies—and that if they stayed permanently, it would be because no Murle would be left alive east of the Pibor River or north of the Lotilla River to oppose them.

The paramount chief continued, mixing a polite request with a veiled threat. "Two *bomas* worth of our children have been stolen," he said and asked the force commander for the mission's help in arranging their return.[1] Otherwise, he said, "in May we will go and get them back."

While I found his casually expressed ethnic hatred to be distasteful, the paramount chief's final words conveyed a sentiment that I could empathize with: "If you come to ask questions, with no action, then we will become frustrated."

But the force commander remained calm as he gave the answer that no longer surprised me. "We can only assist. We can't do much."

This answer didn't seem to satisfy the Nuer leaders, but neither did it seem to surprise them. Soon we were up and out of our seats, posing for the obligatory pictures and moving on to the next meeting where we would ask more questions and ignore the answers.

That meeting was with the local SSPDF officers, but plenty of people surrounded General Tinaikar. Colonel Hanrahan, Andreas, and I dropped back. We elected to skip that meeting and went instead into the marketplace to talk to the local women. Having no translator, we asked the young man who had greeted us in English to help us, and he was happy to do so. As we walked, we asked him where he learned to speak English so fluently, and he told us that he had studied in Malakal and Khartoum. He also said that two of his brothers were down south, fighting with the White Army. Mixed emotions came through as he spoke about them. Clearly he was worried for them. I didn't ask whether he was as concerned for what they were likely doing to the people they met in Murle territory.

With his help, we interviewed some women sitting in the center of town under a roughly constructed shelter whose roof kept the hot morning sun off of us all. "What did they think of the security situation?" Colonel Hanrahan asked.

"We fear the Murle," said one woman, "but maybe since the army is here, they won't come."

Another scoffed. "The army does not fight the Murle. They stay in their barracks," she said.

We asked if the Murle harmed women and children.

"Yes, they kill women and take children. They don't rape, but they will kill you if you resist giving up your child." So far, they say, eight children were kidnapped this year. Those children were valuable; each one could have been sold for thirty cows.

The discussion was cut short when the force commander's aide came looking for us. It was time to cross the river and meet the Ethiopian patrol. While it would have been great to stay longer, talk further, and learn more, our time—as always—was limited. That was why we needed to get observers out into these areas on longer patrols and create a better system for synthesizing what they learned and for sharing it with the rest of the mission.

* *

Reaching the UN camp required us to cross the marshy river on foot. We squelched through the wet grass and mud to the other side, making our way past herds of goats and cows along the riverbank. General Tinaikar uncomplainingly led the way. As a special forces officer, he was surely no stranger to mud on his boots.

The crossing reminded me of all the times I'd heard people say that we couldn't go to this place or that because of the terrain or the roads. But we could have always gone by foot, which was how most people in most places in South Sudan did and how most soldiers throughout most of history had traveled.

When we arrived at the Ethiopian camp, the peacekeepers on patrol—including several women—seemed perfectly content to be camped out under tents. This was what soldiers did. The force commander thanked them for their hard work and admonished them to remain cautious and to stay safe. We drank a bit of coffee with them, then recrossed the river to the helicopter for the long flight back to Bor and, before returning to Juba, our final planned stop —a visit to our temporary base at Anyidi, which now provided protection for Murle civilians displaced from Manyabol and elsewhere. More than a hundred were there already, and their number was rising daily.

* *

In Anyidi we met first with the local elders, who thanked the force commander for the presence of the Rwandan peacekeepers and for their APCs that crouched watchfully around the village, their heavy machine guns facing outward. This was a Dinka village, but the people had been on good terms with their Murle neighbors for some time, they told us. Clearly, however, housing dozens of refugees was putting a strain on their hospitality. One of the men raised the issue of food, toilets, sleeping materials, and non-food items for the IDPs.

The HOFO, Deborah Schein, had joined us for this final leg of our trip. She said that she would see what could be done.

Then the Dinka elders took us to see the refugees, and what had been merely a depressing conversation among equals devolved into a shameful interrogation of the most vulnerable and distressed. We approached a small cluster of dispossessed women sitting in a circle on the ground, some nursing small children, some staring off into the distance at nothing. The force commander and the HOFO asked one of these women how she got here.

She had walked over sixty miles from her village, she told us, while carrying one child and leading another. She had been living here for two weeks now, without bedding, medicine, belongings, or food beyond what little the local community had provided her.

Then they asked her how soon she could leave Anyidi and return to Manyabol, knowing even as they asked the question that her village had been burned to the ground. Telling her that "UNMISS is there, they will provide security," and acting as if UNMISS hadn't also "been there" the day that Manyabol was attacked. As if they themselves had not given the order for our troops to withdraw, leaving the town to be sacked and its citizens scattered. And as if they probably wouldn't be quick to give the same orders again. Rarely in my career had I been more dismayed by the actions of my senior leaders.

As I listened to the conversation, exchanging glances of dismay with Colonel Hanrahan, another woman arrived on the back of a motorcycle. The driver said that she had walked out of the bush and onto the road in front of him several miles east of here. She was old by the standards of South Sudan, where few live past their fifties, and her face was marked with dots in the pattern of ritual facial scarring that Murle women have tradition-ally used as indicators of status, identity, and attractiveness. She had been abducted several days before but had been released by her captors far from her village, far from anywhere.

"How many other women and children were taken?" she was asked.

"I cannot count . . . Many women and children. They took me with my children."

She was alone.

"And the children?"

"They kept them. And they kept the young women. But they sent me away."

She was old and bent. The pain was evident in her face. The Nuer took from her what they valued—her children and her younger, prettier friends and relatives—and left her in the bush to walk to civilization or die of thirst in the blazing sun. She wasn't even worth a bullet.

"Let's go," said the force commander, shaking his head in exasperation. "Otherwise, we'll miss our flight."

We left the refugees of Anyidi exactly as we'd found them, sitting in a clump on a handful of woven mats under a tree. There were around thirty children, some of them naked, almost all barefoot, among a handful of old women and men, too. We gave them nothing—no food, no medicine, no transportation, no hope—exactly as we had been doing since they'd arrived twenty-six days earlier.

* *

The Countess of Wessex was notably absent from this place, where the women and girls of South Sudan most needed to be seen and have their truths spoken about. These hard truths, such as the freedom from the fear of being killed, raped, or abducted by their countrymen, were more important than working alongside them. Women already did most of the work in the subsistence economy in which 95 percent of the population lived, and even men acknowledged the fear that pervaded women's lives.[2] It was not Princess Sophie's fault, of course; her handlers must have known better than to bring her here. The British attaché knew about the situation, and like UNMISS, the United Kingdom didn't want the kind of bad publicity that Abyei had received.

We had a celebrity on hand and the media tools to make this front-page news around the world, but it would have made us look bad, so we kept it quiet instead. Our internal censors tried to keep any words and pictures from even reaching social media.

Visiting dignitaries from rich countries would continue meeting with elites in air-conditioned offices and be shown just enough to make them feel good that they had committed some money to making the world a better place. They wouldn't be allowed to see how little those contributions actually bought for the people of South Sudan.

* *

Back in Juba, I read a report from the International Organization for Migration, the UN agency that tracks the movement of internally displaced persons and refugees. While we were in Yuai and Anyidi, their personnel had been in Pibor, counting. Now 8,491 people from 1,522 families were huddled outside the walls of our base and urgently needed food and shelter. Sixty percent were women and children.

If Princess Sophie had met with these women and girls, I wondered, *would she have been as "filled with confidence," and would we still be doing so little to feed and shelter them?*

57 Death by a Thousand Cuts

We received messages that they were coming, they were
coming. We even informed the UN but they went away.
—PAUL KONYI, EXECUTIVE CHIEF OF MANYABOL

6 March 2020. We were engaged in another planning session, this time
focusing on the coming wet season. But it was not "planning for a rainy
season as usual," General Herlyng noted. The chief JMAC agreed and said
she believed that unusually severe rains would mean that we would be stuck
in our bases. When someone suggested considering what places we could
"sacrifice" from a political perspective, I observed acridly that it already
seemed there was hardly any place in South Sudan that we wouldn't sacrifice. While no one wanted to argue the point, nor did they want to address
it. *No great surprise there,* I thought.

The latest complicating factor to all our plans was a note that the CDF
had sent two days earlier to the force commander stating that troop rotations from China, South Korea, India, Nepal, and Cambodia should be
suspended until further notice. Although the letter did not specifically say
so, the feeling around the table was that this instruction was probably a
response to reports of the new coronavirus, whose impacts seemed to be
centered in Asia. South Sudan, a landlocked country with little trade, was
the last place this new disease seemed likely to show up, but given the poor
state of its medical infrastructure, it wouldn't be good if the virus did. The
CDF, of course, had no authority to make such demands, but the consensus
was that we would hold any Nepalese personnel in the transit housing in
Juba until the issue could be resolved by the mission's political side, while
the leave travel and rotation of individual staff officers from all countries
would continue as usual. The latest of those rotations brought new faces to
both the U5 and the mission's front office. New Zealand's staff officers served
nine-month tours, so we said goodbye to Tracey Tibbs and welcomed her

replacement, Lt. Col. Justin McCleary, as the new deputy. Brent Quin was headed home as well, replaced by Lt. Col. John Gordon. The SRSG's new military adviser seemed like a decent guy, but I didn't have the connection with him that I'd had with Brent. *Then again*, I thought, *that connection hadn't really helped me when it counted—when civilian lives were on the line.*

* *

Meanwhile, reports were beginning to trickle in from patrols in Sector East that had finally reached the villages that had been overrun at the end of February. A hub-and-spoke patrol based out of Likaungole that was meant to start four days earlier and last for two weeks had been canceled because the village was unfit for human habitation. The buildings—many with people inside them—had been burned. The bodies of people and livestock lay in the dusty streets, and the borehole that had provided water was destroyed.

When the SRSG—who had so emphatically declared that it was "bullshit" to think we were responsible for protecting civilians from ethnic violence—finally made a trip together with the force commander, I hoped their findings might be the impetus for changing the way the mission responded to warnings of impending attacks. They visited Pibor together, and Shearer finally saw firsthand the impact of his decision not to deploy peacekeepers before the latest attacks. But the experience didn't seem to faze him, and his responses to the reporters' questions in a news conference a few days later seemed detached and disingenuous.

He noted that eight thousand people were "currently living in make-shift shelters next to the UN base in Pibor," and he acknowledged that "the towns of Manyabol and Likuangole have been almost totally destroyed." He thanked the Indian and Ethiopian peacekeepers "for their rapid response," saying, "This is the kind of nimble and proactive action that we want to be in a position to do more often in future."[1] I wasn't sure what he was talking about, since there had been nothing proactive about our failures in Jonglei, but the question-and-answer session became only more surreal from there.

A reporter asked how bad Shearer thought the situation in Pibor really was. "The situation in Pibor is terrible for those people who have lost their homes," the SRSG replied. "Certainly in Likuangole and in Manyabol, those two towns have been pretty much destroyed." But, he continued, "we will hope that the people are able to go back, even if it is to towns that have been destroyed, they can hopefully go back and begin starting their lives again."

This restated what General Tinaikar and Deborah Schein had previously told the displaced people in Anyidi to do—return to their burned-out villages and start from scratch—with no assurances that either the newly formed government or UNMISS would protect them and despite knowing that the Nuer leadership intended to strike again in the coming months. Shearer's recommendation for people to return home almost certainly put their lives at greater risk.

Another reporter asked what UNMISS would do to restore hope to the hopeless—those who had lost property and family members, and otherwise had suffered in the attacks. The SRSG said we would provide "some non-food items, plastic sheeting, whatever" for those who returned to their burned-out villages.

If Shearer's own children had been stolen, his wife murdered, and his home burned, I wondered, *would he have considered the handout of some plastic sheeting and cookware to be a satisfactory response from the United Nations?* Nobody asked that question, but I would have liked to have heard him answer it.

* *

The latest news from Jonglei was not the only troubling development; the coronavirus that had started out as a minor news story was spreading and quickly. There was now a list of eighty countries where it was known to be a risk to the general population, and the United States was one of them. I met with representatives from our embassy and the WHO, and realized that this contagion had the potential to negatively impact the rotation of our replacements if it got worse.

My week had only one redeeming moment, but even that was tinged with irony. On Saturday I met with Elisabeth and the other volunteers to deliver the books that I'd been collecting for the newly constructed library at the Hope School. A member of the mission's Public Affairs Office was on hand to capture the moment, and at one point, I was asked to hold a book and pose for a picture to encourage reading as a path to success. Only later, looking at the picture, would I realize that the book I'd been handed was *The Hunger Games*.

The dystopian novel that I'd displayed at the library seemed an apt metaphor as the month slowly passed, with a dysfunctional central government, fragmented states, hunger, and death being recurrent themes in both the popular novel and the reality of life in South Sudan outside of Juba.

24. Opening the new library at the Hope School in Juba's POC-3. Author photo.

Within the capital, the big news was that the key issue of apportioning the government ministries between the parties of Kiir and Machar had been decided. Kiir's supporters would control the Finance, Interior, Justice, Information, Education and Instruction, Infrastructure, and National Security Ministries, and Machar would nominate ministers for defense, petroleum, mining, health, and housing. The smaller factions would be put in charge of foreign affairs, transport, agriculture, and disaster management.

Angelina Teny would serve as the minister of defense and Josephine Lagu as the minister of agriculture. All in all, women were appointed to 17 percent of the posts, including the Ministry of Foreign Affairs, although that was less than half of the 35 percent of government positions that the peace agreement said women should hold. Teny's appointment was particularly important, in my opinion. I thought that it might result in General Jok Riak's being replaced as the CDF, thereby potentially improving the relationship between UNMISS and the government, and easing restrictions on our freedom of movement.

* *

But if the political solution appeared to be working at the highest level in Juba, out in the states the people—soldiers and civilians alike—were in dire straits. In the training sites, mass desertions driven by a lack of food were reported at Mas Na Bira in Sector West, near Wau, and at the Maridi training site in the Western Equatorias—the camp that the foreign ambassadors had so recently visited. The commander of the training site at Muom in Unity State had indicated that they were nearly out of food and said that "the soldiers will become very difficult to control if they are not fed." The members of the NUF still had no uniforms to unite them, no pay, and little standardized or formalized instruction. While UNMISS was finally working with the transitional government to distribute stores of food and matériel to the training sites, not much had reached even those locations closest to Juba, and the discontent and desertions that were beginning to manifest in the more distant sites represented a trend that I thought would likely worsen. The NUF remained a notional force, and without efforts toward SSR and DDR, there seemed to be a high risk that many people would return to fighting or banditry.

Jonglei wasn't the only place where intercommunal violence was taking lives. Conditions had gotten bad enough in Tonj that the HOFO had pulled all civilians out of our temporary base there, but the force was staying—which was a first. I suspected the decision was driven by General Tinaikar's realizing that we should have stayed in Manyabol rather than pulling out at the HOFO's direction and leaving the town to be destroyed.

Near Tonj, the village of Wanh Alel—which we had visited in February—had been attacked, just as its elders had feared. Eleven people were dead, fourteen were wounded, and the people who remained had finally given up. The village's executive director told the patrol leader that the community was evacuating in fear of further attacks. Villagers were angry at both their government and at UNMISS for leaving them unprotected, telling our patrol to take the executive director away when they left along with the national flag. Those of Wanh Alel, those who were still alive, expressed their frustration with UNMISS as well. What good were these visits that did nothing to provide security? I, for one, shared those sentiments. We'd had so many opportunities to prevent violence through our presence—we only needed to listen to what the people told us when we traveled the land—and to provide the bare minimum of what they requested. Instead, we had smiled and shaken hands, taken notes and pictures, and left them utterly alone to face their all-too-uncertain futures.

After reading the report, I looked at the pictures that one of the patrol members had taken with my phone in February, particularly the one of me and a pair of colleagues surrounded by smiling women and children, and their men with their ivory bracelets and shouts of "Akol!" I wondered how many of them were still alive, still unwounded. The probable answer was not a pleasant one, and I did not sleep well that night.

58 That Safari Way of Life

I think that safari way of life is one of the best I know
and if I can adapt some of those ideas of adventurous,
full living into normal life I would be more happy.
—DAN ELDON IN A LETTER TO HIS FRIEND JEFFREY GETTLEMAN

13 March 2020. It was Friday the thirteenth, but I was hoping for a little luck in a race against time and trying to board my flight to Kenya before COVID-19 stopped me. A rumor was going around that South Sudan might close its borders in response to news from around the globe about this emergent disease, and if that happened before I left, I'd be fucked.

As the Kenya Airways jet pulled back from the gate and began to taxi toward the runway, I shook my head as repetitive pings from WhatsApp confirmed my fears: notes coming in from the United States and the mission suggested that travel outside South Sudan should be curtailed, but it would all have to be dealt with in Nairobi. I did make a quick voice call to General Herlyng, who was his usual calm self and told me to check in once I'd landed in Kenya. I also exchanged a couple of WhatsApp notes with USMOG staffers and was unsurprised to discover that they would prefer that I cut short my plans.

I intended to advocate for letting things play out, assuming that the curve would flatten, that the hysteria would die down in the next ten days, and that UNMISS would arrange to bring its staff members back into the country in a smooth manner. The worst case, of course, would be that my bosses in the United States or the UN would order me to return, with the first being a strong possibility, the latter an unlikely scenario. The irony was not lost on me that as a U.S. Marine—an ostensible defender of freedom—I was never entirely free myself; many links in my dual chains of command could order me to change my vacation plans at the drop of a hat. *But at least,* I thought, *I'd have one night with Jayde, and that would be better than none.*

* *

Once on the ground in Nairobi, I passed quickly through the eerily empty airport and caught an overpriced cab to the Ngong Treehouse, a lovely collection of bungalows on stilts in the upper-class neighborhood of Karen. It took a while to find the place, but then there was Jayde, her blonde hair curling in tendrils in the Nairobi humidity and a flushed smile lighting her face as she spotted me. Her warm hug melted away the tension that I'd been under for the last six weeks—a weight that I only recognized as it receded. We caught up over dinner and decided to call it an early night.

Jayde had booked us into a lovely bamboo cottage with a large bed downstairs and a twin bed in a loft. She'd claimed the smaller space for herself, so I set myself up downstairs and sent a short email to Col. Eric Larson, who had replaced Colonel Pepper as the commander of USMOG. He replied a few minutes later, saying that he didn't intend to recall me from leave. That set my mind at ease, but I still slept restlessly.

I woke several times when some animal, most likely a tree hyrax, shrieked in the night. The hyrax is a small, furry mammal, about the size of a rabbit, whose nearest relative in the animal kingdom is—improbable as it sounds— the elephant. Hyraxes are notorious for making noises that have been described as "unearthly screams," but I was within a city and inside a sturdy building, so I fell back to sleep fairly quickly. That probably wouldn't have been the case had I been sleeping in a tent on the savanna somewhere.

In the morning, I awoke to the more pleasant sounds of birds and frogs, and I just lay in bed for a while, appreciating that I was in a little slice of paradise in Nairobi. The morning only got better from there. Jayde and I started with coffee and conversation on the balcony. We had a lot planned for our first day, so we skipped breakfast and headed to the nearby Giraffe Centre to meet the locals.

Our vehicle was a RAV-4, which I'd rented from a small local company instead of one of the big international firms such as Avis or Hertz. Doing so was a bit chancy, but I liked supporting a woman-owned, family-run business. A young man named Kevin delivered the car to us at Ngong House, telling us that his mother, Francisca, had sent him. I gave the little suv a quick inspection and was happy to see that it appeared to be in much better condition than some of the ones I'd driven in neighboring Uganda.

The drive to the Giraffe Centre was short, and navigating the Nairobi traffic was a breeze after having spent so many months driving around Juba. It was early on a weekend, and while more cars were on the roads here, at least these roads were paved.

Not many other visitors were at the center yet, so we took our time feeding the giraffes and learning a bit about them. One large female—a towering creature named Daisy—seemed to enjoy my attention, eating food from my hand and leaning down over my shoulder to pose for pictures. But when Jayde handed me the camera and took her turn in the spotlight, Daisy swung her head on her long, supple neck like a club, giving Jayde a hard knock on the noggin. Our guide, Peter, explained that giraffes were very intelligent and had distinct personalities. Daisy did not like women or children— information that would have been good to have a few minutes earlier—and I suspected Peter might have held it back for a bit of entertainment. Jayde laughed off the blow in her good-natured way and tried feeding a smaller, gentler female instead, but Daisy kept butting in, literally and figuratively. Jayde became very good at ducking.

Interacting with the world's tallest land mammal up close was an amazing experience, but we couldn't linger as long as we might have liked. Keen to escape the city and get into the wilderness outside Nairobi, we headed north to Lake Nakuru. The journey was refreshingly uneventful. The roads were good, Google Maps worked offline, and soon we were out of the city, climbing up the mountains of the Aberdare Range.

We saw goats, cows, and sheep by the roadside along with vegetables for sale and, rather incongruously for a sweltering sub-Saharan country, a roadside stand selling fur hats. The roadway made sweeping turns that offered stunningly beautiful views of the Great Rift Valley, dazzling green with forest and farmland. Through the car window, we bought ears of roasted corn from a roadside hawker on the far side of the mountains who had cleverly set up right where road construction created a bottleneck that slowed traffic sufficiently for pedestrian street vendors to ply their trade.

Two hours later, we arrived in Nakuru, making our way into the conservation park and up to the Sarova Lion Hill Lodge in time to catch the lunch buffet. But the real motivation for coming was not the food but the park's incredible wildlife, so we set off in our RAV-4 after politely acknowledging the hotel gatekeepers' stern warning that we had to return by 7:00 p.m., as guests were not allowed to drive in the park after dark. As we drove away, Jayde asked if I knew the reason for this injunction, and I filled her in on my second rule of driving in Africa, which made her laugh.

It didn't take long for us to find the rhinos. These endangered creatures were one of the main reasons I'd wanted to come to this park in particular, as it was also a designated rhinoceros sanctuary. We easily spotted the massive white rhinos grazing in the open grass along the lakeside and, a little farther on, the smaller and more reclusive black rhinos browsing in the bushes. We also saw plenty of antelopes, Cape buffalo, and baboons, as well as some of the small, black-faced monkeys known as vervets—many of them mothers with tiny, cute babies. I fed some of them diced apples from a bag of snacks that Jayde had brought along, and we laughed at their adorable antics.

* *

This park, like many that I'd seen elsewhere in Africa, had marked the junctures of its many dirt roads with blank posts, leaving us to guess exactly where we were on what was a badly photocopied map that did not match Google's satellite imagery. We drove as close as we could to Lake Nakuru itself so that Jayde could photograph the flamingos. She was very excited because they were her mother's favorite birds and somewhat of a family mascot, and she was looking forward to sharing the photos with her parents. A herd of Cape buffalo between the road and the lake gave us pause, but presently a park ranger showed up and offered to escort us safely to the water's edge so that Jayde could get better pictures. We took him up on the generous offer and thanked him afterward, receiving in return a warm smile and a reminder not to stay out past dark.

We drove on in hopes of seeing leopards, lions, pythons, and hyenas, but the farther we went into the bush, the fewer animals we saw. With the sun dropping low toward the horizon, we headed back toward the hotel. Rather than retracing the road we'd just taken, we followed a track on the map that had the advantage of being considerably shorter and taking us alongside a bit of the lake that we hadn't yet seen. And that's how I found myself breaking my second law once again.

Our shortcut led across a bridge, or it would have if the structure had not been washed out. We consulted the photocopied map, dismayed that it only had a passing resemblance to Google's pixelated version, and ultimately took our best guess at which of the little tracks was the quickest route back to the lodge. We were making good time when we hit a massive rut, which was hidden by the long shadows thrown by the trees that lined the track through the lakeside forest. The RAV-4 shuddered at the impact. Obviously the front bumper had been knocked loose.

Painfully aware that I was leaving the safety of my vehicle—in the dark and in a park where lions were a star attraction—I got out and examined the damage with my flashlight. The bad news was that the bumper was definitely off. The good news was that this was clearly not the first time it had happened. Lying on the ground in the dim glow of the headlights and squinting up into the undercarriage of the vehicle, I could see the little loops of rusty wire that had been used before to repair this sort of damage. Their loose twists had been pulled apart by this latest impact. I was able to shove the bumper back into place and twist the wires tightly enough to hold it on again. Luckily for me, I'd managed to get the bumper back in place before becoming "carnivores d'oeuvres" for any large felines.

Despite all the stern warnings, we returned to the hotel after dark but with that particular exhilaration that comes from making it safely through a dodgy situation. Jayde grinned and confessed to me over dinner that as she watched me working in the glow of the car's headlights, she'd had visions of a stereotypical movie scene—the one where the hero, outside the vehicle and unaware of approaching danger, was suddenly struck down and eaten by some horrible creature while the heroine screamed in horror from the safety of the car's interior.

I laughed. Later, as I fell asleep in our little room, with its pair of respectably separate beds, I reflected that Jayde was an awesome traveling companion. Many people would have been considerably less sanguine about our little adventure than she'd been.

The following day, we drove south to Lake Naivasha, the next stop on our journey, while listening to podcasts and chatting amiably about a range of topics. Our object at Naivasha was to visit Hells Gate National Park, where it was possible to bike along the trails due to the absence of large predators, and Crescent Island, where a similar lack of big cats and hyenas meant we could actually walk freely among the herds of giraffes, wildebeests, and zebras.

It was late enough by the time we made it to Hells Gate that we opted to drive around the park rather than bike. Jayde shaved several years off my life by screaming at the shock of a huge black baboon jumping on the hood of the car, demanding treats that we did not have and that I would not have been inclined to hand out if we did. Unlike vervet monkeys, baboons were big and extremely strong. They also possessed incisors as large as those of lions, as we saw for ourselves at very close range.

Besides the aggressive troop of baboons, we didn't see many animals in the park, and we decided to park the car in favor of climbing a grassy green hill and watching the sunset from its summit. I'd stashed a couple of beers in my backpack, and it turned out that Jayde had nicked a whole wheel of brie cheese along with a handful of crackers from the breakfast buffet. I teased her about sustaining the stereotype of Australians, and as we watched the orange hues spread across the horizon, I contemplated asking her then and there if she was interested in being something more than friends.

But I decided to stick with my original plan and wait until we shared a safari tent in the Masai Mara National Reserve. *There would be plenty of time to have that conversation*, I thought, *and it might be better to delay the potential awkwardness if her answer was not affirmative.* We climbed down the darkening hillside in companionable silence, reaching our little SUV just as it began to get dark.

By now, breaking the second law was becoming second nature, but we made it safely to our hilltop Airbnb without incident and headed to bed as soon as we got there in anticipation of an early morning and a long day to come. We had a walking safari on Crescent Island at dawn and then a six-hour drive to the Masai Mara ahead of us, and I wanted to be well rested for them both.

　　　＊ ＊

I woke on my third day in Kenya to the familiar chirruping of birds and to something far less pleasant—the news that the Kenyan president had proclaimed a mandatory quarantine would take effect in forty-eight hours. All inhabitants would be sequestered in their homes for a COVID lockdown. All foreign travelers were ordered to leave the country or be put into fourteen days' isolation. It wasn't entirely unexpected, although I had thought the United States, not Kenya, would be ordering me to leave. And I remembered thinking about the worst-case scenario on the plane. I'd told myself then that one night would be better than none, and I'd gotten to spend a lot more than that with Jayde. Disappointment did not do justice to my feelings, and I dreaded breaking the news to her. I recalled something that the author Paul Theroux had written to the effect that in Swahili, the word "safari" simply referred to a journey and that to be "on safari" meant to be away and out of touch.[1] But in the modern world of cell towers and satellite phones, it was becoming increasingly hard to remain out of touch.

About half an hour later, the two of us sat on the floor together and had an informal crisis meeting to decide what we should do. I hated the idea of cutting short our travels and returning to South Sudan early, and Jayde suggested half-heartedly that we could probably push on. There was a good chance that given the remoteness of our destination in the Masai Mara, the decree wouldn't be enforced. And if it was, oh, well, we would be stuck together in good company in a gorgeous location for two weeks, and she didn't have any place that she really had to be. It was tempting, but I did have responsibilities. Even though my leave balance would have allowed me to extend my stay, the thought of getting stuck outside the mission during this challenging period wasn't something I felt I could risk.

So we gloomily decided the right call was to go back. The drive back to Nairobi airport was very quiet as the full scale of the global pandemic became suddenly much more immediate. Francisca was kind enough to allow us to return the RAV-4 early, and Kevin met us at the airport to pick it up. I wondered how their business would survive with so many tourists leaving Kenya.

One of the things I loved most about East Africa was the hospitality of its people. In the bustle of Jomo Kenyatta International Airport, full of distressed foreigners trying in vain to alter their travel plans, the kindness of strangers enabled us to change ours. My flight had been booked on Kenya's national airline to South Sudan right next door—a low-demand destination—and I easily changed it online. But Jayde's ticket home to Australia was another matter. She was booked on Qatar Airways, and signage in the airport indicated that their local ticketing partner was Swiss International Air Lines.

Not anymore.

The employee manning the Swiss booth, Dennis, told us the sign was old and that Qatar Airways could only be reached by phone. He gave us the number, and we got through only to discover that while they could change the ticket on the spot, they could only accept the substantial change fees via M-PESA, the Kenyan equivalent of PayPal. Of course, neither Jayde nor I had an M-PESA account. Dennis overheard our side of the conversation and offered to help. Jayde and I each maxed out the cash withdrawal on our credit cards, and Dennis took the stack of Kenyan shillings to a money changer, who credited Dennis's M-PESA account. Jayde called Qatar again and passed the phone to Dennis, who gave the agent his M-PESA information, and her ticket was rebooked. Dennis had no reason to take so much time out of his day to help us, and he refused to accept payment for his assistance. It was another example of the hospitality and kindness that I've found to be hallmarks of my interactions with ordinary people in Kenya and Uganda.

Jayde's flight was at midnight, and mine was early the next morning, so we enjoyed a last meal together by the rooftop pool of the Nairobi Four Points Hotel. I was sad to hug her goodbye, annoyed I'd never had the chance to tell her how I felt, and grateful she was heading home and toward safety as the pandemic escalated.

While the departure terminal was again eerily quiet, the flight to Juba was completely full. As I disembarked in Juba, I noticed that the SRSG was among the UN staff also returning from what would be one of the last Kenya Airlines flights to land in Juba for some time.

59 Calling It What It Is

[The Murle] will never be changed . . . they are just like that.
They will never live in harmony with anyone. Really, there
is only one solution . . . some would call it genocide.
—DINKA MAN SPEAKING TO NICHOLAS COGHLAN IN 2013

19 March 2020. The senior national representatives in the force had been given an opportunity to hear directly from the SRSG about the impact of the COVID pandemic on the mission's operations, to discuss issues of personnel movement and patrolling under the current circumstances, and to raise any questions we might have ourselves or on behalf of our contingents. When it was my turn to ask a question, I raised the issue of the recent massacres in Jonglei. "This is a three-part question," I began.

I saw Shearer's lips tighten. I suspected he had a good idea of what was coming, but he'd asked us to share our concerns freely and couldn't very well shut me down before I'd started.

"It's regarding the recent violence in Sector East. First, will we do any sort of review of the decision process that resulted in all those people being killed, displaced, and abducted? Second, what are we doing to get the stolen children back—that's a literal crime against humanity—and third, what are we doing to address the fact that tribal leaders have already indicated they intend to finish what they started in the next thirty to sixty days?"

The SRSG was not happy; it was obvious from the tone of his voice. "Well, first," he said, "I think we should give ourselves credit that it wasn't worse— that more people didn't get killed."

Yeah, just a few hundred, mate. I was making notes with my right hand, but in my lap—out of sight beneath the table—my left clenched into a tight fist as I sought to channel my growing anger.

"So, in answer to the first part, we won't review it now, because we're still in the middle of it. Yes, it's a crime against humanity, but we can't intervene with force. We have to help facilitate these people in working it out." The SRSG looked around the table. "Okay, who has another question?"

He'd completely dodged the topic of how the mission planned to prevent another round of violence before the coming rains would bring fighting to a halt, but now protocol constrained me from saying more. His answers reminded me that David Shearer was a politician, not a humanitarian. I really needed to stop being surprised when politicians lived up to the stereotype.

When the mini town hall meeting ended, I waited with the rest of the lieutenant colonels as the SRSG first, followed by the other senior civilian staff, then the generals, and finally the colonels left the room. When I filed out afterward among my peers, I was surprised to see General Tinaikar standing outside the door.

"Carp," he said, "you were right to ask that question. And the matter should be looked into. If you want to arrange an after-action report, you should do so. It will only be for the force. In time, the mission may do their own."

I thanked the force commander for his support. I also told him that I would arrange to carry out the review and would ask some other officers to join me to provide a fair assessment: the force provost marshal, since there were crimes involved, and those in the Intelligence Branch, which had failed us in this case. He said that sounded reasonable and advised I should do it as soon as possible.

I saluted and headed back to my office to plan the necessary patrols, feeling better than I had since my return from Kenya. *Action*, I thought, *is the best form of anger management.*

60 Everything Ravaged, Everything Burned

Every time civilians are deserted by the UN, rather
than protected, the civilians not only tend to suffer,
but of course the UN's credibility takes a body blow.
—PRINCE ZEID RA'AD AL HUSSEIN

24 March 2020. Overnight, Juba International had been closed to all passenger travel. The UN was still flying internally, though rumors were that this might soon be curtailed as well. In fact, I'd received a call from the provost marshal just twelve hours before telling me that we'd been dropped from the manifest, but I'd asked Sergeant Prasad to sort it out. He'd worked his usual magic. An hour later I had a call from the mission's air movement boss, John Pereira. "Come on down in the morning," he said. "We'll get you on that flight." It was still dark when I arrived at the airport with Colonel Hanrahan and Andreas, but the helicopter was already full of other peacekeepers—mostly South Korean engineers and Indian infantrymen—headed east.

In Pibor, we met three local contacts: the civil affairs rep, Ade, whom I remembered from my previous visit, and the military observers Lt. Col. Bakhtiyar Salimov from Azerbaijan and Lt. Col. Justin Silwenga from Zambia. I was happy to see another familiar face that stood out from and above the rest of the welcoming party. The tall, smiling language assistant Minny-Minny would be accompanying us north once more. Within fifteen minutes, we were in a couple of Land Rovers and headed toward Likaungole with a truck mounting a 7.62mm machine gun and carrying eight Indian soldiers trundling along behind us. Personally, I thought this level of force protection was unnecessary, but the Indian battalion had deemed it appropriate. *C'est la vie*, I thought.

The town of Pibor was much livelier than on my last visit, when the streets were full of armed men, the shops were closing down, and women were carrying their merchandise on their heads to the presumed safety of the area just outside the UN compound. Now the weapons were gone, which meant that the fighters were too. This was a worrying sign, as I suspected that it meant they were massing elsewhere for a revenge attack against the Nuer. *Or perhaps they are out raiding in small groups already.*

Passing the government building, I saw an odd sight that made me smile. Inside the fenced area in front of the building was a tiny group of antelopes: one buck, two does, and a fawn. I recalled that the historian Jared Diamond had written that gazelles such as these couldn't be tamed or kept captive, but he'd never visited Pibor in the dry season, I supposed.

Colonel Hanrahan was in the first Land Rover with Ade and Minny-Minny, while Andreas and I rode with the military observers. They both seem to be good officers, but neither had much knowledge of the local area due to the sector's current policy of rotating observers every thirty days.

The road was as I remembered it from before—hard and dry. It was past midday and we'd had no lunch. Although I was hungry, it would have been unseemly to mention it aloud as most people were hungry most of the time in this country, especially out here.

Dead cattle appeared regularly along the roadside, sometimes in the form of mummified corpses, their skin shrunken tightly from the heat. We saw few living things except for a small herd of six cows attended by four young men, who between them had one M-16-style assault rifle, one AK-47, and four spears. We waved and they smiled. Then we were gone, heading north along the dusty road.

At the Lilibok crossing, the water was gone, and a carcass of what was once a black cow sprawled on the shore. Justin remarked that last week when the force commander had visited, a dead woman was next to the cow and that General Tinaikar had ordered her buried. It seemed his command had been carried out.

We passed the village of Buzenga, which appeared to have been spared by the recent conflicts; its collection of small tukuls were not burned. Two adults and a gaggle of small children were present. The children smiled and waved; the older people did not. It occurred to me that for these people, the coronavirus on which the rest of the world's attention had focused was very far away, and that for them, it might as well not have existed. They were much more likely to die of malaria, starvation, or a bullet.

* *

Arriving in Likaungole, we were greeted by the honorable former county commissioner John Gogol. All the political figures with whom we had met in the countryside since the formation of the new government had identified themselves as "the former." This was a nod to the fact that while their positions had been officially dissolved by an edict from Juba, no one had yet been assigned to take their place, so they remained, unpaid, informally on the job.

The town was quiet, but when the gentle breeze blew from a certain direction, I thought I could smell something rotting—meat. I told myself that it was probably just another cow, similar to the one we had seen by the riverbed. John told us that the ICRC had come to take the bodies of the dead, but there were still two corpses here. It crossed my mind that there must have been an awful lot of bodies if the ICRC couldn't carry them all out in one trip. The dead lay in the shell of a burned hut, wrapped in white plastic bags, and our hosts pointed them out as we toured what was left of the ruined village on the way to our meeting place.

* *

Our discussion took place in a rough sort of longhouse, a charred wooden frame that had been reroofed with white tarps bearing a European Commission logo. About sixty people were in the structure, and some of the men were busy stringing hooks on fishing line when we arrived. Colonel Hanrahan, being from Canada, was no stranger to fishing. She sat down and helped tie on a handful of hooks, which earned her a few smiles and approving nods.

A very old man, the Murle paramount chief, arrived, and the meeting finally began. Several different agendas were in play. My party from Juba was here to collect information on the recent attacks and what could be done to prevent the next one. Ade was intent on getting the paramount chief's assistance in controlling the Murle fighters and returning previously stolen children to the Nuer, while the local leaders had more pressing concerns.

John began by saying they were disappointed in the UN response so far. "We expect more from you. We are already in a bad situation." He then gestured at the people around us. "They have nothing to eat. You cannot force people to work when they have nothing to eat." He clearly referenced previous UNMISS demands that the villagers clean up the wreckage of the village before we would consider putting a temporary base in the area—a base that John insisted was badly needed. "If UN troops were here, we wouldn't lose such numbers—the old men, women, and children."

It seemed this was not the first time that Ade and the UN military observers Salimov and Silwenga had heard this request. Ade sighed, "Is there anything else?"

This brought a bitter laugh from the paramount chief, whose name was Barcho Lual. He then asked rhetorically, "Do you see me as a ghost, or do you see me as a human being?"

No one answered.

"You don't ask the patient who's about to die, 'Where does it hurt?'" Lual continued, gesturing at the people around us. "The situation describes itself by your own eyes." He rubbed his stomach. "Please, feed me. I'm screaming with the pain and I'm half-dead."

None of us said anything, because what could we possibly say?

Lual said that he recalled the 2012 attacks, and in their aftermath, food was brought immediately. He had three requests for us: food, medicine to prevent cholera, and help in mediating the return of the stolen women and children.

Ade spoke, telling Lual that food and medicine would be provided to people in their home locations. He highlighted Manyabol and Pibor as places where supplies had already been delivered and promised that "gradually they are coming with food here."

Lual grimaced and said it would be too late. He was leaving today, he said. He would go south, across the Lotilla River to Jebel Boma, where things might be safe for an old man like him, where there would be food and medicine.

This was bad news for Ade, who had told us that Lual, the paramount chief of Greater Likaungole, was the spiritual leader of all the Murle. Ade had hoped to persuade him to participate in a "peace council" similar to the one Ade had coordinated with the Nuer in Pieri the previous week. I had my doubts about the efficacy of peace councils where only one side of the conflict was invited, but I held my tongue.

Lual seemed to share my feelings and said that he didn't believe that the Nuer had met to talk peace; he thought it was a strategy session for their next attack. As for his people, their children would have to be returned before they would consider negotiations. "For us to have face-to-face discussions with the Nuer," said Lual, "we must have our women and children." He fixed

Ade with a hard stare. "Pass this message: return the children to heal our hearts, and we can have peace."

A young man rose and began to speak. He was the representative of the youngest of the Murle age-sets that were involved in community defense and raids on neighboring tribes.[1] His words echoed those of his elder. "Next week, if you just bring the women and children, we won't try for the cows." He gestured at a few other young men standing at the edges of the small crowd—some holding spears, others with rifles casually slung. "We youths are the ones facing the others. Each one of us has family that has been taken. What will make us attack is if we don't get the children back." He made it clear that there was a fifteen-day window for the return of the stolen women and children, and after that, "someone who is angry" would take matters into their own hands.

When questioned about the most recent attacks, all the speakers—young and old—expressed their surprise about two things. The first was the severity and nature of the violence. They did not mind cattle raids—to their mind, those were normal—but they were shocked that the Nuer had attacked the village. "How can you burn the elderly people in their houses?" asked Lual. The young fighter added, "Cattle you can take, but you don't burn houses and cut down fruit trees!" The second thing that had upset them was the response of the ICRC, which had flown in three planes to evacuate the Nuer casualties but not the wounded Murle, three of whom were still here.

Our hosts took us to see one of these men, who lay in a grass shelter outside the burned remnants of the village, across a muddy field, and toward the edge of the river. The victim was on his back, his leg broken by a gunshot. It had been badly splinted, and Andreas, who was a doctor by profession, shook his head in dismay. On the man's other leg was another wound, a long, bloody trench crusted over by scabbing. Andreas said it was likely a grazing wound from a bullet or perhaps a spear. The man said nothing, seemingly unsurprised and uninterested in us. He just gazed at the hut's far wall and patiently waited for our inevitable departure.

Walking back to our vehicles, I asked John if they feared another attack.

"Yes," John said, "we are not sure of the time, but we think they will come back. The graffiti says they are coming back."

There was little left to say or do, so we headed back to Pibor. Evening was approaching, and tomorrow we had a very long drive ahead of us.

* *

We spent the night at Pibor, and I learned the difference between being stationed at one of the outlying bases as opposed to the large ones such as Juba, Bor, Wau, or Malakal. Here, there was no tukul or café for entertainment or refreshment. There was no cell phone signal, the buildings were in poor repair, and the HESCO walls of the base were crumbling.

At this sort of place, UN personnel and humanitarians no doubt rated a more generous sort of R&R to compensate for the true hardships and dangers they faced, which were far beyond those of Juba. Instead, they received the same rewards as their colleagues in the capital—people who had the benefit of bars, restaurants, hotel swimming pools, and supermarkets both on and off the base. The injustice made me ashamed. I clearly saw that by looking below the surface, the UN didn't truly believe its own declaration: "All human beings are born free and equal in dignity and rights."

After a restless night, we had another early morning, but this time, instead of flying, we were driving 124 miles to Bor and visiting Manyabol and Anyidi on our way. The road was deeply rutted but passable in our sturdy vehicles, and we reached what was left of Manyabol without incident. There, we surveyed ruins that looked similar to those in Likaungole and met with the former regional administrator, Marko Ngare; the former executive chief, Paul Konyi; and the women of the village. We were also expecting to meet with the long-duration patrol that was supposedly based there, but no UN vehicles or blue helmets were in sight.

"They were here on the day of the attack," said Paul, but after the villagers informed them that they had received warnings of an approaching group of Nuer raiders, the UN patrol had pulled out—only an hour before the assault commenced. He said that a new UN force had set up somewhere farther east.

"It would be better if your base was closer to the town center," Marko added with an incongruous smile. In his position, I would have been shouting, but what good would that have done?

Looking around, I wasn't sure why our peacekeepers weren't here, and I became even angrier that we had pulled our troops out last month instead of reinforcing them. The village—or what was left of it—sat on high ground with good fields of visibility and good fields of fire for the heavy guns mounted on our armored vehicles, and it was small enough to be defensible.

Paul and Marko took us to talk with some women who were working to put a sheet of white tarp over a wooden framework. The men translated as we asked the women what they needed. "Dignity kits," said one woman, while another pointed out that there were not enough tarps to roof all the shelters. They addressed themselves to Colonel Hanrahan, apparently happy to see a woman in uniform. They requested the presence of peacekeepers for protection, along with supplies of food and medicine. It had been five days since any food had been delivered, and they were surviving on wild plants and whatever fish they could catch from the Lotilla River, which was several miles to the south. We told them that we would do everything we could to get them what they asked for, and then, as had so many others, we departed, leaving the people of Manyabol to face the future on their own.

Three miles onward, we found the patrol base that the peacekeepers from Bor had established. It was nestled in a clump of small trees off the side of the road. While it seemed to be a comfortable campsite, it wasn't doing much for the people of Manyabol, and it wasn't a particularly good defensive position. When I asked the patrol leader why they were not set up near the village, he told me that his men felt badly about eating hot food, drinking clean water, sleeping in their tents, and relaxing between shifts on guard duty in front of the villagers.

I told him that I understood their sensitivity. Then I said that while I could not give him orders, my advice would be to move the patrol base closer to the village because that was the high ground, and if the UN forces were visible, it would reassure the villagers and deter would-be attackers. "That is what I will recommend to the sector commander and the force commander in my report, anyway," I said with a shrug, "unless I should hear from the operations officer in Bor tonight that you have already taken the initiative to do it yourself."

* *

When we returned to Juba, I turned in a detailed eight-page interim report on my patrol in Jonglei and promised to complete and deliver a more detailed analysis of the conflict as quickly as practical. The interim report listed twenty-six recommendations for improving security, communications, and mobility in Sector East, including establishing a long-duration patrol base at Likaungole, conducting a whole-of-mission effort to ensure the return of the stolen women and children, and preparing for at least one more round of attempted attacks by tribes in the area.

To my great surprise, the report seemed to have an effect. Sector East was authorized to establish a temporary base at Likaungole. It would be coordinated and integrated with the other pillars of the mission, but the force would be the lead. That was a welcome change.

* *

Unchanged was that the coronavirus hadn't been reported in the country yet or in UNMISS. That was good, as South Sudan's medical establishment had a grand total of four ventilators, and UNMISS had received fewer than two hundred COVID test kits.

But everyone was waiting for the other shoe to drop. The widespread belief was that the virus was already in the country but that nothing would be announced until UNMISS had its first case. That would allow the government to say, "See, this is a problem brought in by UN," thus justifying putting additional restrictions on our freedom of movement.

61 Juggling Act

> We have therefore made the assessment that COVID-19 can be
> characterized as a pandemic. . . . Pandemic is not a word to use
> lightly or carelessly. . . . We have never before seen a pandemic
> sparked by a coronavirus. . . . And we have never before seen a
> pandemic that can be controlled.
>
> —DR. TEDROS ADHANOM GHEBREYESUS,
> DIRECTOR GENERAL OF THE WHO

12 April 2020. The shoes dropped quickly, one after another. Citing the need
to protect our personnel and to contain the spread of the coronavirus, the
UN secretary-general directed on 4 April that all troop rotations would be
suspended until 30 June. That represented a significant delay for my planned
return to the United States the following week. Then it was announced that
South Sudan's first COVID case had been recorded in a UN staff member.

USMOG wanted our rotations to go as planned. Several of us had retirements scheduled—myself included—and Colonel Larson's position was
that a mandatory retirement date and a memo from the U.S. secretary of
defense stating that retirements would go on regardless of COVID trumped
UN policies. I had to tactfully explain that getting flights out of the country
was nearly impossible. Even the embassy staff was struggling to move their
people. The secretary-general's order *did* make provisions for exceptional
cases, and the United States was not the only nation that wanted such an
exception made. Norway, Canada, and Australia—all had staff officers that
they wanted to bring in, and the Korean engineers were still anxious to get
their rotation underway.

It became a high-stakes exercise in coordination and conciliation, and a
prime example of the importance of senior national officers during times of
international crisis. All of us were obliged to carry out the wishes of both
our national governments and the mission. In ordinary times, those desires

were generally in alignment, which allowed us to stay focused on our day jobs, but during an emergency, all of us had to start juggling conflicting sets of orders from our two different chains of command and focusing on "the art of the possible."

We also had to contend with South Sudan's own high-level task force on COVID-19. Led by First Vice President Riek Machar, the task force was required to approve all travel into, out of, and through the country. General Herlyng had asked me to handle the mission's coordination with the COVID task force, and I'd cleared the first hurdle of getting the mission to request an exception for twelve staff officers and the entire Korean engineering battalion. Now it was just a matter of waiting for a response. And I had found a new reason to be quite patient and willing to wait as long as it might take.

62 Love in the Time of Coronavirus

The human being is a social beast . . . we need
social distancing, but also social contact.
—GEN. BJØRN GAUTE HERLYNG

29 May 2020. By now, COVID had well and truly hit South Sudan, which had
481 cases reported so far but, thankfully, only six deaths. Deadlier threats
were in the land. A lioness had killed seven people near Rumbek, but lions
were less to be feared than men.

Hundreds of people had been killed, abducted, and sexually assaulted
in the course of just one month, many of them during the government's
ongoing scorched-earth campaign against NAS in Central Equatoria. Also,
Jonglei's director for wildlife conservation, Maj. Gen Mawut Wuoy, noted
that people were killing thousands of game animals for food. If the situation
continued, he warned, the herds might be wiped out, and his game war-
dens were powerless to stop it. "We cannot effectively protect our animals
because we lack funds. There is no means of transport and civilians are
more armed than us."

That was a valid excuse for General Wuoy, I supposed, but the same could
not be said of UNMISS. We failed to stop the violence in the Equatorias
because we continued to allow the government to dictate the movement of
our patrols. "Maybe it's not as bad as Srebrenica, but it's heading in the same
direction," General Herlyng observed. "The history in a few years will show
that there was burning, killing, and rape right outside a UN base." Everyone
knew, still no one did anything. The idea that we needed to intervene was
a dead horse that I continued to beat in our staff meetings but with no
greater effect than before.

If anything, matters seemed worse. In most human conflicts, it was pro-
verbially observed that winners write the history books, but in South Sudan's
on-again, off-again war without winners, I plainly saw that UNMISS intended

to ensure that the historical record reflected a deliberately biased version of events that showed itself in the best light and not as the bystander that it was. I first saw this occurring as I reviewed the draft version of the latest secretary-general's report, where I noted a significant discrepancy between the numbers being reported in the "children and armed conflict" section and those listed in the "monitoring and investigating human rights violations" section.

I brought the matter to the attention of Alfred Orono Orono, the chief of the mission's Child Protection Unit, and pointed out the reason for the mismatched numbers: the child victims of the fighting in Jonglei weren't being counted. I thought it was just an oversight but was shocked when Orono told me that the 194 abducted children and the 25 killed or injured during the fighting in Jonglei from February through May did not need to be listed as having suffered "grave violations against children." He claimed there was a difference between abductions of children as covered by UN Security Council Resolution 1612 and those related to intercommunal violence.[1] The big difference seemed to be that UNMISS would get a pass from the oversight organizations focused on children that might otherwise have taken some action. These 219 dead, injured, and stolen children disappeared from the records. No mention was made of them in the secretary-general's report on children and armed conflict for the period.[2]

Though I brought the matter to the attention of the senior officers from Canada and Norway, the force's legal adviser, and the SRSG's military adviser, nothing changed. The mission seemed intent on ensuring that a few hundred dead and missing children would not tarnish its record on protecting children.

* *

I was beyond frustrated and not really in the mood to be around other people. But earlier in the week, I had accepted an invitation to an Easter weekend potluck dinner, and I figured that it would be rude not to at least show up, bring a dish, and stay for half an hour or so. The pandemic had brought changes to the routine on base. No longer did people gather in large groups at the tukul for weekend parties; instead, they met in smaller groups at their bungalows. Thomas, a tall infantry officer from Norway, hosted the dinner, and I'd arrived carrying a platter of squid that I'd sauteed in garlic butter. Hours later, the food was gone, along with several bottles of red wine and many beers. One of the Australian officers—Jess—had brought a hookah pipe, and sweet, pungent smoke perfumed the porch where we drank, talked, played cards, and listened to songs by Cold Chisel and Missy Higgins.

I'd ended up sitting next to Beatrix, a vivacious redhead from the United Kingdom who worked in JMAC, and I agreed to go hiking with her the following day. We were both training for NORCON—a twenty-two-mile hike run by the Norwegian contingent—and as with many things decided over a bottle of wine, an early morning march carrying heavy packs sounded like a good idea at the time. As the party progressed, I felt a definite tension building between us, and when we left the party together, a kiss in the darkness at the intersection of our paths confirmed that it had not just been my imagination. But we left it at that—a single kiss.

* *

The following morning, I woke up late and was enjoying a lazy stretch when I realized that I was late for the planned hike. I threw on my uniform and boots, grabbed my pack, and headed to the meeting point. Beatrix was not there, nor was anyone else. We had not been the only people at the party who'd claimed they planned to hike off their hangovers, but I was twenty minutes late, so I figured perhaps they had left without me. I took a swig of water, tightened the straps on my pack, and stepped off onto the red dirt of the road, determined to make the best of it since I was already awake. My phone buzzed with a WhatsApp message from Beatrix.

"Well, fuck. Did you make it?"

I replied that I'd only just made it to the starting point and asked if she still wanted to hike.

"I'll come. I'm hungover as fuck, though."

That spirit was one of the things I'd found so attractive about her. We spent the next ninety minutes hiking twice around the perimeter of the camp, a distance of about six miles. Then we spent the afternoon making lunch, making love, and reading chapters aloud from *The Sisters Brothers*, a novel in which cattle theft, artisanal gold mining, and violence committed by armed civilians were features of society in the western United States, circa 1851.

* *

Deep conversations were something I enjoyed sharing with Beatrix, and one of the things we talked about was the comparisons to be made between

South Sudan in the present and the American West in the late 1800s. Both had a lot in common: ethnically motivated attacks by non-state groups, scorched-earth campaigns by government forces against tribal groups (often for the purposes of gaining access to resources), cattle as a form of cash and source of conflict, widespread access to firearms, and so on. Levels of violent death were high in both cases. We hypothesized that improved infrastructure—railways, roads, communication links—along with education and increased restrictions on firearms (especially rapid-fire weapons) were responsible for the significant decline in violence in the western United States from 1870 to 1930. We felt that if UNMISS did more to pave roads, promote education, and disarm the population, the mission would become more effective in protecting civilians.

＊ ＊

My final month in the mission was a surreal time. Work was perhaps as tedious as it had ever been and filled with extra administrative burdens from both USMOG and the mission—the price I paid for the privilege of being the senior American at the end of an unusual rotation. But my evenings, early mornings, and weekends were filled with the joy of being unexpectedly and passionately in . . . something. Love? Perhaps. Beatrix and I didn't put a name to what we had.

We had a shared love for literature; that was certain. After moving on from *The Sisters Brothers*, I read her passages from Italo Calvino's *Invisible Cities* while we lazed about in bed. Later she read me chapters from *The War of Don Emmanuel's Nether Parts*, Louis de Bernières's incredible work of magic realism, as I cooked breakfast: coffee, eggs, sauteed green vegetables, and toasted French bread.

Hours spent with Beatrix were many things. We laughed watching *Rick and Morty*, cried when a beloved character in a novel died tragically. We talked about our reasons for choosing lives of military service, and I thought her answer was fantastic.

"When I was a girl," she said, "I always wanted to be a knight. People told me that I couldn't, but now I have a sword and I serve the Queen, so I think that I've rather proved them wrong."

We talked about plans for the future—hers to live on a canal boat, mine to travel the world in a tiny van—but we didn't address the question of whether those futures might include each other. Instead, I simply delighted in the unexpected pleasure of her company, living fully in the present whenever we were together.

* *

The waiver from UN Headquarters to bring in a small contingent of staff officers was approved, and the high-level task force gave its authorization as well. The Australians decided on waiting to rotate their officers, while the American, Norwegian, and Canadian officers got as far as Addis Ababa before being blocked from boarding the Ethiopian Airlines plane for the final leg of their trip into Juba.

Although their paperwork was all in order and Riek Machar himself had signed their approvals, the NSS officer who controlled Juba's airport thwarted their arrival. So they went into quarantine in Ethiopia, while I worked with the mission staff and the international community to get them past this newest obstruction. Our officers weren't the only ones impacted. An UNPOL officer, six UNMISS civilians, five ICRC workers, and nineteen MSF volunteers also had their travel delayed.

Two weeks and much negotiating later, my replacement—Lt. Col. Sean Moore—along with the rest of those whose transit through Ethiopia had been interrupted, finally made it into Juba. The new arrivals went straight into quarantine—again—which delayed my own departure by yet another two weeks. I wasn't bothered. It was a pleasant reprieve from having to face my own quarantine in the United States and from dealing with the realities of leaving first Beatrix and then the Marine Corps. In my journal, I wrote: "It occurs to me to wonder if this is the end of the last big adventure—the last time that I'm a part of something greater than myself."

63 Such Sweet Sorrow

> It wasn't necessary for me to say much to Phil. He understood
> how guilty I felt abandoning my troops before the mission
> was over, how guilty I felt that I had failed so many people
> and that Rwandans were still dying because of it.
>
> —GEN. ROMÉO DALLAIRE

8 June 2020. My last day in the mission seemed to move too quickly at times and too slowly at others. Beatrix had arrived after midnight and tumbled into bed laughing. "I've been dancing for three hours," she said by way of explaining her damp body, and we were soon snuggled up and sleeping. My alarm went off before dawn, and while Beatrix slept, I finished cleaning and packing and taking care of all the small details to put the little bungalow in order for my successor. I managed to get back into bed for a little cuddling and kissing before getting shaved, showered, and dressed for work.

At the end of his morning meeting, General Tinaikar honored my departure with a heartwarming speech. The quote that stood out in my mind was his observation that "it's not easy to be a nonconformist in any organization—but especially not the military." He went on to praise me for always speaking up and for being "the conscience of the force," and then he gave me a fatherly hug. It was—at least for me—a very touching moment. When the force commander went to his meeting with the SRSG, I was left to say farewell to General Herlyng, who handed me one of his personal coins and a small book titled *Brown Cheese Please*, which he said would help me understand Norwegians a little better.

For tea, I held an impromptu ceremony at the tukul, where I gave out the force commander's commendation letters to Maj. Himadri Roy and Sergeant Prasad and received small going-away gifts from them: chocolates, coins, and a little statue of a meditating elephant. There were hugs and handshakes all around.

One of my colleagues was mysteriously absent. When I texted, "Elevenses?" she replied in the affirmative.

It was past 11:30 a.m. before I made it to Beatrix's place for lunch, carrying bags full of frozen goods and vegetables to gift her. I had to be back at my house to sign over equipment by 12:30 p.m., so we ate the delicious shrimp and noodles that she'd prepared, hugged and cuddled and kissed, and then hugged some more. Neither of us were crying—we were laughing instead—but a shadow of sadness was definitely in our smiles.

We had no time for a more intimate farewell. Instead, I blew a kiss and walked back to my house for a flurry of last-minute packing and cleaning. I also needed to change into my travel clothes and to sign my pistol, ammunition, and some communications gear over to Sean.

Soon I was squeezed into the passenger seat of our SUV, making the drive from UN House to the airport for the last time. Sergeant Prasad was at the wheel; Emm and Christopher—who were leaving with me—were in the back seat. We passed boys leading cows and a young man carrying goods for sale—some shirts and a pair of wallets. *What are the odds*, I wondered, *that he will sell some? Will he eat if he doesn't?*

I looked out the window for signs of hope for the future. There were more paved roads now than when I arrived, more bricks being made. It was not much of a sign, but it would have to be enough.

* *

Ethiopian Airlines flight 355 was running late. As I waited for its arrival in an almost-empty terminal, I was again conscious of a sense of loss, a sense of unfinished business. Usually at the end of a deployment as a Marine, you rotated home with your whole unit, all of your colleagues. But now I was leaving my unit in South Sudan and, with it, many friends—and a woman with a strong hold on my heart.

Moreover, I felt as if I were leaving a part of myself behind in a country that deserved much better than I'd been able to give it. A country of crushing human poverty and of great natural wealth. A country of red dirt, brown rivers, green trees, and blue skies as far as the eye could see. A country of bright dresses and brighter smiles. A country of sad donkeys pulling dilapidated water carts, weary militiamen riding battle-scarred technicals, and corrupt politicians in gleaming new Escalades. It was everything all at once, and I felt as if I was leaving it forever.

The past three months had been a rollercoaster. Hundreds of people were dead, hundreds more were missing, and those losses weighed heavily on my conscience—all the more so because my own life seemed so charmed. I'd traveled widely, found love, and done all I could to save lives, to help the less fortunate, and to ensure that the mistakes we'd made would not be repeated. But had it been enough?

Sitting in silence, I contemplated the answer to that question, reviewing everything that had happened since I'd gone toe to toe with the SRSG and lost the battle to convince him to make "robust, proactive, and nimble" something more than empty words. The Roman philosopher Cicero once mused on whether his country was to have "peace without honor, or war with its calamities," and it seemed to me that the people of South Sudan and the military forces of UNMISS had managed to have both at the same time—with the civilians bearing all the calamities and the UN sacrificing our honor on the altar of political expedience.

* *

On the last leg of the flight to Dulles, I wrote in my journal: "It's now hitting me that my mission, and a really big part of my life is coming to an end, and with it a realization of how lucky I was to have the group of friends that I did. I wonder if I will ever have that again."

PART 4

The Long Road Back

64 The Bitter End?

Memoirs end in the middle. You can't just say "they
all died," or "they lived happily ever after."
—DR. ELISABETH MCKETTA

6 November 2021. This story could have ended when I stepped onto the
Ethiopian Airlines DHC-8 in Juba for the long flight back to the United
States. My assignment was over, and once out of South Sudan, I technically
had no further obligations to the people there.

I'd left the U.S. contingent better than I'd found it from a logistical perspective, having helped to improve the C2 structures of the force and to
lay the groundwork for patrols that were better supported with women
and language assistants, that were better equipped for the terrain and the
weather, and that went where they were most needed and stayed there
longer. That's what had been written in my performance evaluations, at
any rate, along with glowing recommendations from colonels and generals. "I would enthusiastically recommend his promotion to Colonel at the
earliest opportunity . . . a great nominee for another assignment with the
UN . . . a strong officer who could continue to serve in Multinational and
Joint Positions."

But in my mind, in all the ways that counted, my time in South Sudan
had been a failure. I had set out to aid others with a genuine if naive belief
that through my diligent efforts, I could help the people of South Sudan
attain their most basic human rights. I wasn't required to raise their standard
of living, but I was charged with preventing them from being murdered,
abducted, or starved to death; with keeping them from being sexually
assaulted and tortured; and with helping support the creation of political
and social institutions that might give them some agency in their own lives.
That was all. Yet, I felt that I had failed to achieve even that much. I realized
that I could not consider the journey on which I had embarked in 2019 to

be complete until I could point to some positive change, some progress, in the core mandate area—the protection of civilians. But how?

Writing candidly about what I'd seen and done and what I believed still needed to be accomplished was something I could do. After all, I was an experienced writer. Throughout my career, I'd often written in professional forums about topics such as gender integration in the U.S. Marines and had won acclaim for my book on military ethics. But while in uniform, I had also found my freedom of speech was curtailed on politically sensitive topics such as the U.S. military's 2015 attack on the MSF hospital in Kunduz, Afghanistan.

There, an American AC-130 gunship had pounded the medical center with heavy weapons for over an hour, ignoring the desperate text messages and phone calls from doctors on the ground. It was a mistake, said American generals, politicians, and lawyers, and not a war crime as the Geneva Convention defined it. Personally, I felt the deliberate destruction of a civilian hospital and the murders of forty-two medical staff, patients, and their family members were more than just "a mistake."

"You are officially cleared to submit that to the *Washington Post*," a military lawyer had told me after he reviewed the editorial I'd written on the Kunduz massacre. "That's my official opinion. But you shouldn't expect to ever get promoted again if it gets printed."

I'd thought hard about it and had decided at the time that I could still do more good inside the system than outside it. Then I'd put the draft aside and put the mask back on, once again the good soldier, once again the good dog.

But now I was retired. Now I was off the leash.

65 For the Record

> Overall, a break remains in the "chain" of activities designed to
> protect civilians. . . . Interpretation of mandates by mission leaders
> is a critical element in how robustly or conservatively protection of
> civilians is approached. . . . The effectiveness of mission leadership
> varies. . . . The chain remains broken with regard to the use of force.
> —UN OFFICE OF INTERNAL OVERSIGHT SERVICES REPORT, 2014

23 June 2020. I had clicked the blue "send" button in Gmail and closed the
book on my final task for the force headquarters, having written my full
report on the massacres in Jonglei that included a list of recommendations
for how such tragedies could be prevented in the future. The report was
nineteen pages long, and its concluding sections highlighted the issues
UNMISS needed to address. The root of the problem as I saw it was that the
SRSG didn't believe that intercommunal violence was "our job to prevent";
thus, there appeared to have been no mission-wide mobilization to engage
with key leaders in all three communities.[1] I wrote:

> Until the most senior levels of Mission and Force leadership realize that
> intercommunal violence is the leading threat to civilians, and thus the
> major focus of our mandated tasks, we can expect to see the planning
> for and response to such attacks marginalized. . . . At the earliest signs
> of mobilization (which existed for at least 2 weeks prior) a massive effort
> by all Mission pillars should have been made to intervene with Lou Nuer,
> Dinka Bor, and Murle leadership to eliminate the perception that violence
> and crimes against humanity could be visited on the people of Jonglei
> State with impunity.

I highlighted that intelligence and information gathering remained stove-
piped—that the JMAC, the Intelligence Branch, and the Joint Operations

Center did not cooperate sufficiently—and that for once, the only party preventing UNMISS from conducting aerial reconnaissance was UNMISS itself.

The South Sudanese government hadn't attempted to prevent us from flying in Jonglei. Instead, our own internal Risk Assessment Committee had repeatedly denied requests from the force to conduct reconnaissance flights to locate the White Army and discover what was happening in the vast savannas between Akobo and Pibor. Risk assessment is important in aviation. I had spent most of my own career in that branch of the military and understood the consequences of failure all too well. But risk is calculated based on the severity and likelihood of an incident, and the mission's own matrix had deemed the likelihood of our helicopters being shot down as "highly unlikely" given that no such attacks had occurred in sixteen years. So while the severity of such an event would have been catastrophic, when going by our own standards to judge the overall risk, conducting such flights would have fallen well within acceptable criteria. We had no excuses.

The report also noted that the force itself had several problems to address. We had failed to perform minor engineering projects, such as bridging the Lilibok crossing, and to procure vehicles that would enhance our mobility. Also, in areas where refugees or armed militias were able to move on foot, our well-trained infantry had no excuse for being unable to do the same— even without taking into account our massive advantage in aircraft and tracked vehicles.

> It is less than 8 kms [5 miles] from the Lilibok Crossing to Likaungole, but our mechanized forces treat a stream that is regularly waded across by civilians as an insurmountable obstacle.

Further, I pointed out that we didn't seem to be learning from our most recent mistakes. History instead continued to repeat itself with deadly results for the civilians we were mandated to protect.

> While this report is focused on the February violence, a failure to reform our processes and procedures since then has led to another round of intercommunal violence; the Murle counterattacks in May and Dinka Bor attacks in June were both predicted by the reports and documents used to create this report, but little was done to take action, and once again, Early Warning was ignored and aerial reconnaissance foregone.

I ended the report with the observation that "had the Mission and the Force actually acted in a 'proactive, robust, and nimble' manner at any point in the lead-up to these events, it is likely that significant death and damage could have been avoided." I then provided seven concrete recommendations to improve matters. These recommendations seemed to me no more than common sense, a bare minimum upon which to build a more resilient mission:

1. Participate in standing up the "Whole of Mission Approach in addressing major POC issues" as previously discussed with Chief CAD [Civil Affairs Division], with the following caveats:
   a. The "Mission Task Force" should not be a single entity stood up when violence happens, but there should be an active working group for, at a minimum, the GPAA [Greater Pibor Administrative Area] and Tonj/Lakes that meet regularly to review developments and execute programs to prevent violence from occurring.
   b. These should be "action officer level" groups (for Force, LtCols—for other pillars, a civilian/police equivalent).
   c. Performance should be measured based on monthly/weekly statistics for violence against civilians, including killings, abductions, and rapes.
   d. Product of the working group should be 1-2 slides, similar in format to the example in this report from SEAST [Sector East], showing the locations of the major actors, and noting what is being done and what needs to be done.
2. Perform a review of the SEAST Contingency Plan for Intra-communal violence. If no such plan exists, direct that it be developed immediately. It is not enough that the Sector have such a plan; the Field Office must have one as well—much as there are Mission-level plans for contingencies in Juba, there should be the same in Sectors; with specific triggers for hand-off from civil/police to military control of crisis. This should also be done for SWEST, certainly, and potentially for SUNITY and SNORTH as well.
3. Task an officer in FHQ to develop a review like this one for the dry-season violence in SWEST, which was more sporadic and less organized than the 2020 Jonglei Massacre but has still cost the lives of hundreds

of civilians, and a review will likely show similar trends; that we knew well in advance where the violence would happen and failed as an institution to put the required Force presence into the specific villages where UN presence would have deterred violence.

4. Task an officer in FHQ to update this report, or use it as a basis for an expanded report encompassing the follow-on attacks in May and June, with especial attention to what actions, if taken in March/April following the investigations of CAD, FHQ, and HRD could have forestalled the subsequent attacks.

5. Direct a full review of the current Aviation Risk Management (ARM) Process be conducted by a cross-cutting team, to include MSD [Mission Support Division] and other relevant parties. Specifically, the composition of the Risk Assessment Committee must be examined, as well as whether the current written procedures are being followed.

6. Engage with the Mission, specifically the Child Protection Unit, Gender, and HRD to determine what will be done to extract the hundreds of abducted women and children from sexual slavery, forced marriages, etc.

7. Engage with the Mission to reform the current structure of HOFO as "Area Security Coordinator," with a mechanism to ensure that military crises are handled in a more appropriate and successful manner.

I forwarded the document to General Tinaikar, General Herlyng, and Colonel Hanrahan, with a note of apology for taking so long to finish the write-up. I added a postscript:

While I have left the Mission, I remain with you in spirit—I know this is a challenging time in the world as a whole, and in South Sudan in particular. I know there are no easy answers in Jonglei, but I am hopeful that you will be able to leverage some of the observations and recommendations in this report to make the best possible decisions vis-à-vis this troubled area in the weeks and months to come.

General Tinaikar replied, "Thanks a lot, Ed. Appreciate your efforts and more, the passion you bring to your work."

Colonel Hanrahan wrote back as well, saying that she hoped the mission would take heed of the recommendations. "Though targeted towards Jonglei, for the most part," she wrote, "these recommendations would be relevant in the whole of the country."

Those replies gave me hope that all the work—the days spent on the ground interviewing victims of the violence and the long hours researching and writing the report—had not been in vain and that, finally, the mission would learn from its mistakes of the past.

66 August and Everything After

> For years this Marine has stood the watch. . . . For years he stood
> watch so that our fellow countrymen could sleep soundly, in safety,
> knowing that this Marine would stand the watch. Today we are here
> to say—the watch stands relieved. Relieved by those you have led,
> guided and trained. Marine, you stand relieved. We have the watch.
> —"THE WATCH"

13 August 2020. I had donned my uniform for the final time and stood in front of Colonel Larson and a small group of my USMOG colleagues in a nondescript conference room in the Taylor Building as Koz read out the final lines of the poem that U.S. Marines have long used to bid farewell to those departing the service. Along with my camouflage fatigues and combat boots, I had worn the N-95 mask that had become ubiquitous in this time of COVID. The gathering was small, the ceremony short, and as the final bars of the "Marines' Hymn" played, I left the profession of arms, which had been my home for almost three decades. I found myself again a civilian—a title I had not carried for twenty-nine years—and the very sort of person that I had, until very recently, a mandate to protect.

Now I had no one to protect but myself, and that was an odd feeling. Additionally, with this transition out of the formal leadership roles that I had occupied for almost three decades, I wasn't responsible for anyone else either. I felt very much alone in the world. My correspondence with Beatrix had waned over time since my return to the States. In one of my recent journal entries, I'd written that I felt "a sense of what the loss of her friendship would be like, and recollections of thoughts on whether happiness—whether home—might be a person and not a place." But I didn't tell her about those thoughts. Instead, I wrote in an email:

I've been feeling a tad blue lately, nothing I can really put a finger to, probably missing the mission and my friends in general and you in particular if I'm being quite honest.... But I think I can be just a bit manic-depressive at times, and I'm probably on a down period.... I think I get this way around times of change, when everything's a bit in limbo.

I received no answer. That didn't do much to lift my mood, but in fairness, not much seemed to be doing that these days. Also in fairness, cheering me up wasn't her responsibility; she had a real job in the mission. Anyway, the difficulty sleeping and concentrating were attributable, I thought, to my change of routine.

When I was filling out my disability assessment paperwork, the caseworker from the Veterans of Foreign Wars asked me if I wanted to fill out the additional form to be evaluated for post-traumatic stress disorder (PTSD). "No, thanks," I replied. "I don't think that's an issue for me."

* *

What continued to be an issue for me was the feeling that I had unfinished business in South Sudan. I had applied for some jobs with humanitarian agencies such as the Danish Refugee Council and hadn't been hired right away, but they asked to keep my résumé on file for future consideration. While I continued to look for a way back to South Sudan, I planned to live quietly on my retirement and disability pensions, focus on volunteer service work, and do some solo traveling as I sought to catch up with family and friends in the United States and around the world. The places I most wanted to visit were not, in general, big cities but the wild places, where the greatest threat to life and limb was not my fellow humans. That was good, since the COVID pandemic had revealed that in many countries, self-interest and science denial were combining to make ordinary people a threat to themselves and those around them.

My odyssey began with a visit to my sister Charli in Amherst, Massachusetts, where I again crossed paths—more by accident than design—with Jayde, who was on a road trip from New York to Maine with a friend. They stopped in Amherst to join Charli and me for a weekend rafting trip, and by the end of the visit, Jayde had decided to join me on my planned journey's next leg, which was to explore Alaska. A month later, on the porch of a log cabin overlooking a pasture full of reindeer, I finally got around to asking her the question I'd meant to voice on the Masai Mara seven months earlier: did she want to continue our travels as something more than friends? It took a while for her to give a definitive answer—almost two months in fact—but when she did, the answer was yes.

* *

In the meantime, Jayde and I had gone our separate ways. I hiked the Grand Tetons, volunteered with Team Rubicon in Hurricane Laura recovery efforts in Texas, and visited family around the country. I also finally admitted to myself that I'd unlikely be able to renew a romantic relationship with Beatrix despite never actually raising the question with her. I should have initiated the conversation face-to-face months before, but I hadn't. And when Jayde finally decided to take a chance on me, I chose to let go of what might have been and focus on what could be, allowing myself to be completely open to sharing my life with another person.

I did spend the next twelve months traveling, but it was not the solo trip that I had planned. While I often found myself in wild places—the Amazon jungles, the mountains of Croatia, and the forests of Estonia—I was not alone. It turned out that home was indeed a person and not a place, a person who listened to my stories and encouraged me to tell them, a person who—like me—was interested in leveraging the power of the written word and electronic media to change the world for the better. I told Jayde that I wasn't sure what I was going to do next. I might want to return to the UN as a volunteer or work for a humanitarian organization. I wondered aloud whether getting a doctorate in peace and conflict studies would be a better option or whether I should focus on some more technical aspect of development and help build the infrastructure that I believed would be key to ending the violence.

"Whatever you decide," she said, "I'll support you."

67 Admiring the Problem

UNMISS needs to be restructured to have oversight
responsibility of the DDR process since it has direct
impact on the peace and security of the country.
—BRIG. GEN. TAEF UL HAQ, SECTOR UNITY COMMANDER IN 2020

15 December 2020. The report of the Independent Strategic Review of UNMISS
was released while I was getting ready to fly to Germany for another Christmas with my niece. Hoping to see signs of progress, I made it a point to
occasionally check the UN's web page where the secretary-general's updates
and other reports were posted. I wanted to know if my report had made
a difference and whether things were improving for the people I had left
behind. I was keen to find out what changes El-Ghassim Wane, the veteran diplomat who led the review, would recommend in the way UNMISS
implemented its mandate, especially regarding the protection of civilians.

The report listed several important barriers to a successful mission in
South Sudan. It noted the government and other actors violated the mission's
freedom of movement, naming this "the single most important factor limit-
ing the Mission's ability to carry out its mandated activities"; yet, the report
offered no recommendation to enforce the mission's right to move without
government interference. It also mentioned the poor infrastructure—"only
200 kilometers [124 miles] of paved road in a country roughly the size of
France"—but made no recommendations to improve the roads and bridges.[1]

The report spent a whole page talking about *how* the force was conducting its patrols without noting that despite concepts that sounded good
on paper—such as hub-and-spoke deployments and integrated patrols—
civilians were not actually being protected. They were, in fact, dying in
ever higher numbers.

Those numbers clashed with the kind words that General Tinaikar had
sent me in an exchange of holiday cheer. "Hub and Spoke has caught on,"

he wrote, "and our presence in the field has started making a difference. This is your singular contribution to the Mission."

If that was my singular contribution, I would have hoped to see that it was actually doing more to end the violence against civilians, but it wasn't. More disturbingly, the independent review had attempted to shift the blame for any failures of the patrolling plan away from the leaders of the mission and on to the troop-contributing countries, stating that "much of the contingent-owned equipment that is deployed with troops is underutilized because much of it is not fit for the environment. Moreover, many troop-contributing countries are unable to operate as self-sustaining units when deployed to remote areas."[2]

I had personally seen Mongolian, Ethiopian, Nepalese, Bangladeshi, Ghanaian, and Indian troops deploy successfully to remote areas, so this assessment rang false to me. Yes, more types of specialized equipment would help, and both my colleagues in the Logistics Branch and I had worked hard to get them, but such equipment, while nice to have, was not a necessity. In my experience, the biggest obstacle to implementing effects-based patrols was not the lack of equipment but the lack of political will among mission leaders. That included the will to make better use of equipment already in the mission—such as the ATVs that served as personal transports at UN House and the boats that sat unused by the Indian battalion in Bor—and, more importantly, the will to push past government checkpoints and to use our engineering assets to build bridges and pave roads.

I was happy to see that the report did highlight several other issues—particularly that aid workers had "raised concerns about the consistency of the UNMISS response to emergencies in which humanitarian actors requested the protection of their personnel and compounds at field locations."[3] Those concerns were valid. In 2020 nine civilian aid workers had been killed in South Sudan: three in one incident, two in another, and the rest dying alone. But unlike the attacks on the humanitarians living in the Terrain Compound in 2016, these later attacks provoked no public outcry, no international media coverage, and no investigations.

Why? Probably because those people were local hires, South Sudanese nationals. Their government didn't care, their employers preferred to keep quiet, and the UN certainly had no interest in highlighting that it was failing not only to protect civilians but also to fulfill one of its other core mandate tasks—to create conditions conducive to the delivery of humanitarian assistance. In fact, more than 450 incidents of humanitarian operations being constrained were reported in 2020, illustrating another case where things were getting worse, not better.

The last big disappointment was the report's recommendation that UNMISS should not play an operational or logistical role in supporting either SSR or the process of DDR. The report did so despite noting that "the majority of South Sudanese stakeholders consulted during the review process advocated an increased technical assistance role for UNMISS, in particular for security sector reform, disarmament, demobilization and reintegration, and the rule of law, as well as support for building roads, constructing other types of infrastructure and providing other types of direct and material support."

Indeed, while Wane acknowledged that "security sector reform and certain aspects of disarmament, demobilization and reintegration were vital to the success of the peace process," he refused to recommend that UNMISS play any significant role, seemingly ignoring the historical successes of peacekeepers in implementing DDR and SSR in Liberia, Sierra Leone, and Côte d'Ivoire.[4]

I felt a familiar anger rising again. How could this sort of thing go unquestioned? There didn't seem to be much that I could do about it, so I threw myself into a sufficiently overwhelming workload so that I would have little time to think about the problems in a country and a mission where I no longer had any real influence.

* *

I enrolled in two separate graduate degree programs—a writing program through Harvard University and a philosophy program at the University of Melbourne. I told myself that the work toward these two degrees could help me process my experience in South Sudan and Afghanistan. The latter also would prepare me to challenge the centuries-old ethical framework of "just war" that I had seen abused by my own country and others to rationalize making wars that were not just and, in most cases, supposedly not even considered as wars. The former course of study, I thought, would enable me to better communicate what needed to be done to repair the damage in South Sudan and elsewhere. But the reality was that I had pivoted unconsciously to one of my preferred responses to dealing with anger and a perceived lack of control—that is, engaging in overwork.

68 Changing the Guard, Rewriting the Histories

It was whitewashed, it was unbelievable. . . . I mean, the UN
has a hard time criticizing itself, but . . . I was shocked when
I read that thing, because it was so not true, so fabricated.
—UN OFFICIAL QUOTED IN MARK MILLAR'S
THE PEACEKEEPING FAILURE IN SOUTH SUDAN

30 June 2021. When I heard that David Shearer had stepped down as the SRSG in January, I thought that perhaps things would change for the better. I'd believed that the unwillingness to put UNMISS boots on the ground to protect civilians in the central, western, and eastern regions of South Sudan through the long, bloody years of 2019 and 2020 could be traced directly to his personal belief that most of the 3,552 civilians killed in South Sudan during that period were, as he had put it, "killed in intercommunal violence, which isn't our job to prevent." I was hopeful that under the leadership of the new SRSG, Nicholas Haysom, things would change. But unfortunately, it seemed that would not be the case.

＊ ＊

I was in the middle of my second semester in Harvard's creative writing program when the UN released its official report on the violence in Jonglei, which covered January through August 2020. I wanted to find out if the mission had learned anything from my own report of June 2020 and if it had any concrete plan to do better.

The report was authored by the UN Office of the High Commissioner for Human Rights (OHCHR) and UNMISS, which should have been a red flag. When the organization tasked to protect civilians was allowed to write the report about how thousands of civilians were killed on its watch, I knew the account was likely to be biased, but I had no idea it would be as bad as it was.

The thirty-six-page report documented 738 murders, 39 rapes, and 686 abductions of women and children, noting also that many of the abductees would be "subjected to forced marriage and sexual enslavement."[1] It made eight recommendations to the government of South Sudan, to the ethnic militias in Jonglei, and to the international community, but it made no recommendations that UNMISS itself change its approach.

The report also included information on the final wave of attacks that had taken place between June and August 2020—after I had left the mission—again by the same coalition of Nuer and Dinka fighters that had ravaged the Murle villages in February 2020. I had warned the mission to expect these attacks in my interim report on 27 March 2020, but as with all the previous attacks, UNMISS peacekeepers were absent and were deployed only after the damage had been done. The penultimate section of the official report, titled "Responses to armed violence," documented the political, military, and judicial actions that the government of South Sudan had taken and was clear that none of these instruments had functioned satisfactorily.

"Overall, the response of Government forces did not meet the standards of what can reasonably be expected in these circumstances, and failed in their duty to protect Dinka, Murle and Nuer communities from human rights abuses committed by community-based militias. . . . The lack of action by South Sudanese authorities to protect the human rights of individuals living in Jonglei . . . amounts to a human rights violation."[2] Yet the section was silent on the extent to which the UNMISS response failed to meet the standard of what might reasonably have been expected and, in fact, that it had not even met the standard at which the mission had performed in 2012, when Hilde Johnson had less than half the number of peacekeepers at her disposal than David Shearer had in 2020.

Instead, the mission congratulated itself for visiting Pieri the month after the February attacks to ask the prophet Dak Kueth and the White Army leaders to mediate with the Murle; for hosting a mediation forum in Juba during September 2020—again, only after the final wave of violence had ended—and for obtaining the release of a grand total of nineteen abducted women and children. That figure represented a mere 3 percent of those kidnapped into sexual slavery by the Nuer and Dinka fighters. The report also stated that "in early January, UNMISS peacekeepers adopted a nimble, robust and proactive approach to deter rising violence in the Greater Jonglei region. Between 9 January and 22 April, at least 10 long-duration patrols were carried out in Gumuruk, Manyabol and Likuangole."[3]

By rolling up all the patrols conducted in a four-month period that included the quiet months of March and April (after the Nuer and Dinka militias had completed their attacks and retreated north) but that excluded the months of May through August (when the Murle carried out a revenge attack in Pieri and the Nuer and Dinka again struck Anyidi, Gumuruk, and Likaungole), the report made it sound as if UNMISS peacekeepers had been active in attempting to protect civilians rather than merely deploying after the attacks to count the dead and offer empty words of condolence to the living. The mission had cherry-picked its statistics to make it sound as if it had actually done something to prevent the violence rather than deliberately avoiding conducting reconnaissance, pulling back the very patrols that could have prevented the destruction of Manyabol, and failing to deploy proactively to areas such as Likaungole, Kermath, and Pieri.

Further, the report claimed that peacekeepers had been faced with "mobility challenges and a lack of passable roads. This was compounded by scarce air assets [sic] availability for timely insertion of UNMISS troops in affected areas."[4] But this was patently untrue. During the period in question, our air assets had been at the same readiness percentages as previously; only our own unwillingness to fly had prevented their use.

I had personally been on the roads in those regions at the time that the violence was occurring, and while the roads were rough, they were certainly not impassable. Indeed, thousands of armed militia and tens of thousands of refugees had managed to travel those same areas on foot and without any of the logistics support that our peacekeepers had.

The report was a lie.

Appended to the document was a copy of the government's reply to the findings. As I read it, I found that I could not argue with several items in its response, which called for "UNMISS to be more engaged, particularly, one of its core mandates is to protect civilians. . . . The Government also urges UNMISS and the UN in general to always go beyond condemnation and reporting and take practical measures to resolve the violence."

The South Sudanese also asked that UNMISS do the exact same thing it should have been doing all along—"to put down early warning and prevention mechanisms, to avoid recurrence of any violence between the communities in Greater Jonglei. . . . Part of this early warning and prevention mechanism . . . [would be] to carry out constant air surveillance in the area."[5]

Clearly, UNMISS leadership again not only had been bystanders to atrocities but also, even when they were presented with reports that documented the problems, did nothing to change their approach and would both whitewash the public-facing documents and avoid taking any responsibility for the deadly outcomes of their failures to act.

But more worrying was that other UN officials—the high commissioner for human rights and the secretary-general himself—made no attempt to hold the mission accountable. Indeed, they did not even recommend any changes in the policies that had cost so many hundreds of men, women, and children their lives, their dignity, their freedom. No one in the organization—no person, no agency—was willing to criticize or even discuss the deadly flaws within UNMISS. As a result, the changing of the guard in the mission's headquarters did nothing to improve civilian protection for the South Sudanese.

＊ ＊

The new SRSG, Nicholas Haysom, was still using Shearer's "bumper sticker"—the phrase "nimble, robust, and proactive" had appeared in his speech on 28 May and in his press conference on 3 June—but as with his predecessor, the slogan was mere words, never action. As a result, the first six months of his tenure saw 1,042 civilians killed in the same manner, in the same places. Likaungole had been attacked again, with 90 killed and 133 women and children abducted, only two months after the report on the 2020 attacks had been released. The mission would never learn from its mistakes if it would never admit to making them and if the secretary-general would not hold it accountable for its performance on protecting civilians.

＊ ＊

In the face of this information, I could not in good conscience remain silent. I could not let a handful of UN bureaucrats create a false chapter in the history of the world's newest nation. Wanting to put the record straight helped spur me to begin writing *Blue Helmet*. I set to work with the simple hope that I could make the world take notice of the slow-moving crisis in South Sudan before too many more lives were lost.

69 Post-Traumatic

Car parks make me jumpy—
and I never stopped the dreams
Or the growing need for speed and Novocain.
—COLD CHISEL, "KHE SANH"

26 July 2022. In due course, I had completed my writing program at Harvard, found an agent, and, with her help, began to polish the proposal for this book, but some of her recommendations grated on me. "All stories that succeed have a 'Hero's Journey,'" she noted in one of her comments. "Explain yours here."

My first reaction was anger. I wanted to tell her that in the real world, not everyone was a hero, and not every journey ended with the protagonist still alive and triumphant. I knew I could point to the reports showing that thousands of journeys had ended in violent and preventable deaths during my own tour in South Sudan, and many thousands more had occurred since then. I hadn't succeeded either in persuading my own leaders to take action or in getting their successors to learn from our mistakes with the reports I'd written.

General Tinaikar had finished his assignment to UNMISS in January 2022, noting in his farewell address that whether the motivation was political or intercommunal, "violence is violence. We cannot sit idle when people are being killed. . . . When people are dying, it's not possible to rely on long bureaucratic procedures. . . . The UN system can be slow in its response to crises that flare up. Our collective job, when we hold positions of leadership, is to remove as many of these roadblocks as possible and prioritize our resources to protect people."[1]

He also said that it was an ongoing process, but I saw no sign that the process then in place was working. History continued to bloodily repeat itself in South Sudan and would keep doing so there—and elsewhere—until those who attacked civilians and those who stood by while they did so faced some sort of accountability. Of course, South Sudan wasn't the only place where a lack of accountability and a lack of adherence to the principles of the UN Charter and humanitarian law were taking innocent lives.

* *

Nine months earlier, I'd watched my last war—the one in Afghanistan—end ignominiously. Eleven of my fellow Marines died at the Kabul airport while doing their part to make the best of a hastily organized airlift to evacuate Americans from the country during the fall of Kabul. That was bad enough. Worse was to find out, three days later, that my country had retaliated for their deaths by deliberately killing seven children with high explosives and shrapnel.[2] Afterward, our top general had stood in front of reporters and declared that we had gone through "the same level of rigor that we've done for years. . . . The procedures were correctly followed, and it was a righteous strike."[3]

I was angry then, too, at the final pointless killings, that it all seemed to have been for nothing, and that, in all likelihood, no one would be held accountable. I was also angry that U.S. contingency plans to evacuate from Afghanistan did not include the local staff. As with so many national staffs employed elsewhere—including South Sudan—they were left to fend for themselves.[4] But anger hadn't helped me then, and it wouldn't help now. Besides, I knew that my reaction was partly just a symptom of the diagnosis that I'd recently received—chronic PTSD.

What *had* helped me in dealing with the diagnosis was admitting the underlying cause for some of the issues that I'd been struggling with since leaving the military—"feeling irritable or having angry outbursts"—and acknowledging which of my long-held behaviors were negative coping methods and which ones were positive. Some of my natural tendencies, such as seeking out wild places, seemed to fit into the second category. "Spending time in nature," the U.S. Department of Veterans Affairs (VA) called it.

But solo hiking through mountainous bear country in Wyoming and Croatia could also have been considered dangerous behavior, or a negative coping strategy. When I found myself halfway up the side of an active volcano in Iceland at midnight, alone, and knowing that any false step on the rain-slicked scree would result in a fall of hundreds of feet, I knew that I had to try something else, because the overwork wasn't working and because getting hurt or killed wouldn't be just my problem anymore.

I had a partner to think about—Jayde—so I ignored the inner voice that demanded that I push on, the same voice that exhorted me to reach the summit and look over the lava escaping from Fagradalsfjall or die trying. Instead, I began a slow, careful retreat down the side of the volcano, moving away from danger and toward evaluation and treatment. As I descended past the most treacherous part of the slope, I mentally reframed my decision. It was as Maj. Gen. Oliver Smith said at the Battle of the Chosin Reservoir during the Korean War: "Retreat, hell! We're not retreating; we're advancing in a different direction."[5]

* *

Worldwide, ptsd affects about 6 percent of people who have been exposed to disturbing events such as those associated with war, physical violence, sexual violence, accidents, and the deaths of loved ones. In South Sudan, studies showed that 40 percent of the South Sudanese population suffered from ptsd, along with 24 percent of associated aid workers and un staff. Chronic stressors increased the likelihood of its onset, and besides the endemic political instability, the most significant source of chronic stress for the un staff in particular came from threats at checkpoints and other restrictions on their freedom of movement.

Yet, despite the massive amounts of trauma, the country had only three psychiatrists, and the sole psychiatric hospital in Juba had a mere twelve beds. When they were full, sufferers were taken to the city's prison. Beyond the capital, medical aid organizations did what they could, but it wasn't much. Even for those in the un or humanitarian organizations, there was demand for more assistance. In a survey of staff from un agencies along with national and international aid organizations, better access to mental health services was the number 1 response to an open-ended question asking how staff support services could be improved.[6] Among the local staff, mental health services were considered twice as important as increased salaries and equity in benefits. But there was another side to the coin: even when such services were available, many people did not seek treatment or acknowledge the problem.

I was one of those people. The events I'd borne witness to in South Sudan were just the latest in a lifetime of accumulated stressors that I'd locked away and tried to forget. From beatings as a child—sometimes to uncon-sciousness—to mortar attacks in Afghanistan, I'd endured a full one-third of the traumatic events that were known to be triggers, and I'd thought I was doing okay. As with many veterans, I'd never admitted to myself or the military doctors that my experiences had affected me in any way—at least not until that hair-raising moment in Iceland caused me to check in with a nurse at a VA clinic. I gave him honest answers to such questions as was I "avoiding thinking or talking about some of my military experiences?" And was I "trying to avoid feelings related to those experiences?"

Yes and yes.

Yes, I felt emotionally numb, distant, and cut off from other people.

Yes, I had difficulty concentrating and difficulty sleeping.

I spoke with psychologists and was prescribed drugs by psychiatrists, but neither had much impact. Newly emergent alternative therapies leveraging psilocybin and similar substances seemed to help, as did fostering animals and working with my hands while rebuilding houses and volunteering in COVID vaccination operations with Team Rubicon. With diagnosis and treatment, I did much better. I was able to put aside my anger and refocus that energy on doing something to help myself by helping others. Writing was a well-documented therapy for past trauma, and my experience in UNMISS, my military credentials, and my education as a writer made me uniquely qualified to put a suitable ending on a story that might, I hoped, bring some sort of meaningful change to both South Sudan and the UN itself.

70 Good Offices

To exercise good offices, confidence-building, and facilitation in
support of the mission's protection strategy, especially in regard to
women and children, . . . to facilitate the prevention, mitigation, and
resolution of intercommunal conflict through . . . mediation and
community engagement . . . as an essential part of preventing violence.
—UN SECURITY COUNCIL RESOLUTION 2459
ON THE UNMISS 2019 MANDATE

1 January 2023. Part of the story I wanted to tell was to acknowledge the
good that had come out of my year in South Sudan. I felt compelled to
remind myself and tell the world that the presence of blue helmets in the
country *had* accomplished something worthwhile, even if we could have
done so much more.

The battalions of UNMISS—the individual women and men in uniform—
had done everything that was asked of them. They had scraped 3,100 miles of
dirt roads—the same roads that their predecessors had been diligently scrap-
ing for almost a decade—into passable conditions. One of their number—
Sgt. Xudong Wang—paid the ultimate price during these operations and
was posthumously awarded the Dag Hammarskjöld Medal for his sacrifice.[1]
The troops had watched their road repair efforts dissolve in the rains, but
they had not complained; instead, they had continued to carry out their
patrols—some 51,708 of them. If most of those patrols consisted merely of
standing guard in a watchtower overlooking their own base or its adjoining
POC site, well, those orders had come down from on high. As the secretary-
general or the Security Council had never questioned them, who were the
peacekeepers themselves to say it was not the best possible use of their time?

The peacekeepers also defended the 188,000 displaced people living in
UN-administered protective camps, and they defended the UN's own bases.
If people could make it within sight of those walls, they were safe. Wherever

I went and whenever I had spoken with Nuer leaders, they'd thanked the UN for what it had done to protect Nuer civilians in Juba, Bor, and Bentiu during the worst of the violence in 2013 and 2016. They never chided us for failing to do more to protect their people from the atrocities perpetrated by government forces in places such as Leer in 2015 and Koch in 2018.[2]

Those failures to protect civilians were not the fault of the peacekeepers themselves. Had they been asked to do more, had they been allowed to do more, had they been funded to do more—I am confident that they would have. When they were ordered to create austere bases in distant villages, they did so uncomplainingly, and while those bases stood, they, too, were pockets of protection in a dangerous land. Peacekeepers were not allowed to go certain places, but where their leaders let them go, they went, and violence was less likely when they were present.

The peacekeepers' efforts facilitated the delivery of $1.2 billion of humanitarian assistance that benefited 5.3 million people. Another 1.9 million people went unsupported; however, that was not the fault of the peacekeepers or the humanitarians but of the international community, which had not fully funded the UN's Humanitarian Response Plan for South Sudan.

That lack of support could be attributed to several reasons. Others who'd worn the blue helmet previously had cited indifference, self-interest, and racism. I agreed but thought another factor was at work as well—one linked to the fact that humans aren't wired to respond well to large but slow-moving threats.[3]

71 Slow-Moving Crisis, Widespread Problems

> The international community, through an inept UN mandate
> and what can only be described as indifference, self-interest and
> racism, aided and abetted these crimes against humanity.
> —LT. GEN. ROMÉO DALLAIRE

11 September 2023. At the end of the latest round of violence in South Sudan, the cumulative count of civilians killed at the hands of armed men since the country's civil war ceased in September 2018 exceeded eight thousand dead, which was on par with the number of Bosnian men and boys that Serbian forces murdered in the notorious Srebrenica massacre. That horrifying event occurred in large part because a UN peacekeeping battalion failed to protect the Bosnian civilians who had taken shelter in the small town where the peacekeepers had their base. The Dutch peacekeepers allowed Bosnian Serb soldiers to separate out the men and boys, who were subsequently murdered en masse. The women and girls were merely deported to Serbia but often after being raped or seeing their male relatives murdered and mutilated. These crimes against humanity—for which the Bosnian Serb commander, a general named Ratko Mladić, was sentenced to life in prison in 2017—took place over twenty days in July 1995; their impact was magnified because they happened in such a small area and in such a short span of time. Likewise, one of the distinguishing features of the Rwandan genocide had been the relative speed at which it had happened. General Dallaire had called it "one of the fastest, most efficient, most evident genocides in recent history."[1]

The repeated attempts at ethnic cleansing on the savannas of eastern South Sudan and the other threats against civilians in the country represented a slow-moving crisis. In theory, that allowed for many more opportunities to intervene, but it also seemed perhaps less dramatic because any single incident's death toll was substantially less than the thousands murdered at Srebrenica and at the various massacre sites in Rwanda. Over time, though, slow-moving crises kill more people than fast-moving ones. Earthquakes, tsunamis, and hurricanes make the news, but simple exposure to the elements kills more people in the course of a year. Daniel Gilbert, a professor of psychology at Harvard, had pointed out a similar problem in another context, noting in a 2010 lecture that "many environmentalists say global warming is happening too fast. No, it's happening too slowly. It's not happening nearly quickly enough to get our attention."[2]

* *

However, after one round of raids by Nuer and Dinka militias, something different happened. When 308 people were killed and 299 were abducted during another wave of attacks in Jonglei that began on Christmas Eve, 24 December 2022, hundreds of media reports documented the violent deaths of civilians. Unfortunately for the victims and their families in South Sudan, the news wasn't about them.

Instead, it was about Ukrainians—people who resembled many of the reporters from Europe and the United States, people who lived in apartment buildings and on neat little farms, people who also weren't supposed to be dying violently. Fewer Ukrainian civilians were killed in the months of December 2022 and January 2023 combined than were killed in Jonglei during the sixteen-day period from 24 December 2022 to 9 January 2023; yet, the white faces of the dead in Europe received all the media attention and their country most of the world's aid.

The hundreds of South Sudanese victims, still living and dying in the land that *TIME* forgot, had been ignored again—as had the dead in Ethiopia, where the deadliest civil war of the twenty-first century had just ended after two years and an estimated six hundred thousand civilian deaths.[3] That civil war had also gone largely unremarked upon by the same news outlets that reported daily on Ukraine, even though officers who served as UN peacekeepers were among those murdered or "disappeared" without a trace.[4] It was hard not to see in the media's focus that human life and dignity in Africa seemed to have very different value than it did in Europe, and it was hard to resist the effects of the mass media barrage. I found myself very tempted to go to Ukraine as a volunteer, and if it weren't for the steadying influence of my marriage to Jayde, I might well have joined the thousands of other veterans from around the world who had done so.[5]

* *

Not only did the dead in South Sudan go unreported, but also the living there received such different treatment. In 2022 over $9 billion in humanitarian aid poured into Ukraine, a nation approximately the size of South Sudan but ten times richer on a per capita basis. At the same time, the humanitarian appeal for South Sudan was only $1.7 billion, but about a third of that requirement went unmet. In a period where the world at large—and the United States in particular—was able and willing to pour billions of dollars' worth of humanitarian aid into a conflict zone in a wealthy European nation, countries somehow found it impossible to provide a fraction of that to one where 18 percent of the population was suffering "emergency" levels of food insecurity—only one step below famine—and where the WFP was forced to halve its rations in 2021. It was hard not to ascribe this discrepancy to the "indifference, self-interest and racism" that General Dallaire had pointed to as reasons the world did so little during the Rwandan genocide.

But I believed other issues were also at play. As noted, the UN and its member states were rarely held accountable for their failures, and far from being transparent, the organization did its best to obfuscate its formal reports, making it harder for journalists and academics to see the problems. This contributed to a lack of awareness, driving a vicious cycle.

* *

The problem of accountability appeared in many forms within UN peacekeeping operations. Some of them I had experienced firsthand, such as when UNMISS failed to report the hundreds of children killed and abducted in Jonglei as having been the victims of grave violations of human rights. These 219 dead, injured, and stolen children *did* appear in the secretary-general's report for that period in paragraph 52 of the section on "monitoring and investigating human rights violations"—a paragraph that described the total numbers of killings, abductions, and other grave violations. But in the same section—in paragraph 62, which specifically focused on child protection—the report stated that only 27 children had been victims of killings, abductions, rape, and maiming. It went on to specify that children were at greatest risk in Western Equatoria, Upper Nile, Northern Bahr el Ghazal, Unity, Central Equatoria, and Eastern Equatoria States but *not* Jonglei.

This shocking misrepresentation of the facts allowed the UN to unabashedly claim that grave violations had gone down rather than up, with Special

Representative of the Secretary-General for Children and Armed Conflict Virginia Gamba saying that she was "encouraged by the significant decrease in grave violations against children in South Sudan since the last report of the Secretary-General."[6] But that decrease only represented a lack of honest reporting, not a lack of crimes against children. In fact, if the lost children of Jonglei had been counted in 2020, the numbers for child abductions would have been nearly triple what was reported. But their lives didn't seem to matter, and it appeared no one would challenge the UN on it. The problem was not only that UNMISS had under-reported serious human rights violations but also that the people in charge of this key program had ignored that the true extent of the violence directed at children was written in black and white on the report's previous page. Neither the secretary-general nor his special representatives seemed to have actually read the reports. Apparently, no one on the Security Council did either.

* *

Misrepresenting facts was neither new for UNMISS nor limited to statistics on violence. While researching that aspect, I'd stumbled across another place where the UN hid its dirty laundry in plain sight—namely, the archives for its internal dispute tribunal, where staff members could challenge unfair practices. The example that caught my attention was a case of wrongful firing in 2013. That an employee had been unfairly terminated didn't stand out to me; the way in which senior mission staff had behaved when asked to explain themselves did. The judge who ruled in favor of the plaintiff and against the mission put it this way:

> It begs belief that the witness who was interim Chief of Staff at UNMISS, among other previous and subsequent high positions held, would actually claim that the leadership of a United Nations peacekeeping mission held meetings at which it took far-reaching decisions in respect of the mission's mandate and personnel but kept no records of its discussions and decisions. Not only is such a claim preposterous, irresponsible and mischievous, it goes to show the extent to which a highly placed officer of the Organization is prepared to go to deceive the Tribunal in order to cover up an inexcusable and arbitrary act.[7]

That "highly placed officer" was Ian Sinclair, who would go on to hold ever more senior positions in the UN. It seemed that even when senior leaders were publicly identified as having behaved inappropriately, they were rewarded with promotions and shielded from repercussions.

Moreover, I discovered that the same problems I'd observed close at hand in UNMISS were not anomalous. The UN's track record in the DRC, Mali, the CAR, the Abyei Administrative Area, Ethiopia, and Sudan all had serious issues. The UN also withdrew its mission from Darfur despite the protests of the women and minority groups, who warned that death and displacement would follow. Both did in 2023 when civil war broke out between rival military leaders.

Member nations were a big part of the problem. In countries with major UN missions, checkpoint economies flourished. Weapons were smuggled into conflict zones while natural resources were smuggled out or exploited in sweetheart deals, and many of the countries that benefited simultaneously sent their peacekeepers to those same conflict zones. Countries that did send peacekeepers appeared to get a free pass for the atrocities committed by other members of their militaries at home and in neighboring countries.

Some permanent member (P5) states of the Security Council failed to pay their share of the costs of peacekeeping; others sent their soldiers and mercenaries to sexually assault and massacre civilians under the nose of UN missions in places such as Mali and the CAR. The permanent members of the UN Security Council were also the top profiteers in the global arms trade, exporting the same weapons and ammunition used to kill civilians and peacekeepers. What could be done about the systemic lack of accountability for both those who failed to act and those who acted badly?

72 How to Change the World

> To be able to measure success or failure accurately, and then hold
> our leaders to account, is one of the principles of democracy—
> its absence should be an issue of concern for every citizen.
> —JAYDE LOVELL

30 June 2023. In writing this final chapter, I was worried that the scale of
the identified problems might seem so large that readers would conclude
that nothing could be done about them. The failure to protect civilians,
the corrupt checkpoint economy, the unequal treatment of national staff
and of refugees, the traffic in weapons and looted resources, the failure to
account for true numbers of grave violations against children victimized
during armed conflict—each of these issues would merit its own book to
examine the detailed solutions required. But all of these problems have
common roots, and the path to solving them begins with the implementing
three simple principles: *transparency*, *accountability*, and *awareness*.

A spirit of transparency, to me, means presenting the data in a way that
is *accurate*, *clear*, and *valid*, and that *serves the greater good*. The UN has a
problem meeting such standards. Regarding accuracy, its senior leaders
can and do make statements that are objectively false, as was the case with
Ian Sinclair. In many reports, the data lacks clarity; instead, it is presented
in such way as to mask the scope of serious issues. For example, when
Alfred Orono Orono stated that children killed in armed conflict between
tribal militias had not *technically* suffered grave violations according to a
particular Security Council resolution, his statement—while accurate—
was not valid. Only unreasonable persons would agree that children killed
with bullets, burned alive in a hut, or hacked to death with machetes by
large groups of armed men attacking their village had not suffered a grave
violation of their human rights as a result of armed conflict, and hiding
these stories behind technicalities reflects a spirit of deception rather than

transparency. In such a case, a responsible UN official should have acted to report the actual number of victims and should have noted that the standard for counting such victims needed updating to reflect the realities of modern warfare. Doing so would have highlighted the final element—working to serve the greater good.

In this case, that "greater good" would be ensuring that the UN member states understand the actual number of children harmed by armed conflict so that they can determine whether UN programs to reduce or eliminate that harm are working. By providing invalid data in an official report, UNMISS masked the true extent of the problem, leading Virginia Gamba to applaud a significant decrease in harm. Given the truth, or even checking the math in reports from her staff against other human rights data that was readily available within the UN, she should have voiced alarm at the growing numbers of children being killed, injured, and abducted, and called for additional resources to address these violations of international law. When grown men and women put their own career interests before the interests of vulnerable children, I think anyone would agree that we have a problem.

This failure to act in the spirit of transparency while ostensibly serving the greater good was also exemplified by the case of Operation Sangaris, when members of the French military sexually abused children in the CAR. After the children reported the abuse to UN officials in 2014, the report was

> passed from desk to desk, inbox to inbox, across multiple United Nations offices, with no one willing to take responsibility to address the serious human rights violations. Indeed, even when the Government of France became aware of the allegations and requested the cooperation of United Nations staff in its investigation, these requests were met with resistance and became bogged down in formalities. Staff became overly concerned with whether the allegations had been improperly "leaked" to the French authorities, and focused on protocols rather than action. The welfare of the victims and the accountability of the perpetrators appeared to be an afterthought, if considered at all. Overall, the response of the United Nations was fragmented and bureaucratic, and failed to satisfy the core mandate of the United Nations to address human rights violations.[1]

Every UN official who saw or heard of the report first should have kept in mind the greater good—that is, the safety and dignity of the people under their protection. Their initial response should have been, "How do we aid the victims, bring the perpetrators to justice, and put mitigations in place to make sure this doesn't happen to anyone else?" Instead, their default reaction was an attempt to silence and punish the one person who finally did take action, to hide behind claims of immunity and confidentiality, and to trust in the relative impunity often granted to senior members of the organization to shield them from personal consequences. Most disturbingly, when their misdeeds were finally brought to the public's attention, the three senior UN officials who *were* found to have acted improperly by the UN's own investigation showed absolutely no contrition for their actions; instead, they denied personal responsibility and made written statements claiming that they had done nothing wrong in covering up the matter.

Improving transparency in UN peacekeeping and throughout the organization is strongly linked to the second key principle of accountability. The word "accountability" stems from the Latin root word *computare* (to count); basically, it means holding people responsible for the numbers. This can be understood in terms of a simple rubric. If a peacekeeping mission has a mandate to protect civilians, then it should understand how to measure its successes and its failures in plain numeric terms. Leaders who deliver success should be encouraged to continue doing so, and those who do not first should be cautioned and then should be replaced. We do not expect that a chef who cannot cook an edible meal will remain employed very long, nor do we expect that businesses that fail to yield a profit or hospitals that kill more patients than they cure to remain open. Why, then, should we continue to tolerate UN missions whose performance of their core mandate—to protect civilians—get worse with each passing quarter?

Another key element in an overarching organizational framework of accountability is being clear about *who* should do the accounting, especially in cases where plainly something has already gone very wrong. Independent investigations, by impartial experts who are free from conflicts of interest, should be required for any future incidents similar to the ones General Cammaert noted in our conversations in 2019—those in Malakal, South Sudan, and in Semuliki and Kamanyola, the DRC. Retroactive investigations, in the context of South Sudan, should look at the attacks in Jonglei and Central Equatoria during 2020 and those in Leer, Adidiang, and Aburoc during 2022 where UN forces based nearby failed to prevent the deadly violence or to intervene once it began. The reports must contain, at a minimum, an assessment of whether there was early warning of the attacks, what was done to prevent them, and what the response was when preventive measures failed, as well as recommendations on what must be done differently in the future to improve.

Notably, I am not the only one to advocate for this approach to addressing the complex problems of peacekeeping. The UN itself has acknowledged that a lack of transparency and accountability is problematic. Its peacekeeping website states, "Mandate implementation is hindered by slow, unresponsive service delivery, micro-management by governing bodies, a trust deficit with Member States and with staff, inadequate resourcing of and ineffective implementation of mandates and a lack of transparency and accountability."[2]

In light of the systemic abuses in humanitarian and development programs in 2006 and 2007, the United States led a UN Transparency and Accountability Initiative; yet, as this book has shown, the problems persist. UN Security Council Resolution 2436 of 2018 highlights the importance of special investigations to accountability and performance. Also, the 2023 Policy on the Protection of Civilians in United Nations Peacekeeping notes that in situations where civilians have been killed or sexually assaulted in proximity to a UN base—or in a situation where the mission knew or should have known about an imminent threat to civilians and failed to respond within their capabilities—an inquiry or after-action review must be undertaken.

But it is not enough to allow missions to investigate their own failures and then to accept without question their reports' assertions that all blame lies with other parties—as has been the case with many ex post facto reports on violence in South Sudan—or to accept their assessments that no remedial action is required on their part. The POC policy clearly states that "remedial or corrective measures must be taken to avoid reoccurrence and/or improve the POC response of the mission."[3] Even independent reviews are only valuable to the extent they comply with the principles outlined in this chapter. When the UN hired former UNMISS SRSG Ellen Margrethe Løj to lead the 2018 independent review of its struggling mission in Mali, her "lack of leadership and preparedness" in Juba in 2016 was overlooked. To make matters worse, the UN did not publish her whole report on the situation in Mali. Instead, it "portrayed a selective and inaccurate summary of Løj's recommendations in the secretary-general's report to the council: it made no reference to the two options that conflicted with these political interests and instead framed the third option as the review's main recommendation."[4]

Clearly, in spite of demanding accountability and transparency from its missions, the UN Security Council and the General Assembly does not require it. So if the UN will not hold itself accountable, then how can ordinary people such as you and I persuade them to change? To hold its peacekeeping missions to its own existing standards of accountability and transparency, and to improve its organizational culture to embrace and operationalize the definitions of transparency and accountability that are laid out in this book? That is where the concept of *awareness* comes in.

* *

My wife introduced me to someone who had an answer to the question of how individuals can force large organizations to change their behavior. Jennifer Jacquet is an associate professor at New York University whose specialty is breaking down barriers to changing large organizations, and the UN certainly seems to count. Jacquet's 2015 book *Is Shame Necessary? New Uses for an Old Tool* highlights the useful role that an uncomfortable sensation—shame—could play in changing the way that powerful groups operate.

In her framing, the mechanism of shame has already been responsible for successfully increasing accountability and transparency in some other areas of UN operations. The UN didn't take action to prevent sexual abuse in conflict zones on its own; in fact, it went to great efforts to avoid doing so until it was shamed into action in 2015. That spring, *The Guardian* newspaper revealed that senior UN leaders had attempted to suppress reports of the abuses in the CAR by discrediting Anders Kompass, the UN staff member who passed evidence of the crimes to French police.[5]

Those efforts to cover up the atrocities would certainly have succeeded if Kompass hadn't stood his ground and if an advocacy organization had not launched the "Code Blue Campaign" to demand action on the issue. Only after Code Blue took the issue to *The Guardian* did a storm of negative publicity force the UN secretary-general to finally take action. Ban Ki-moon ordered an independent review, which determined that three senior members of the UN—Babacar Gaye, the SRSG for the CAR mission; Renner Onana, the chief of the Human Rights and Justice Section in that same mission;

and Carman Lapointe, under-secretary-general for the Office of Internal Oversight Services—had all "abused their authority." It concluded, "The fact that the problem persists despite several expert reports commissioned by the United Nations over the past 10 years serves only to exacerbate the perception that the United Nations is more concerned with rhetoric than with action."[6]

While shame following exposure *could* be an excellent motivator for change, it also has limitations. As Jacquet points out, "An audience is a prerequisite for shame"; it only works if large segments of the world are able to see the transgressions. In the UN's case, that required three things: insiders, such as Anders Kompass, who were willing to highlight the problems; advocacy and media organizations willing to spread the message; and a concerned public willing to speak out against the reported injustice. Thankfully, with the internet, it is easier than ever before for everyday citizens to show that they're paying attention and sharing what they learn. Social media is an easy platform for sharing and shaming, with a potential audience of over five billion people.[7] And while the word "shame" has negative connotations, its use is also reflected in the "audience effect." When people believe they're being watched, they often choose to engage in fewer bad behaviors, such as wasting energy, and in more good ones. The WHO, for example, leveraged the power of this effect to create better health outcomes for patients after discovering they were more likely to take their medication if someone simply watched them swallow it.

Regarding the United Nations, the internet also gives everyone the ability to be its audience—that is, to bear witness to the UN's actions and to spread the word if those actions are inconsistent with the ideals of its charter. Also, anyone with an internet connection can access most UN reports, but in many cases, those documents are unhelpfully obtuse, with the important details obfuscated behind acronyms and confusingly worded, or simply hidden in appendixes. Meanwhile, some of the most important items, such as the investigatory reports of the Office of Peacekeeping Strategic Partnership, remain hidden from public view.

Requiring clear writing for these reports and access to all of them in the spirit of transparency would help. But until then, the public will need experts to translate these reports into easy-to-read articles and infographics, insiders willing to share those documents of public interest that have been suppressed, and journalists with a platform to shine the spotlight where it is most needed.

Through such efforts, we create the awareness needed to inform and expand the audience, and to leverage the power of shame to shape the way that the UN approaches peacekeeping. It's also how we start to rein in the global arms trade in which UN member states—including the United States, Russia, China, and France—supply the weapons used by non-state actors, tribal militias, and state perpetrators of mass violence to kill both civilians and the peacekeepers sent to protect them.

* *

Part of my own work going forward therefore will be through the non-profit organization World Without War (www.worldwithout.org), to which I intend to donate my royalties from this book. Its mission includes assisting members of the UN, military, and humanitarian communities to bring safely and confidentially to light serious issues in peacekeeping. World Without War also seeks to help both ordinary citizens and professional journalists find the stories that need telling, to translate raw data into accurate pictures, and to equip them with the questions that need to be asked.

For instance, why have civilian deaths been consistently rising in South Sudan since the signing of the peace treaty in 2018? Why have hundreds of abducted children disappeared, not only from their homes but also from the statistics on children affected by armed conflict? Simply asking these questions frankly and in a public forum may itself be an impetus for change.

But in many cases, just getting people to ask "why" will not be enough. We must also ask the question of "how." Once an issue can no longer be ignored, how do we begin to fix it? My personal recommendations for what must be done to address the specific issues that I saw during my year as a UN peacekeeper are detailed in appendix A. But I don't have all the answers, and I am wary of those who claim they do. Therefore, another element of my own future work will be to help create and participate in forums where these important topics can be examined by a wide range of people. We cannot simply rely on "experts" because they do not always have the answers. If they did, then we wouldn't have any problems!

My hope is that in the years to come, by investing my own time and money in working to improve these problems and by encouraging others to join me, together we will see the sort of positive change in South Sudan and other conflict zones around the world that will let me rest easy when the final bugle sounds. I invite you to add your voice to mine. We live in a world where a small effort by large numbers of concerned citizens around the world can make a real difference in the lives of those living in conflict zones, and I truly believe that is a difference worth making.

Afterword

My great hope was that by the time I finished writing *Blue Helmet*, things would have changed for the better. But that has not been the case.

In 2023 the world watched the UN Security Council abrogate its primary responsibility "for the maintenance of international peace and security," with the United States using its veto to prevent action being taken against Israel, as thousands of children and other civilians were killed in Gaza, many with U.S.-made weapons. Russia also continued to block action being taken against its own attacks on civilians in Ukraine. No matter that the civilian dead included hundreds of the UN's own staff in the Gaza Strip, the organization showed itself incapable of acting to uphold the Universal Declaration of Human Rights when faced with aggression by state actors.

Meanwhile, the problems in and around South Sudan have worsened, as has the state of peacekeeping operations in general. The civil war in Sudan, brought on in part by the too-early dissolution of the UN mission in Darfur, has sent waves of refugees over the border, further destabilizing both South Sudan and neighboring Ethiopia. In 2023 the WFP reported the largest funding deficit in its entire history, coming up $14.5 billion short of what it needed to feed the world's most vulnerable, with its director stating that "47.3 million children, women and men faced starvation without life-saving assistance."[1] Some 2.3 million of those people were in South Sudan, suffering what the WFP called the "worst humanitarian crisis since independence," with the famine-stricken people who did receive rations getting only 70 percent of the calories needed to remain healthy.[2] The U.S. government's Prosper Africa program has resulted in $86 billion of investments in forty-nine African countries, but not a single dollar was invested in South Sudan, in the DRC, or in Libya.[3] As noted previously, the United States and its Western allies spent tens of billions of dollars supporting Ukraine with military hardware and other aid even while their purchases of Russian commodities, ranging from nuclear fuel rods to petroleum products, poured tens of billions of dollars into Russia's own war machine. But none of the permanent members of the UN Security Council were willing to fund the shortfalls in the WFP budget for South Sudan or, for that matter, for Afghanistan, Syria, Haiti, Somalia, Sudan, Yemen, and the DRC.

The picture in peacekeeping, and in UN humanitarian operations in general, is—if anything—even worse. As I write this, 234 of my UN colleagues have been killed since the beginning of Israel's assault on the occupied Palestinian territories. It is the highest number of UN aid workers killed in a conflict in the history of the United Nations, yet the organization can muster nothing more than hashtags on social media. If ever there was a time for a chapter VII intervention, November 2023 was it.[4] Instead, the United Nations Children's Fund simply counts the rising thousands of children killed by Israeli shrapnel and joins the rest of the UN in wringing its collective hands. Indifference, self-interest, and racism aided and abetted these crimes against humanity, just as General Dallaire once said.

Where peacekeeping missions had been closed down prematurely—in Haiti and in Sudan—chaos has reigned. While the killings of thousands of children by Israel in the occupied Palestinian territories were shocking in terms of their scale and speed, at least the world was aware of them. The deaths of thousands more children over the course of the year in twenty-four other conflict-ridden countries went largely unreported outside of confusingly worded UN reports. Fourteen of those countries were on the African continent, and in South Sudan, once again, the numbers of children killed was drastically understated in the secretary-general's reports. Whereas the UNMISS HRD annual report suggested that 224 children were killed in 2022, the secretary-general reported only 46, meaning over 79 percent of the killings of children in South Sudan went unreported in the UN's annual report on children and armed conflict.[5]

In 2023 the UN mission in Mali was ordered out of the country, and the mission in Sudan proved incapable of protecting civilians. The government in the DRC asked that the UN mission there be withdrawn by the end of 2024, and a proposed deployment of Kenyan police forces in a new UN mission to Haiti was halted. Around the world, UN missions continued to fail the world's most vulnerable populations despite the best efforts of the individual peacekeepers, UNPOL officers, and civilian staff. Many nations—including the United States—also failed to pay their full assessments for peacekeeping, and the total shortfall for this key UN budget line was $1.35 billion in 2023.[6] Over 20 percent of the total required budget for peace-keeping went unpaid in a year where over a hundred times that amount was spent to finance major wars.

Clearly the crisis in peacekeeping—which I believed from my boots-on-the-ground perspective in 2020 could not possibly get any worse—has grown even direr, yet I remain confident that UN peacekeeping holds the key to restoring and maintaining stability around the world. The challenges to our current world order will grow in the coming decade; the pressures of climate change and population growth make them a certainty.

The world can no longer afford to spend $2.4 trillion per year on weap-ons—a sum that has been steadily increasing by $47 billion each year since the turn of the century.[7] Nor can it dismiss overnight the 27 million women and men who currently serve in militaries throughout the world.

But we *can* refocus that great store of human capital in the service of peace and the support of development. Armies are good at building roads; in fact, soldiers built many of the world's earliest paved road networks. Armies, by their nature, also have doctors, drivers and pilots, engineers, and trained administrators. They know how to employ logistics and communications and computer networks, and they follow the orders of their civilian leaders. What they do not know, they will happily learn.

Professional soldiers are prepared to fight—and equipped to do so—but that is not what any of us wants to do. As Gen. Douglas MacArthur said, "The soldier above all other people prays for peace, for he must suffer and bear the deepest wounds and scars of war."[8]

In closing, I beg of you, the reader, to answer our prayers. Do whatever is in your power to encourage the leaders of your nation to put its resources toward development and peacekeeping, to expand its contributions of personnel to UN peace operations and increase its donations to the WFP, to use its diplomatic power to encourage the peaceful resolution of long-standing conflicts, and to use the words of the Universal Declaration of Human Rights as its guide. This standard requires us to recognize the dignity and the equal rights of all humans—even those whom today we may consider adversaries—and to seek solutions that give all people the freedoms from fear and want, and that promote social progress and better standards of life.

Ask your leaders to use their "might for right" and to abandon the long-held practice of using their positions of political and military strength to attack others with impunity. Instead, ask them to use their powers in such a way that they could stand proudly and without a qualm in front of the most moral leaders of the modern age—Mahatma Gandhi, Dr. Martin Luther King Jr., Mother Teresa, Albert Einstein—and recite your nation's military record in times of peace and of war. Ask them to lead so that such a recitation would not include vengeance as a motive, assassination as a political expedient, or the torture of prisoners or the killings of civilians. Ask them to change so that the record would instead list people saved from famine and rescued from natural disasters, development projects completed, and natural resources preserved. Ask them to accrue a record that reflects the best of what soldiers can do when employed in the service of peace—not the worst of what they will do when unleashed in war.

Acknowledgments

I begin this section in an untraditional fashion by acknowledging those things that are missing from this book. They include a more in-depth discussion of cattle culture and what can be done to eliminate the violence that continues to plague this element of South Sudanese society at the time of publication. Missing, too, are properly in-depth discussions about the disastrously cascading effects of climate change and about the potential for education to bend the arc of history in South Sudan. Much more could and should be written about the role of women and elders and about the UN country team and the humanitarian organizations that work in South Sudan—particularly about what they are doing well and what they could be doing better.

I'd also like to acknowledge the many people who are missing from this book, colleagues who made my time in UNMISS so memorable but whose names do not appear in the main text. Kristin, Palle, Shawn, Scott, Squizzy, Lauren, Gulnoz, Rune, Pauline, Arve, Guarav, Raymond, Benny, Ganzorig, and all the rest—I promise you a book of your own one of these days. You all deserve it—there are so many vignettes that I did not have room to include here but that still shine brightly in my memory.

Now, returning to what is more customary, I would like to acknowledge the invaluable assistance of the many people who have helped me bring this book to life, starting with my wife, Jayde Lovell. Thanks for all your patience, encouragement, and help, my love! You make me happier than John Farnham when "You're the Voice" topped the charts in 1986. A massive thank you to Kristin Deasy, Sheena Thomas, Emelye Lovell, and Bec Susan Gill, the beta readers who helped me transform a very rough draft into its final form; to Rebecca Rhodes for her discerning review; and to Maj. Gen. (Dr.) A. K. "Tony" Bardalai (Indian Army, ret.) for both his insightful foreword and the example he has set as a former soldier and fellow blue helmet who has taken up the pen to continue working in the cause of peace.

My sincerest thanks go to Taylor Gilreath, Sara Springsteen, Tom Swanson, and the rest of the team at Potomac Books. I'd also like to thank Dr. Elisabeth McKetta and " Professor Catherine Eaton along with my "tribe" in the Harvard Extension School's Creative Writing program: Esther Hamer, Shazia Ilyas, Maurice Haeems, Kelsey C. M. Kelleher, Dr. Becky Konkle, Elisa Maiz, Bailey Merlin, Asi White, and Keywanne Hawkins. I'm grateful for Wendy Keller, the agent who helped me find the best home for this book, and for the team at ReAgency, who truly exemplify their motto of "marketing for good."

Thanks go as well to Vicky and George for letting me use their lovely guest cottage as a writing retreat when the going got tough, to Pop for the best advice I've ever gotten, Nan for the caramel cake, Alan Workman for the cricket lessons, and to Vicki Chamlee for her indispensable efforts in copyediting this book.

Finally, I close this section by acknowledging that *Blue Helmet* represents only one perspective on the situation in South Sudan during a time when there were about 10 million other unique, personal perspectives to consider.

Appendix A

Ways to Improve the Protection of Civilians

Standardize Best Practices. Within the UN Department of Peace Operations, best practices regarding the command and control of military and police forces should be standardized and implemented across all missions. In particular, UN political and military boundaries should align so that one military commander and one senior civilian have mirrored geographic areas of responsibility. Also, in times of crisis, it must be made clear when and to what extent crisis management becomes the purview of the military commander.

Improve Reporting. The periodic reports of the secretary-general should include not merely statistics on civilian deaths, injuries, sexual trauma, and abduction but also a simple explanation of what was done to prevent such incidents. Did early warning reports highlight the incident area? If so, were UN patrols or temporary bases in the area, and if not, why not? If so, why did they fail to prevent the violence? What will be done to ensure the incident does not recur? Subsequent reports should also highlight whether the planned improvements from the previous report have been implemented and shown effective.

Publicize Incident Investigations. In countries with active peacekeeping missions, incidents that result in the violent deaths of peacekeepers, humanitarians, or civilians should be investigated and reported on by an outside agency, and the results should be published publicly.

Implement Accountability for Senior Staff. Accountability for the performance of individual peacekeepers and units is improving, but similar accountability protocols must be implemented for the more senior civilian and military leaders responsible for crisis management up to and including the SRSG. If a situation is handled well, these leaders should be recognized for their achievement. If failures occur on the scale of Malakal and Juba in 2016 and of Abyei and Jonglei in 2020, then those leaders must be publicly reprimanded or removed from their posts. This accountability should also be implemented—particularly with the srsg and the force commander—in cases where even in the absence of a single major crisis, a mission has failed to successfully implement its key mandate tasks over a period of six months despite taking the remedial steps noted in item 2.

Act on Available Information. Leaders at all levels must listen and act. The srsg and the force commander must listen to the jmac and the Intelligence Branch, and if the latter identifies a "hot spot," then forces must be deployed *before* conflict erupts. Patrol leaders also must listen to local leaders. If the locals say there is a threat of violence or they require a peacekeeping presence, then they must be believed, and troops must be deployed in the short term while a whole-of-mission engagement with the Civil Affairs Division, Political Affairs Division, and so on takes action to address the underlying cause of the latent conflict in the area.

Improve Mobility. Experts should consider mobility requirements for each mission. Where necessary, they should strategically reinforce the standard equipment of deploying battalions with specialized ground and riverine equipment, just as it is standard to provide air support.

Institutionalize ddr. Disarmament of both former combatants and the general populace is a critical part of peacebuilding. It cannot be ignored or abdicated to local governments and military organizations. Best practices in disarmament suggest that given the lack of trust inherent in most post-conflict settings, a third party should oversee such efforts. un missions are the most logical choice in countries where they are present.

Fund Tactical qips. Quick impact funds must be made available to battalion and company commanders. These leaders should be taught both to listen carefully to what local leaders ask for and to take action to implement improvements at the ground level.

Improve Local Infrastructure. Where transportation infrastructure—particularly roads and bridges—is not already in place and of a standard to support year-round travel, its construction must be prioritized. There is simply no excuse for a mission with engineer units specifically tasked with bringing equipment capable of building sealed roads to spend a decade in-country and not make substantive improvements to this defining feature of a modern economy.

Develop Holistic Trauma Mitigation Plan. The effects of conflict-related trauma must be addressed for the civilian population and for the peacekeepers, UNPOL officers, and civilian staff of the mission who are directly exposed to known risk factors for PTSD, including threats of violence and dealing with the aftermath of conflict—for example, corpses, wounded survivors, and so on. Resources should also be made available to the humanitarians who are exposed to these risk factors.

Appendix B

Policy Recommendations for the United States

Training. During pre-deployment training, USMOG needs to brief senior U.S. military observers (SUSMOS) about the personalities of key mission personnel and about the leaders of the parties to the conflict. There should also be a greater focus on understanding the in-country situation. This can be accomplished through asynchronous learning, but a "body of knowledge" should exist that covers the relevant military orders, the political climate in the mission and the country, the interactions of local ethnic and religious influences, the historical major incidents—their reports and repercussions—and an understanding of U.S. policy goals vis-à-vis the particular mission.

Embargoes. Ensure embargoes don't prevent the United States from supporting security sector reform and disarmament, demobilization, and reintegration. While it is important to cut off lethal aid to governments and non-state militaries engaged in civil wars or human rights violations, this move should not prevent engagement in SSR and DDR—specifically, providing uniforms and training in topics such as human rights.

Military Support of the Civil Sector. Encourage South Sudan to create a "Corps of Engineers" and a "River Guard," and mentor both through cooperative engagements with the U.S. Army Corps of Engineers and the U.S. Coast Guard. The U.S. Army also has medical and veterinary units that could model effective practices in human and animal medicine that would be highly relevant to addressing the needs of South Sudan and to employing its soldiers for noncombat, internal civil-military cooperation.

Define U.S. Policy Goals. This point ties into training (discussed above). The United States should have targets for mandate tasks and other items of interest—for example, protecting civilians, reducing sexual abuse, and improving the development and professionalization of the host nation's military. All of these should have target metrics of success, and senior U.S. military representatives in UN missions should be required either to account for how their actions are driving improvement in the metrics or, if progress is not being made, to provide recommendations for high-level interventions by the State Department, the Department of Defense, the U.S. ambassador to the UN, and so on.

Appendix C

Resources and Recommended Reading

Extensive resources on South Sudan and the UN, on peacekeeping and arms control, and on SSR, DDR, and the protection of civilians can all be found on www.worldwithout.org, which represents part of my personal commitment to raising awareness and to facilitating both research and action. That site includes links to a wide array of audiovisual and digital assets, as well as to a more comprehensive list of recommended readings on topics raised in this book. The following list, however, is a good place to start for readers interested in getting a more nuanced perspective on specific issues.

For military engineers in service of civilian infrastructure: U.S. Army Corps of Engineers, "A Brief History," accessed 22 July 2024, https://www.usace.army .mil/about/history/brief-history-of-the-corps/introduction/. This online history gives a great perspective on how a military engineer corps can be used for infrastructure improvements during peacetime.

For understanding the treatment of different classes of persons displaced by conflict: Concern Worldwide, "Refugee vs. IDP vs. Migrant . . . What's the Difference?" 22 April 2022, https://www.concern.net/news/refugee-idp -migrant-difference. This web page gives a good explainer concerning forcibly displaced persons.

For alternative approaches to peacekeeping: Nonviolent Peaceforce, "Case Studies of Unarmed Civilian Protection," March 2016, https://nonviolentpeaceforce .org/wp-content/uploads/2022/04/UCP_Case_Studies__v5.3_LQ.pdf. This sites provides a good case study.

For more on the Nuer White Army, a unique and challenging community militia: Human Security Baseline Assessment, "My Neighbor, My Enemy: Inter-tribal Violence in Jonglei," *Sudan Issue Brief* no. 21 (October 2012), https://www.smallarmssurvey.org/sites/default/files/resources/HSBA-IB21 -Inter-tribal_violence_in_Jonglei.pdf.

Notes

DEDICATION

The number of fatalities, according to the United Nations' data on fatalities during peacekeeping operations, is available here: United Nations Peace-keeping, "Fatalities: Total Fatalities since 1948," accessed 17 November 2024, https://peacekeeping.un.org/en/fatalities. This figure was current as of 31 August 2024.

1. THE WORST DAY

1. While English has been the official language since South Sudan gained inde-pendence in 2011, few people outside of the country's elites spoke it. Instead, the lingua franca was "Juba Arabic," which lacked a specific written form but was used throughout the country as a way for people whose first language is their tribal mother tongue to conduct trade, undertake negotiations, and administer local governance. See United States Agency for International Development, "Language of Instruction Country Profile South Sudan" (Washington DC: USAID, 2021), https://pdf.usaid.gov/pdf_docs/PA00XFMT.pdf.

2. The United States contributed 25 percent of the UN's budget for peacekeeping in 2019 but had not paid its full assessment since 2017. As of 2024, the United States still owed $1.1 billion in unpaid peacekeeping assessments, resulting in funding shortfalls for peacekeeping missions. See Congressional Research Service, "United Nations Issues: U.S. Funding of U.N. Peacekeeping," *In Focus*, 9 April 2024, https://sgp.fas.org/crs/row/IF10597.pdf.

3. From 2015 to 2018, South Sudan was considered the most dangerous country for humanitarian workers, according to the UN, and independent assessors ranked it as one of the world's three "least peaceful" countries in the world, along with Afghanistan and Syria.

2. ORIGIN STORY

1. I had always thought that "Service before self" was the motto of the U.S. Army Air Corps with which my dad flew during World War II, but the U.S. Air Force didn't adopt it as one of its core values until 1995, long after my

father's military service. I have come to believe that he picked up the saying during his two years in India because it has long been the official motto of the Indian Army.

2. My exemplar in this regard was America's most-decorated Marine, Lt. Gen. Smedley Butler. Disillusioned by the corruption and disregard for human life he witnessed throughout his career, Butler alarmed the establishment when he published *War Is a Racket*, an attack on the nascent military-industrial complex that existed in 1939.

3. BIG MEN, STRONG WOMEN

1. Interestingly, Garang's vision had always been for a unified Sudan, one where the southern states stood on an equal political footing with those in the north. But without Garang to advocate for this vision in the 2011 referendum on whether to stick together or stand apart, the people of the southern Sudan voted overwhelmingly to form their own nation.

5. AFRICA WANTS TO KILL YOU

EPIGRAPH: U.S. Embassy in South Sudan, Juba, "South Sudan—Travel Advisory—Level 4: Do Not Travel," 28 June 2018, https://ss.usembassy.gov/south-sudan-travel-advisory-level-4-do-not-travel/.

7. THROUGH AMERICAN EYES

EPIGRAPH: International Crisis Group, "Salvaging South Sudan's Fragile Peace Deal," *Africa Report*, no. 270 (13 March 2019), https://www.crisisgroup.org/africa/horn-africa/south-sudan/270-salvaging-south-sudans-fragile-peace-deal.

1. John Bolton, "Remarks by National Security Advisor Ambassador John R. Bolton on the Trump Administration's New Africa Strategy," delivered at the Heritage Foundation, Washington DC, 13 December 2018, https://trumpwhitehouse.archives.gov/briefings-statements/remarks-national-security-advisor-ambassador-john-r-bolton-trump-administrations-new-africa-strategy/.

2. Throughout this book, unless stated otherwise, quotes are taken from my contemporaneous notes.

10. A SHORT HISTORY OF PEACEKEEPING

1. General Dallaire stated that the order to abandon Tutsi civilians to the *génocidaires* had come from the top and acknowledged that he disobeyed a direct order to remain and attempt to help: "Boutros Boutros-Ghali, the secretary-general of the United Nations, personally called to order me and my remaining troops to withdraw for fear of further UN casualties. I refused." See Roméo Dallaire, *The Peace* (Toronto: Random House Canada, 2024), 20, Kindle edition.

2. The UN's operation in Somalia disintegrated in 1993 after the retired U.S. admiral in charge of the operation authorized an assassination-by-airstrike attempt against a leading Somali political leader. That attack failed to kill its target, but it did kill many civilians, sparking a major uprising against the UN forces in the Somalian capital. The Battle of Mogadishu culminated in several U.S. helicopters being shot down, an event that was later dramatized in the movie *Black Hawk Down*. The result was the end of that UN operation, and Western militaries were reluctant to involve their forces in future UN operations on the African continent.

3. Ivan Lupis and Laura Pitter, "The Fall of Srebrenica and the Failure of UN Peacekeeping," *Human Rights Watch*, 15 October 1995, https://www.hrw.org /report/1995/10/15/fall-srebrenica-and-failure-un-peacekeeping/bosnia-and -herzegovina.

4. I learned that the term "refugee" was a misnomer; to be considered refugees, they would have had to cross an international border. The inhabitants of these camps were "internally displaced persons" (IDPs). Semantics, I thought, until I discovered that IDPs had fewer protections under international law. Their government was supposed to protect them, but that government's attempts to kill them had driven them from their homes and into these camps in the first place.

11. DISASTROUS PASSIONS

1. Emma McCune was a British aid worker who became Riek Machar's second wife. In 1993 she died in a traffic accident in Nairobi while pregnant with their unborn child.

12. LOUDER THAN WORDS

EPIGRAPH: Lauren Spink and Matt Wells, *Under Fire: The July 2016 Violence in Juba and UN Response* (Washington DC: Center for Civilians in Conflict, 2016), 53, https://civiliansinconflict.org/wp-content/uploads/2017/09/civic -juba-violence-report-october-2016.pdf.

1. What "Action for Peacekeeping" failed to address was the complete lack of accountability for mission leaders who failed to achieve results on even those elements of their mandates that were spelled out with absolute clarity, such as the injunction to "to use all necessary means to protect civilians under threat of physical violence, irrespective of the source of such violence."

2. I was neither the most influential nor the most patient person to finally arrive in Juba that month. Rebecca Nyandeng also returned to South Sudan's capital in May as a member of the "opposition in government," having been tasked by President Salva Kiir to lead a committee on expanding the ruling party's political bureau.

13. BOOTS ON THE GROUND

1. The National Salvation Front is universally referred to as NAS, which is not an acronym or abbreviation but simply the formulation of the Arabic word for "people," ناس or *naas*, in Juba Arabic. This militarized political organization is based in Central Equatoria and led by Lt. Gen. Thomas Cirillo Swaka, a renegade SPLA officer who had served as a deputy chief of staff in the government's forces until his defection to found NAS in 2017. He cited corruption, ethno-centric politics, and the failure of the Kiir regime to maintain order and deliver economic development to the people of South Sudan as his reasons for rebellion. The use of NAS as the movement's nom de guerre was meant to reinforce the idea that his organization fought on behalf of all South Sudanese people.
2. USMOG referred to the latter position as the senior U.S. military observer, while the UN called it the senior national representative. These officers were responsible for the administrative and training requirements for all officers from their respective countries and for the coordination of official activities such as VIP visits.

14. CONTINGENCY PLANS

1. "Greening the Blue" was the UN's roadmap to achieving a neutral impact on climate change. Peacekeeping generated more than half of the UN's total greenhouse gas emissions during my year in South Sudan, with UNMISS being the second-biggest contributor to those emissions.

15. FREEDOM OF MOVEMENT

1. This problem was not unique to South Sudan. It had occurred previously in other peacekeeping operations, most notably in Bosnia, and with similarly damaging effects on the ability of UN peacekeepers to carry out their mandate. See Mark Cutts, "Humanitarian Operation in Bosnia, 1992–95: The Dilemmas of Negotiating Humanitarian Access," Working Paper no. 8 (Geneva: United Nations High Commissioner for Refugees, May 1999), 13, https://www.unhcr.org/us/media/humanitarian-operation-bosnia-1992-95-dilemmas-negotiating-humanitarian-access-mark-cutts.
2. Ethiopia returned to a state of civil war in 2020. The conflict, which lasted two years and cost hundreds of thousands of civilian lives, triggered high levels of internal instability that still existed in mid-2024.
3. UNMISS, "Conflict-Related Violations and Abuses in Central Equatoria, September 2018–April 2019," 3 July 2019, 23, https://unmiss.unmissions.org/sites/default/files/final_-_human_rights_division_report_on_central_equatoria_-_3_july_2019_0.pdf.

16. THE LAY OF THE LAND

EPIGRAPH: United Nations Environment Programme, *Greening the Blue Helmets: Environment, Natural Resources and UN Peacekeeping Operations* (New York: United Nations, 2012), 27, https://operationalsupport.un.org/sites/default /files/unep_greening_blue_helmets_0.pdf.

1. The name also distinguished the government forces from the South Sudan People's Liberation Army-in-Opposition (the SPLA-IO), with whom they had been formally at war just one month previously.

2. While the 2018 peace agreement had been signed by Salva Kiir and Riek Machar in September, the local SSPDF and SPLA-IO forces in Western Bahr el Ghazal had continued to carry out ambushes and raids in the vicinity of Wau until November 2018. See United Nations Security Council, *Report of the Secretary-General on the Situation in South Sudan*, S/2018/1103, 10 December 2018, 5, https://undocs.org/S/2018/1103.

3. Track 1.5 diplomacy is often defined as "unofficial interactions between official representatives." See Jeffrey Mapendre, "Track One and a Half Diplomacy and the Complementarity of Tracks," *Culture of Peace Online Journal* 2, no. 1 (2000): 69, https://peacemaker.un.org/sites/peacemaker.un.org/files /TrackOneandaHalfDiplomacy_Mapendere.pdf.

4. United Nations Human Rights Council (UNHRC), "Report of the Commission on Human Rights in South Sudan," 31 January 2020, 27, https://undocs.org/en /A/HRC/43/56.

5. In South Sudan, the monsoon season normally ran from April to November. The year 2019 marked a change in the historical pattern, with the rains coming earlier and leaving later and with more water accumulating, leading to unprecedented flooding.

6. To be fair, the U.S. government also believed that it could erase the wrongs it did when it killed civilians in Iraq and Afghanistan, and it made "condolence payments" of $2,500 for each human life. That was the equivalent of just five cows at 2019 prices in South Sudan.

17. EASY BUTTONS AND HARD TRUTHS

1. The UN defined such situations as "very dangerous locations where staff are directly targeted as a result of their association with the United Nations or where premises are targeted, causing imminent threat to staff; where there is war or active armed conflict and where staff are at high risk of becoming collateral damage." See the International Civil Service Commission, "Rest and Recuperation (R&R) Framework," accessed 20 May 2024, https://icsc.un.org /Home/RestRecuperation.

18. AN OUTSIDER LOOKS IN

1. The Office for Peacekeeping Strategic Partnership is an internal oversight organization that functions as a sort of inspector general for peacekeeping operations. Its reports are neither made public nor historically shared with any but the top-ranking members of the peacekeeping missions and UN Headquarters.

2. I was disappointed to discover that Cammaert's assessment of this visit—in contrast to his previous reports—was not made public. It was another unfortunate example of the UN's lack of transparency and was particularly galling since General Cammaert was one of the few authors of UN-sponsored reports to ever suggest that UNMISS itself needed to make improvements.

21. THE AGONY OF JMAC

1. Lauren Hutton, "Prolonging the Agony of UNMISS: The Implementation Challenges of a New Mandate during a Civil War" (The Hague: Netherlands Institute of International Relations Clingendael, 2014), 20, https://www.clingendael .org/sites/default/files/pdfs/Prolonging%20the%20agony%20of%20UNMISS %20-%20Lauren%20Hutton.pdf.

2. Hutton, "Prolonging," 27.

22. COORDINATED ASSESSMENT

EPIGRAPH: United Nations Security Council Resolution 2459, adopted at its 848th meeting, Geneva, 15 March 2019, 7–9, https://www.securitycouncilreport.org/atf /cf/%7B65BFCF9B-6D27-4E9C-8CD3-CF6E4FF96FF9%7D/s_res_2459.pdf.

1. United Nations Security Council Resolution 2459, 2.

2. UNHRC, "Report of the Commission," 30.

3. The UN's own investigation of the UNMISS response to the 2016 violence in Juba stated that "[the] Force did not operate under a unified command. . . . [An] Incident Commander, commanding all the forces at UN House . . . [was ordered] to retain an explicit and ultimately confusing command link to Sector South headquarters in Tomping. . . . This confused arrangement, in combination with the lack of leadership on the ground, contributed to incidents of poor performance among the military and police contingents at UN House." See Maj. Gen. Patrick Cammaert, "Annex: Executive Summary of the Independent Special Investigation into the Violence in Juba in 2016 and the Response by the United Nations Mission in South Sudan," 1 November 2016, 3–4, https://www.securitycouncilreport.org/atf/cf/%7B65BFCF9B-6D27-4E9C -8CD3-CF6E4FF96FF9%7D/s_2016_924.pdf.

4. A common operating picture is a near-real-time display of information streams from multiple sources that enables officers in command roles to make effec-

tive decisions based on an up-to-date understanding of the situation on the ground.

23. ORDERS IN WORK

1. Cammaert, "Annex: Executive Summary," 3; and United Nations, "Troubled by Report's Findings on July Violence, Secretary-General Pledges Greater Accountability by United Nations Mission in South Sudan," 1 November 2016, https://press.un.org/en/2016/sgsm18245.doc.htm.
2. "Head of UN Peacekeeping Mission in South Sudan to Step Down in November," *UN News*, 23 October 2016, https://news.un.org/en/story/2016/543412. The "lack of leadership" and "preparedness" Løj was responsible for in UNMISS did not keep the UN from hiring her again; in 2018 she was chosen to lead an independent strategic review of the UN's mission in Mali.

24. UNITY!

EPIGRAPH: UNHRC, "Report of the Commission," 32.

25. WOMEN, PEACE, AND SECURITY

EPIGRAPH: Susan Sebit, "From Where I Stand: 'Young Women's Inclusion in Peacebuilding Will Create Sustainable Peace,'" UN Women, 8 August 2019, https://www.unwomen.org/en/news/stories/2019/8/from-where-i-stand-susan-sebit.

26. RHYTHM AND THE RAINS

1. That model called for a company-size force of about 130 to 150 peacekeepers to deploy into the field for a week or two, establish a base in an unstable area, and conduct short, day-long patrols radiating outward to project security into a large area, gather information, and support the activities of humanitarians.
2. The predominance of the Auswegian influence was a function of numbers: Norway, Denmark, and Australia had about twice as many officers assigned to UNMISS as the United States did. An engineering company from the United Kingdom was in Bentiu, but only seven British officers and a similar number of Canadians served as staff in the force.
3. The Nairobi-based company formerly known as "African Expeditions" has operated since 2018 as AFEX Kenya Ltd. (https://www.afexgroup.com/about-us.html).

27. THE TIGERS OF SOUTH SUDAN

1. I knew that my experience was not unique, but I was surprised to discover later that even General Tinaikar had been harassed in this way, with his convoy being

held up and cocked weapons pointed at them during a nighttime encounter in December.

28. INCONCEIVABLE

1. Ardern had won Shearer's seat in the New Zealand parliament after he resigned to take the lead role in UNMISS in 2017, and she had gone on to lead the Labour Party to victory that same year, serving as her country's prime minister from 2017 to 2023.

2. The White Army was a Nuer militia that came into existence in the early 1990s and played a significant role in both the struggle for independence and the civil wars that followed. The White Army was distinctive for its autonomy and lack of formal military hierarchy. Its men used bravery and weight of numbers to make up for their lack of heavy weapons, and they periodically mobilized outside the context of state-sponsored warfare to attack neighboring tribes, to steal cattle and women, and to inflict revenge on those who had raided their villages in the past.

3. This shortfall existed for three reasons. Many of the forces originally planned for the additional Regional Protection Force element, which the Security Council demanded in the wake of the 2016 debacle, were supposed to come from Kenya, but it pulled its troops from UNMISS after the firing of General Ondieki. Delays in bringing in the approved forces gave the South Sudanese government time to change its mind and to take political steps to block the deployment of several key units, including tactical helicopters and reconnaissance UAVs. And the mission chose to use the funds earmarked for those units and other elements—including 850 standard peacekeepers plus more engineer and transportation units—to fund additional civilian staff positions instead.

29. UNMISS INACTION

1. Malong was emblematic of the complex military-political intrigues in the country. Like many of his generation, Malong had been fighting since the 1980s and had served as the governor of Northern Bahr el Ghazal State during the restive years between 2008 and 2014. A popular and powerful Dinka leader, he had become the highest-ranking officer in the government forces until 2017, when he was sacked by Salva Kiir, who may have seen him as a rival. Escaping house arrest on the pretext of illness, Malong had then formed his own opposition movement, which, unlike Machar's SPLA-io, had not signed up to the current peace treaty and so remained a legitimate target for all military forces that *had* made peace.

2. The Buya and Toposa are two ethnic groups that occupy adjoining areas in

the state of Eastern Equatoria. Both are pastoralist communities, and while they had previously lived in peace, conflicts had arisen over access to water sources and grazing fields that led to small-scale raids to steal cattle and carry out revenge killings.

3. Alahayi Nemaya and Dawit Kahsay, "UNMISS-Supported Centre Set to Empower Women in Wau," United Nations, 20 August 2019, https://unmiss.unmissions .org/unmiss-supported-centre-set-empower-women-wau.

4. Elysia Buchanan, "No Simple Solutions: Women, Displacement and Durable Solutions in South Sudan" (Nairobi: Oxfam International, 2019), 20, 15, 19, https://oxfamilibrary.openrepository.com/bitstream/handle/10546/620857 /bp-no-simple-solutions-women-displacement-south-sudan-030919-en.pdf.

5. Had the cantonment process been properly implemented, it would have been a form of DDR—the very thing that South Sudan desperately needed and for which senior leaders such as General Wang had advocated. Unfortunately, without support from UNMISS or the international community, it ended up being just another way for South Sudanese elites to siphon money into their own bank accounts.

31. THINGS FALL APART

EPIGRAPH: Maj. Chris Young was a Canadian tank officer who served with UNMISS as an observer in the Equatorias in 2016–17. His account of the problems surrounding SOI and freedom of movement was something I wish I had read before my own deployment instead of afterward. See Chris Young, "Canada and South Sudan: Coming to Grips with 'Juba Good,'" *Canadian Army Journal* 18, no. 1 (2020): 59–71, https://publications.gc.ca/collections/collection_2020 /mdn-dnd/D12-11-18-1-eng.pdf.

1. Only much later would I discover the reason the government of South Sudan sought to block UNMISS from stationing Rwandan peacekeepers in Yei was not its proximity to the border with Uganda itself but with the DRC. Yei sat on the main gold smuggling route between the conflict-stricken province of Ituri in the DRC (where Uganda and Rwanda were engaged in a proxy struggle for control of resources) and regional illicit gold hubs in Uganda. With the South Sudanese government closely aligned with Uganda and the SSPDF involved in the gold trade, they had no desire to allow Rwandans into this area. See Marcena Hunter and Ken Opala, "Tarnished Hope: Crime and Corruption in South Sudan's Gold Sector" (Geneva: Global Initiative against Transnational Organized Crime, May 2023), 4, 12, 24, https://globalinitiative.net/wp-content /uploads/2023/05/Marcena-Hunter-and-Ken-Opala-Tarnished-hope-Crime -and-corruption-in-S-Sudans-gold-sector-GI-TOC-May-2023-.pdf.

32. NO COUNTRY FOR YOUNG MEN

1. "Those of" is an expression used by the South Sudanese to denote allegiance to a group. To them, my colleagues and I were "those of UNMISS."
2. Nick Turse, "Ghost Nation," *Harper's Magazine*, July 2017, https://harpers.org /archive/2017/07/ghost-nation/.

33. STRONG MEDICINE FOR TANKS

1. Rwandan forces fought in two wars and a pair of smaller campaigns in the DRC between 1996 and 2009, while Ethiopian troops had been at war with Eritrea and fighting against Islamist forces in Somalia during roughly the same period.

34. RIEK MACHAR VERSUS THE WORLD

1. "Communique on the Occasion of the Tripartite Summit on the Revitalised Agreement on Resolution of the Conflict in Republic of South Sudan," State House, Entebbe, 7 November 2019, https://www.peaceagreements.org /viewmasterdocument/2248.
2. "UN Security Council Visit to South Sudan Sunday 22nd October 2018 Press Conference," Juba International Airport, UNMISS press release, 20 October 2019, https://reliefweb.int/report/south-sudan/near-verbatim-transcript-un -security-council-visit-south-sudan-sunday-22nd.
3. "Machar Threatens to Opt Out of Unity Government," Radio Tamazuj, 21 October 2019, https://web.archive.org/web/20191021150257/https://radiotamazuj .org/en/news/article/machar-threatens-to-opt-out-of-unity-government.
4. "Machar Leaves Juba, Rebuffs Unity Government Call," Radio Tamazuj, 22 October 2019, https://web.archive.org/web/20191022133729/https://radiotamazuj .org/en/news/article/machar-leaves-juba-rebuffs-unity-government-call.
5. "UN Security Council Visit."
6. "UN Security Council Visit."
7. Duop Chak Wuol, "Opinion: The UN Security Council's Misguided Approach to Peace in South Sudan," Radio Tamazuj, 21 October 2019, https://web.archive .org/web/20191022145131/https://radiotamazuj.org/en/news/article/opinion -the-un-security-council-s-misguided-approach-to-peace-in-south-sudan.

35. UNTIL THE FIRST BULLET FLIES

EPIGRAPH: Lauren Spink and Matt Wells, *Under Fire: The July 2016 Violence in Juba and UN Response* (Washington DC: Center for Civilians in Conflict, 2016), 83, https://civiliansinconflict.org/wp-content/uploads/2017/09/civic -juba-violence-report-october-2016.pdf.

36. JUBA SOCIAL CLUB

EPIGRAPH: Quoted in Bruce Morris, "David Shearer: Life in Hell-Holes," *Mt Albert Inc*, 11 April 2018, https://www.mtalbertinc.co.nz/david-shearer-life-hell-holes/.

37. NONWORKING GROUP

1. The Arabic root word for *khawaja* means "master." Its connotation ranges from ironically humorous to mildly pejorative depending on the circumstance. While the term was traditionally applied mainly to Caucasians, in recent years it has been used to refer to any foreigner who appears noticeably non-African.

38. FRIENDSGIVING

EPIGRAPH: Emilio Manfredi et al., "Interim Report of the Panel of Experts on South Sudan Submitted Pursuant to Resolution 2471 (2019)," United Nations Security Council, 22 November 2019, 21, https://www.undocs.org/S/2019/897.
1. "Angry Demonstrators Storm UN Camp in DRC after Deadly Attack," *Al Jazeera*, 25 November 2019, https://www.aljazeera.com/news/2019/11/25/angry-demonstrators-storm-un-camp-in-drc-after-deadly-attack.

39. CLASH OF CLANS

1. Small Arms Survey, "National Small Arms Assessment in South Sudan," United Nations Development Programme, accessed 10 December 2023, https://www.undp.org/sites/g/files/zskgke326/files/migration/ss/South-Sudan-National-Small-Arms-Assessment---Web-Version.pdf.

41. UP THE CREEK

1. General Cammaert led the inquiry into the disaster at the Malakal POC camp on 17–18 February 2016. The UN refused to share his full findings and recommendations and only released an abbreviated "Note to Correspondents" after the violence in Juba later that year. See UN Headquarters Board of Inquiry, "Note to Correspondents: Board of Inquiry Report on Malakal," United Nations, 5 August 2016, https://www.un.org/sg/en/content/sg/note-correspondents/2016-08-05/note-correspondents-board-of-inquiry-report-malakal.
2. Médicins sans Frontières, "MSF Internal Review of the February 2016 Attack on the Malakal Protection of Civilians Site and the Post-Event Situation," June 2016, 25, https://www.msf.org/sites/default/files/malakal_report_210616_pc.pdf. Emphasis in original.
3. When I shared this observation with the force commander, his reply was, "It's the value of life. . . . Very cheap here it seems. No report, no public notice,

no investigation. I hope that someone, somewhere has at least felt a sense of loss—a basic human trait. If not, then we are indeed in a sad space."

42. A LONG DECEMBER

EPIGRAPH: See Christopher Holshek, "U.S. Military Observers and Comprehensive Engagement," *Small Wars Journal*, 10 February 2011, 1, 5, https:// smallwarsjournal.com/blog/journal/docs-temp/673-holshek.pdf.

1. At least temporarily. When I was helicopter-borne in 2019, musing about the power of time to change nations and people, Russia had annexed Crimea five years earlier, and there was little news coverage of its proxy war against Ukraine in the Donbas and of the atrocities that its citizens employed as Wagner Group mercenaries had committed in Africa. Reporting changed in 2022 at least with respect to the civilians killed by Russian forces in Ukraine. The hundreds of African civilians tortured and killed by Russian mercenaries in the CAR and in Mali still received scant attention, let alone meaningful action to protect them from the depredations of Wagner, which the United States has designated as a transnational criminal organization and the United Kingdom has listed as a terrorist organization.

2. These fees actually ranged from $500 to $2,000, as spelled out by the government's regulations in the "Financial Act, 2019/2020 FY," Ministry of Finance and Economic Planning, Government of the Republic of South Sudan, accessed 10 December 2023, https://www.mofep-grss.org/wp-content/uploads/2019/12/FY -2019-2020-Financial-Act.pdf. For the presidential decree, see the President, Republic of South Sudan (RSS), "Republican Order No. 29/2017 for the Free, Unimpeded and Unhindered Movement of Humanitarian Assistance Convoys in the Republic of South Sudan, 2017 A.D.," 9 November 2017, https://docs .southsudanngoforum.org/sites/default/files/2017-11/Order-Humanitarian %20assistance.pdf.

43. THE FAR EDGE OF THE EMPIRE

1. Gbudue *was* the last of the Azande kings when I visited Yambio and Lirangu in 2019, but that changed on 9 February 2022, when his great-grandson Atoroba Peni Rikito Gbudue was coronated as the new king of the Azande. Like other modern monarchs, King Atoroba renounced direct participation in politics and voiced his intention to focus on cultural and social development for his people instead.

45. HUB AND SPOKE

1. Since 1802 the U.S. Army Corps of Engineers has played a vital role in America's development, surveying, mapping, building roads, and becoming the

nation's lead agency for flood control. It constructed not only military bases but also facilities for the postal service and the National Aeronautics and Space Administration, and since the 1960s it has served as a leading environmental preservation and restoration agency.

46. NOT ALL LIVES

1. UNISFA, "Summary of UNISFA Mandate," United Nations Security Council Resolution 2469, 2019, https://unisfa.unmissions.org/mandate.
2. Lela Gilbert, *Baroness Cox: Eyewitness to a Broken World* (London: Lion Hudson, 2008).

47. A SAD STATE OF AFFAIRS

EPIGRAPH: Guterres made this remark in a speech to regional leaders in Addis Ababa, Ethiopia, on 27 January 2018. "UN Chief Warns African Bloc against Conflicts of Interest in South Sudan," Voice of America, 27 January 2018, https://www.voaafrica.com/a/united-nations-chief-warns-african-bloc -against-conflicts-interest-south-sudan/4227880.html.

1. Richard Jale and Priscah Akol, "Peace Soldiers Die from Poor Conditions despite Release of Funds," Eye Radio, 23 January 2020, https://www.eyeradio .org/peace-soldiers-die-from-poor-conditions-despite-release-of-funds/.

49. MAYBE JUST ONCE

EPIGRAPH: Machar was the executive director of Malek County and made his public plea via Radio Tamazuj, an independent media service that broadcast on shortwave radio and the internet. It operated from exile after the NSS forced the closure of its office in Juba. See "Communal Fighting Leaves 9 Dead in Western Lakes," Radio Tamazuj, 6 February 2020, https://web.archive.org /web/20200207133748/https://radiotamazuj.org/en/news/article/communal -fighting-leaves-9-dead-in-western-lakes.

50. RECONCILIATION AND RUMORS OF WAR

EPIGRAPH: UN Office of Internal Oversight Services, "Evaluation of the Imple-mentation and Results of Protection of Civilians Mandates in United Nations Peacekeeping Operations," 7 March 2014, 7, 19, https://digitallibrary.un.org /record/767929?ln=en&v=pdf.

1. The UN uses the spelling "Likaungole," but place names in South Sudan often bear various spellings. This town's name is sometimes represented as Lekongole, Likongole, and Lekaungole. And sometimes it doesn't appear at all, including on Google Maps circa 2023.

2. David Yau-Yau was one of the thirty-two governors who found themselves suddenly "former governors" when Salva Kiir reverted to the "Ten Plus Three" solution. The territory he controlled as the governor of the now-defunct Boma State had its capital in Pibor. But Yau-Yau was more than just a politician; he had risen to prominence by twice leading successful armed rebellions against government forces in Jonglei. Each time he accepted amnesty for himself and his troops, and each time he got a better deal, which led to him becoming the sole prominent Murle political leader during the 2019–20 period.

3. United Nations Peacekeeping, "South Sudan's President Makes Surprise Announcement to Return the War-Torn Country to 10 States," 15 February 2020, https://peacekeeping.un.org/en/south-sudans-president-makes-surprise-announcement-to-return-war-torn-country-to-10-states.

51. PEACE ON PAPER, ARMY ON THE MOVE

EPIGRAPH: Shearer asked this rhetorical question in a paper he published in 2001 and argued that mercenaries rather than peacekeepers should be used in places such as South Sudan. See David Shearer, "Privatizing Protection," *Global Policy Forum*, August/September 2001, https://archive.globalpolicy.org/pmscs/40933-privatising-protection.html.

1. The authors of a study published three months earlier found that when "peace-keeping units get locally deployed to violent post-war areas . . . they reduce the level of civilian harm almost immediately." See Anup Phayal and Brandon C. Prins, "Deploying to Protect: The Effect of Peacekeeping Troop Deployments on Violence against Civilians," *International Peacekeeping* 27, no. 2 (September 2019): 311–36, https://doi.org/10.1080/13533312.2019.1660166.

2. Nick Turse, *Next Time They'll Come to Count the Dead: War and Survival in South Sudan* (Chicago: Dispatch Books, 2016), 116.

53. THIS IS IT, YOUR EXCELLENCY

1. Ugali is a dense porridge made of corn meal and is a staple dietary item in East Africa.

2. "Silencing the Guns 2020," *African Union*, accessed 3 July 2023, https://au.int/en/flagships/silencing-guns-2020.

54. CRIMES AGAINST HUMANITY

EPIGRAPH: Wardwell was an American aid worker with Nonviolent Peaceforce, and the incident he described was from the fighting in Unity State in 2014. See Turse, *Next Time*, 85. The bird was the same species that I saw in Bor, and the massive scavengers would enjoy a bounty of human flesh in Jonglei State during the period of 18 February to 18 March 2020.

1. The weapon was very likely a Chinese-made M-16 clone known as a CQ-5.56.

55. COME TO COUNT THE DEAD

1. Hutton, "Prolonging," 20.
2. Victor Lugala, "East African Locusts Meet Unexpected Fate in South Sudan," *Gurtong*, 27 February 2020, https://web.archive.org/web/20200228123142/http:// www.gurtong.net/ECM/Editorial/tabid/124/ctl/ArticleView/mid/519/articleId /22030/East-African-Locusts-Meet-Unexpected-Fate-In-South-Sudan.aspx.

56. POTEMKIN WOULD BE PROUD

1. A *boma* is the smallest administrative division in South Sudan and consists of about 4,500 people. The assertion that nine thousand children had been stolen was obviously hyperbole, but Murle raiders *did* abduct Nuer children. They usually did so in small-scale raids over the course of any given year rather than in a massive assault such as the ones the Nuer and Dinka periodically launched in retaliation.
2. Throughout my travels across the country, I saw scores of men carrying guns, yet I never saw a man carrying water or firewood, or doing any real physical labor that was not military in nature. Nicholas Coghlan, who served as the Canadian ambassador to South Sudan from 2012 to 2016, recounted speaking to women much like those I met in Yuai and Anyidi. The women told him, "We build the houses, . . . we help with the food distributions, we do the cooking, we look after the goats. We fetch the firewood. We look after the gardens." When asked what the men did, the women appeared puzzled and amused. Finally one said, "They make babies." Left unsaid was that many of those babies were made without consent. "There is no specific area where women feel unsafe because they are unsafe everywhere," replied a Dinka man to UN researchers conducting a 2020 survey of gender-based violence. "Rape, physical violence and bullying (when a lady wants to talk, she is shut out by men) of women is common here." But it was unfair to say that men only made babies; men also made war. See Nicholas Coghlan, *Collapse of a Country: A Diplomat's Memoir of South Sudan* (Montreal: McGill-Queen's University Press, 2017), 167–68, Kindle edition; and Steven Chimwemwe Iphani, "'A Boy Should Be a Fighter': Addressing Harmful Masculinities Driving Cattle-Related Violence" (Geneva: International Organization for Migration, 2020), 19, https://publications.iom .int/system/files/pdf/A-Boy-Should-be-a-Fighter.pdf.

57. DEATH BY A THOUSAND CUTS

1. United Nations Peacekeeping, "Near Verbatim Transcript: Media Briefing by the Special Representative of the Secretary-General and Head of the United

Nations Mission in South Sudan, Mr. David Shearer, Juba," 9 March 2020, https://peacekeeping.un.org/en/near-verbatim-transcript-media-briefing -special-representative-of-secretary-general-and-head-of.

58. THAT SAFARI WAY OF LIFE

1. Paul Theroux made this observation in his book *Dark Star Safari: Overland from Cairo to Cape Town* (New York: Hough Mifflin, 2004), a memoir of his 2001 trip through East Africa.

60. EVERYTHING RAVAGED

1. Age-sets are an important aspect of Murle culture. Men will usually belong to their set throughout their lives. Age-sets offer social support but can also be a vector for violence.

62. LOVE IN THE TIME OF CORONAVIRUS

1. United Nations Security Council Resolution 1612, titled "On Children in Armed Conflict," requires a monitoring and reporting mechanism to "collect and provide timely, objective, accurate and reliable information on the recruitment and use of child soldiers in violation of applicable international law and on other violations and abuses committed against children affected by armed conflict." I could find nothing in this document to suggest that the abductions in Jonglei did not fall under "on other violations and abuses committed against children affected by armed conflict," but my protests went unheeded. The full text of the resolution, which the Security Council adopted on 26 July 2005, can be found here: https://digitallibrary.un.org/record/554197/files/S_RES _1612%282005%29-EN.pdf?ln=en.
2. United Nations Security Council, "Report of the Secretary-General on Children and Armed Conflict," A/75/873-S/2021/437, 6 May 2021, https://undocs.org/en /A/75/873.

65. FOR THE RECORD

EPIGRAPH: UN Office of Internal Oversight Services, "Evaluation," 12, 17, 20.
1. This occurred despite the UN report's clearly stating that mandates concerning the protection of civilians *did* cover threats due to "tribal and intercommunal conflict and conflict over land and resources," as well as threats from organized militaries and criminal elements. See UN Office of Internal Oversight Services, "Evaluation," 17.

67. ADMIRING THE PROBLEM

1. El-Ghassim Wane, "Report on the Independent Strategic Review of the United

Nations Mission in South Sudan Pursuant to Security Resolution 2514," 15 December 2020, 43, 42, https://www.securitycouncilreport.org/atf/cf/%7B65BFCF9B -6D27-4E9C-8CD3-CF6E4FF96FF9%7D/s_2020_1224.pdf.

2. Wane, "Report," 45.

3. Wane, "Report," 49.

4. Wane, "Report," 56, 57.

68. CHANGING THE GUARD

EPIGRAPH: Mark Millar, in *The Peacekeeping Failure in South Sudan: The UN, Bias and the Peacekeeper's Mind* (New York: Bloomsbury, 2022), was quoting a UN staff member's reaction at reading the official report of the 2014 attack on the POC site at Bor, where forty-two adults and eleven children were killed as the mission stood by and responded only after the attackers—who numbered fewer than fifty armed men—had been allowed to kill and loot at will for thirty minutes. I had felt the same sort of incredulity after reading the official report on the 2020 attacks in Jonglei.

1. OHCHR and UNMISS, "Armed Violence Involving Community-Based Militias in Greater Jonglei, January–August 2020," March 2021, 19, https://www.ohchr .org/sites/default/files/Documents/Countries/SS/Jonglei-report.pdf.

2. OHCHR and UNMISS, "Armed Violence," 16–17.

3. OHCHR and UNMISS, "Armed Violence," 18.

4. OHCHR and UNMISS, "Armed Violence," 18.

5. OHCHR and UNMISS, "Armed Violence," 32, 33.

69. POST-TRAUMATIC

1. United Nations Peacekeeping, "An Officer and a Gentleman Bids Farewell: Lieutenant General Shailesh Tinaikar, UNMISS Force Commander," 21 January 2022, https://peacekeeping.un.org/en/officer-and-gentleman-bids-farewell -lieutenant-general-shailesh-tinaikar-unmiss-force-commander.

2. A *New York Times* investigation would show that the target of the strike was simply an aid worker going about a normal day, and Gen. Kenneth F. McKenzie Jr., the commander responsible for the killings, stated that "I will stress this was not a rushed strike. The strike cell deliberately followed and observed this vehicle and its occupants for eight hours while crosschecking what they were seeing with all available intelligence." But the building that the DOD originally claimed was an ISIS hideout was actually the headquarters of a U.S.-based NGO, whose location would have been on-file with the U.S. Embassy and the U.S. military. Clearly, if the strike cell had used "all available intelligence," then they would have known where their target worked and, after tracking him for that period, should have had the time to cross-reference the organization's staff

roster with home addresses and family status, especially given that the U.S. military had biometric data on 80 percent of the Afghan population. See Azmat Khan, "Military Investigation Reveals How the U.S. Botched a Drone Strike in Kabul," *New York Times*, 6 January 2023, https://www.nytimes.com/2023/01 /06/us/politics/drone-civilian-deaths-afghanistan.html; and Gen. Kenneth F. McKenzie Jr., "Pentagon Press Briefing," U.S. Central Command, 17 September 2021, https://www.centcom.mil/MEDIA/Transcripts/Article/2781320/general -kenneth-f-mckenzie-jr-commander-of-us-central-command-and-pentagon -pres/.

3. Gen. Mark Milley was, admittedly, half right. That "level of rigor," applied over twenty years of drone strikes, had killed over four thousand civilians, including hundreds of children. Unlike the lost children of Jonglei, the Afghans' deaths *were* counted in the statistics of grave violations against children; yet, the powerful Western nations that had killed them with impunity faced no consequences. See Rebecca Kheel, "General Acknowledges 'Others' Killed in Drone Strike Targeting ISIS Car Bomb," *The Hill*, 1 September 2021, https:// thehill.com/policy/defense/570402-top-general-acknowledges-others-killed -in-drone-strike-targeting-isis-car-bomb/.

4. In South Sudan, local staff members were routinely abandoned in the face of advancing armies, and those who survived expressed surprise and sorrow at the way they had been treated. One locally recruited NGO employee recalled, "We who had a contract with MSF, we were told 'this is your community, remain here.' That left scars in our minds. You are contracted by an organisation, why do they leave you like that? There was nothing that protected us." See Xavier Crombé and Joanna Kuper, "War Breaks Out: Interpreting Violence on Healthcare in the Early Stage of the South Sudanese Civil War," *Journal of Humanitarian Affairs* 1, no. 2 (19 August 2019), https://doi.org/10 .7227/JHA.012.

5. "The Battle of the Chosin Reservoir and the medal of Honor," National Medal of Honor Museum, 23 June 2022, https://mohmuseum.org/chosinreservoir/.

6. Hannah Strohmeier, Willem F. Scholte, and Alastair Ager, "How to Improve Organisational Staff Support? Suggestions from Humanitarian Workers in South Sudan," *Intervention* 17, no. 1 (April 2019), https://www.researchgate .net/publication/332274922_How_to_improve_organisational_staff_support _Suggestions_from_humanitarian_workers_in_South_Sudan.

70. GOOD OFFICES

EPIGRAPH: United Nations Security Council Resolution 2459, 8.

1. The posthumous award for peacekeepers killed in the line of duty bears the name of Dag Hammarskjöld, the second UN secretary-general, who died on

a peace mission in 1961. Others who directly supported the UNMISS efforts to aid the people of South Sudan died unheralded. John Simon, a civilian who worked to unload the tons of food that we shipped monthly up the Nile to sustain our base in Malakal and support WFP food distribution, was killed when two of the barges assigned to Operation Lifeline caught fire on 9 October 2019.

2. Notably, we received no such thanks from the Equatorian people we met with in Yei and Lasu, where government forces had been carrying out horrifying atrocities since 2017 without UNMISS forces intervening.

3. This fact has been documented in the literature of neuroscience and psychology. See Greg Harman, "Your Brain on Climate Change: Why the Threat Produces Apathy, Not Action," *The Guardian*, 10 November 2014, https://www .theguardian.com/sustainable-business/2014/nov/10/brain-climate-change -science-psychology-environment-elections.

71. SLOW-MOVING CRISES

1. Roméo Dallaire, *Shake Hands with the Devil: The Failure of Humanity in Rwanda* (Boston: Da Capo Press, 2022), preface, Kindle edition.

2. Daniel Gilbert, "Global Warming and Psychology," Harvard Thinks Big, 2010, 9:12–9:20, https://vimeo.com/10324258.

3. The numbers of civilians killed in Ethiopia's civil war dwarfed the civilian casualties inflicted during the Russian invasion of Ukraine (around 10,500 as of February 2024) and Israel's invasion of Gaza (at least 12,000 as of May 2024). While neither of those invasions was a civil war, they make for useful comparisons in terms of the degree to which the international community and its media platforms focused on the killings of civilians in Europe and the Middle East versus those in Africa. Notably, while UN agencies regularly published civilian casualty statistics for Ukraine and Gaza, they never did so for Ethiopia. They have so far failed to provide an official accounting, stating only that the parties to the conflict "perpetrated violations and abuses in Tigray on a staggering scale. These included mass killings, . . . rape, . . . [and] deliberate starvation. . . . These amount to war crimes and crimes against humanity." See David Pilling and Andres Schipani, "War in Tigray May Have Killed 600,000 People, Peace Mediator Says," *Financial Times*, 6 July 2023, https://www.ft.com/content/2f385e95-0899-403a-9e3b-ed8c24adf4e7; Office of the United Nations High Commissioner for Human Rights, "Two-Year Update: Protection of Civilians—Impact of Hostilities on Civilians since 24 February 2022," 2024, 2, https://www.ohchr.org/sites/default/files/2024-02/two -year-update-protection-civilians-impact-hostilities-civilians-24.pdf; United Nations Office for the Coordination of Humanitarian Affairs, "Hostilities in

the Gaza Strip and Israel: Flash Update #165," May 2024, https://www.unocha
.org/publications/report/occupied-palestinian-territory/hostilities-gaza-strip
-and-israel-flash-update-165; and Office of the United Nations High Commissioner for Human Rights, "Comprehensive Investigative Finding and Legal
Determinations: Report of the International Commission on Human Rights
Experts on Ethiopia," A/HRC/54/CRP.3, 13 October 2023, 83–84, https://www
.ohchr.org/sites/default/files/documents/hrbodies/hrcouncil/chreetiopia/a
-hrc-54-crp-3.pdf.

4. Katharine Houreld, "Ethiopian Guards Massacred Scores of Tigrayan Prisoners,
Witnesses Say," *Washington Post*, 4 December 2022, https://www.washingtonpost
.com/world/2022/12/05/ethiopia-tigray-massacre-killing-prisoners/.

5. Jayde and I had married on 13 August 2021. The ceremony was held in the tiny
coastal village of Store Heddinge, Denmark—about an hour from Copenhagen—
with my friend Martin serving as our witness. It was another memorable Friday
the thirteenth and, by complete coincidence, exactly seventy-four weeks since
she and I had met in Kenya at the beginning of the COVID-19 pandemic.

6. Office of the Special Representative of the Secretary-General for Children and
Armed Conflict, "South Sudan: Grave Violations against Children Declined
following Revitalized Peace Agreement and UN Engagement with Parties, but
More Remains to Be Done," 11 January 2021, https://childrenandarmedconflict.un
.org/2021/01/south-sudan-grave-violations-against-children-declined-following
-revitalized-peace-agreement-and-un-engagement-with-parties-but-more
-remains-to-be-done/.

7. Andreyev v. Secretary-General of the United Nations, United Nations Dispute
Tribunal, case no. UNDT/NBI/2011/089, 29 November 2013, 15, paragraph 68,
https://www.un.org/en/internaljustice/files/undt/judgments/undt-2013-152
.pdf.

72. HOW TO CHANGE THE WORLD

1. Secretary-General, "Report of an Independent Review on Sexual Exploitation and Abuse by International Peacekeeping Forces in the Central African
Republic," United Nations General Assembly, 23 June 2016, https://undocs.org
/en/A/71/99.

2. United Nations Peacekeeping, "Reforming Peacekeeping," accessed 3 July 2023,
https://peacekeeping.un.org/en/reforming-peacekeeping.

3. United Nations Department of Peacekeeping, "Policy: The Protection of Civilians in United Nations Peacekeeping," 1 May 2023, 20, https://peacekeeping
.un.org/sites/default/files/2023_protection_of_civilians_policy.pdf.

4. Daniel Forti, *Independent Reviews of UN Peace Operations: A Study of Politics
and Practice* (New York: International Peace Institute, 27 October 2021), 9,

https://www.ipinst.org/2021/10/independent-reviews-of-un-peace-operations
-a-study-of-politics-and-practice.

5. Code Blue, "The UN's Dirty Secret: The Untold Story of Anders Kompass and Peacekeeper Sex Abuse in the Central African Republic," 29 May 2015, http://www.codebluecampaign.com/press-releases/2015/5/29-1.

6. Secretary-General, "Report of an Independent Review," 13.

7. Stacy Jo Dixon, "Number of Global Social Network Users 2017–2028," Statista, 17 May 2024, https://www.statista.com/statistics/278414/number-of-woroldwide-social-network-users/.

AFTERWORD

1. World Food Programme, *Annual Performance Report for 2023*, Rome, 5 June 2024, 4, 14, https://docs.wfp.org/api/documents/WFP-0000159843/download/.

2. World Food Programme, *South Sudan Annual Country Report 2023*, 2023, 3–4, https://docs.wfp.org/api/documents/WFP-0000157757/download/.

3. "Results," Prosper Africa, accessed 3 June 2024, https://www.prosperafrica.gov/results/.

4. United Nations Charter, chapter VII, "Action with Respect to Threats to the Peace, Breaches of the Peace, and Acts of Aggression (Articles 39–51)," 26 June 1945, https://www.un.org/en/about-us/un-charter/chapter-7.

5. In fact, the problem is far worse than shown, as four different official UN sources of data on children killed by armed actors in South Sudan in 2022 do not come close to adding up. Claims were made that the number is as low as twenty-eight for the entire year, while others show forty-nine being killed in the course of a single forty-five-day period in Unity State. The analysis shown is based on the following reports: United Nations Mission in South Sudan, "Annual Brief on Violence Affecting Civilians: January to December 2022," February 2023, https://unmiss.unmissions.org/sites/default/files/infographics_-_annual_brief_on_civilian_casualties_-_infographics_20230216_f_0.pdf; and United Nations Security Council, "Report of the Secretary-General on Children and Armed Conflict," A/77/895-S/2023/363, 5 June 2023, 22, https://www.securitycouncilreport.org/atf/cf/%7B65BFCF9B-6D27-4E9C-8CD3-CF6E4FF96FF9%7D/S_2023_363.pdf.

6. United Nations, "Without Faster Collection Rate of Unpaid Assessments, United Nations Liquidity Crisis Risks Worsening in 2024, Management Chief Warns Fifth Committee," 9 October 2023, https://press.un.org/en/2023/gaab4428.doc.htm.

7. South Sudan recorded the second-highest percentage increase in military spending globally in 2023. Its spending rose by 78 percent to reach $1.1 billion despite remaining under a UN arms embargo for the purchase of lethal military

equipment. The largest percentage increase was in the DRC. See Nan Tian et al., "Trends in World Military Expenditure, 2023," Stockholm International Peace Research Institute, April 2024, https://www.sipri.org/sites/default/files/2024-04/2404_fs_milex_2023.pdf.

8. Douglas MacArthur, speech to the Corps of Cadets at the U.S. Military Academy, West Point NY, 12 May 1962, https://penelope.uchicago.edu/Thayer/E/Gazetteer/Places/America/United_States/Army/USMA/MacArthur/1962_speech_to_the_Corps.html.

Index

Abdelbagi, Hussein, 208

abduction, 87, 152, 237–38, 252, 267, 279, 293, 314; of children, 58, 246, 280, 302, 314–15, 354n1; as a conflict driver, 247–49, 272–73; efforts to release victims of, 271, 303; first-hand accounts of, 249, 251; of women, 58, 302

Aberdare Range (Kenya), 261

Aburoc, 319–20

Abyei Administrative Area, 91, 191–92, 208, 252, 316, 331

accountability, 59, 319; importance of, 317; lack of, 91, 191, 212, 307, 314–16, 318–20, 341n12; reports calling for more, 341n23; ways to improve, 317, 321, 331–32. *See also* shame; transparency

"Action for Peacekeeping," 41, 98, 341n1

Addis Ababa (Ethiopia), 135, 142, 207, 283, 351

Addis Ababa Agreement (1972), 18–19

Adewumi, Adewuyi "Ade," 230–31, 269–73

Adidiang, 319–20

Adok, 190. *See also* Nile River

aerial patrols, 210

aerial reconnaissance, 206, 233–34, 292, 304

AFEX compound, 105, 185

Afghanistan, 10, 12, 32, 35, 48, 53, 100, 301, 308, 339n1; American attacks

on civilians in, 290, 307, 343n6, 355n2, 356n3; American withdrawal from, 307; deployment to, 48; WFP budget shortfall in, 326

Africa, 13, 21–23, 33, 37; dangers in, 21–23; disparity of media attention to, 25, 59, 191–92, 300, 313, 350n1, 357n3; U.S. policy on (2018–20), 27–28

African Development Bank, 124

African Union (AU), 115

age-sets, 273, 354n1

AK-47. *See* assault rifles

Akech, Daniel, 14

Akobo, 116–19, 133, 139, 164, 171, 188, 210, 241, 243

akol (elephant), 217, 258. *See also* elephants

Alam, Mohammad Jahangir, 110, 206, 228, 242

al-Bashir, Omar, 32, 91

Al Jazeera, 191, 220

all-terrain vehicles (ATVS), 204, 211, 300

ammunition, 66, 151, 152, 156, 169, 316; black market cost and sources of, 66, 156; supply of, as ceasefire violation, 151, 169

Antonietti, Patrick, 28

Anyidi, 227–29, 250–52, 304

APCS. *See* armored personnel carriers (APCS)